Coming Out Proud to Erase the Stigma of Mental Illness

Stories and Essays of Solidarity

Patrick W. Corrigan
Jon E. Larson
Patrick J. Michaels

Instant Publisher
Collierville TN

D0902365

ISBN: 978-0-578-15856-3

Printed in U.S. by Instantpublisher.com

Table of Contents

Preface

Stigma robs people of rightful opportunities that undermine their work, housing, health, and citizenship goals. One of the most effective ways to erase stigma is by people with lived experience telling their stories of recovery: **COMING OUT**. Being in the closet with mental health experiences often leads to shame. **COMING OUT** replaces shame with a sense of authority and empowerment. Erasing shame is not enough, however. **COMING OUT** promotes affirming attitudes and behaviors: that people with even the most serious of mental illnesses recover and do so by actively choosing their goals and their treatment plans. This is a book about people **COMING OUT**, standing up and proudly hailing their life journey, highlighting challenges and accomplishments in the process.

It's hard to be courageous in the face of failure; and that is how people with mental illness are often wrongly framed by psychiatric professionals. Everyone, with disability or not, experiences challenges at work, in relationships, and with health. And everyone fails at times when facing some of these challenges. People do not recover by making their world risk free. People do not land a better job, move to a nicer neighborhood, build more intimate relationships, or enjoy fewer medication side effects if they do not entertain and pursue the risky option. Best achievements come the hard way: falling flat, picking one's self up, and moving on. Risk and failure is part of human agency. "Saving people" from risks is taking away their dignity. The stories in this book help readers put failure and accomplishment into perspective.

Standing up in the crowd with stigmatized experiences is courageous. We know from history that people of courage are ultimately those who replace injustice with opportunity:

people of color; men and women; people of all sexual orientation; young and old; and people with disabilities, including those that come from psychiatric disorders. The authors of this book are our heroes. We are a varied lot coming from different parts of the world, with different challenges and paths to recovery, and different styles in telling our story. Hence, as editors, we decided to stay very close to each person's voice because people disclose their stories in very different ways. Celebration of diversity is essential to coming out.

> One isn't necessarily born with courage, but one is born with potential. Without courage, we cannot practice any other virtue with consistency. We can't be kind, true, merciful, generous, or honest.
>
> Maya Angelou

Who should come out? There are excellent examples, well known in American culture, including film stars like Rod Steiger, Patty Duke, and Margot Kidder; sports celebrities like Brandon Marshall; political leaders like Patrick Kennedy, and news reporters like Mike Wallace. These are beacons of integrity that inspire the public to pause and be mindful of ways we stigmatize. Although these leaders provide the clarion call for people to stand up, heroes are like the authors herein; what Elckerjick called EVERYMAN in his 15th century play. Real stigma change occurs when co-workers, neighbors, family, sports team members, and others come out. It makes the public stop and think, "You are just like me." We are not, however, seeking to pass as everyone, show ourselves as normal. Mental illness and recovery are part of many of our identities;

passing as normal is another way of being in the closet. We call for solidarity here. We ask other people to stand with us as we are.

Our courage does not arise from the battlefield with the Shakespearean hero. There is not a key moment where authors stood, gave voice, and triumphed; stigma did not slink away. The stigma wars are ongoing and ordinary. They occur every day, everywhere, among almost everyone. Ordinary might not seem courageous. But it is the person who toils daily towards some goal that describes the true human enterprise. Slamming the door of the closet might get attention and have momentary impact. But being out makes the person an everyday beacon of truth.

> Umbrella, light, landscape, sky;
> There is no language of the holy.
> The sacred lies in the ordinary.
>
> Deng Ming-Dao
> Tao master

This book began as a journey. Jon Larson, Patrick Michaels, and I advertised for authors to tell their stories in April 2014 and received more than 100 replies of interest. We asked people to go beyond stories of recovery to add their experience with the ideas of coming out, pride, and solidarity. Jon, Patrick, and I entered into partnership with prospective authors, exchanging drafts of their stories. Editorial feedback was not presumptuous; never did we suggest a specific message be omitted or added. Instead, we attempted to dialogue with authors, perhaps inquiring about a message in order to accentuate his or her voice. Some essays flowed well. Others required exchange between author and editor until the author was in a good place. Some authors may have decided to pull their essay if they were unhappy with its final product. As editors, we excluded no pieces. By the way; we do not see this text as one and done. Stigma will be erased as the mass of people who are out grows. The Coming Out Proud program and this text are meant to start the process.

We thank many people who helped and inspired us. Jon, Patrick, and I have worked with people with lived experience and others in sharing our Coming Out Proud program. In the process, we have worked and been inspired by Sara Abelson, Maya Al-Khouja, Khatera Aslami, Jennifer Boyd, Carl Blumenthal, Blythe Buchholz, David Castro, Rachel Del Rossi, Malia Fontecchio, Michael Gause, Kristin Kosyluk, Magdalena Kulesza, Richard Krzyzanowski, Jonathon Larson, Robert Lundin, Keith Mahar, Glen McClintock, Sue McKenzie, Dinesh Mittal, Keris Myrick, Ingrid Ozols, Janice Parker, Mike Pietrus, Nicolas Rusch, Annie Schmidt, Lindsay Sheehan, Heather Stuart, Alessandra Torres, Kelechi Ubozoh, Suzette Urbashich, Steve Valdez, Eduardo Vega, and Stephanie Welch. Special thanks to Katherine Nieweglowski for significant help in editing the manuscript and Maya Al-Khouja for designing front and back covers.

Patrick W. Corrigan
January 12, 2015

To men and women of vision and courage
who each day herald the call for solidarity.

What's There to be Proud of?
Patrick W. Corrigan

Nervous breakdowns, failures, hospitals, broken promises, cracked relationships: what is there to be proud of? I don't come easily to the notion that pride defines the experience of many people who identify themselves with mental illness and in recovery; it has been a 20 year journey for me. However, I am certain Coming Out Proud is an important

Patrick W. Corrigan

vision for many. In this essay, I review evidence that supports my beliefs, some that reflects my research, others represent my lived experience. At the scientist level I know pride is a meaningful product of recovery. At the personal level, I have experienced accomplishment and am more authentic by coming out with dignity.

I have been studying the stigma of mental illness for more than 15 years, having written six books on the topic as well as more than 100 peer-reviewed articles. I head the National Consortium on Stigma and Empowerment which has been supported by the National Institute of Mental Health for 15 years. I am a licensed clinical psychologist who has set up rehabilitation programs for people with mental illness seeking to help them with vocational, independent living, and health goals. During this time, I have also been beaten by the stigma of mental illness. I am a person who has struggled with and often overcome by significant symptoms of depression anxiety. I know what it means to be crippled by panic on one hand -- overwhelmed by stress, not being able to calm down -- and overwhelming sadness on the other -- literally glued to my chair and unmotivated. I have tried a variety of meds for more than 25 years, some helpful, others that cause wicked side effects. I know the embarrassment of going to an emergency program and having to recount my history to the psychiatry resident for the tenth time. I know the shame of being hospitalized, having my teenage children, Abe and Liz, visiting dad, terribly confused by what was happening. My parents are blue-collar trades people; the mental hospital was as foreign to them as a trip to Singapore. I remember once, when being admitted to a hospital for physical reasons, telling Abe and Liz, "This time; Daddy's not nuts!" I attended conferences for years on mental health and stigma, knowing the issues applied to me, but not standing up and out as a person with mental illness. Stigma is not just a scholarly thing for me; it's personal.

What is Stigma?
Stigma is stereotype, prejudice, and discrimination. Public and self-stigma hamper the lives of many people with mental illness. Public stigma occurs when the population endorses stereotypes about mental illness (people are dangerous, incompetent, and responsible for their mental illness) and discriminates as a result. Many of the employment, independent living, and health goals of people with mental illness are blocked by a public that endorses prejudice. Employers do not want to hire people with mental illness or provide them with reasonable accommodations. Landlords do not want to rent quality units or provide access to full support systems. Health care providers offer a lower standard of treatment. Research on this last point is particularly sobering. A study by Ben Druss from Emery University examined the practice of primary care providers in

the VA. Druss tested the degree to which veterans were referred to cardiologists if they presented symptoms consistent with heart trouble. He found that 100% of patients were referred to cardiac care clinic unless the primary care doctor knew the patient had a mental health history. In that case, only about 50% of patients labeled with mental illness were referred. These were not ignorant people discriminating against individuals with mental illness, these were physicians who should be fairly well-educated about psychiatric disorders. This was not an irrelevant result but, rather, a case of life and death!

Public stigma concerned me personally. The Illinois Department of Professional Regulation asked about my mental health history when I applied for my license in 1990. "Yes or no? Have you ever been diagnosed with mental illness?" I was not going to admit my history fearing the licensing board might throw up hurdles. I could not practice in the state without the license. (Might I be risking action by the State admitting my response to the 1990 application?) Nor did I let my colleagues know. Although wounded healers are common metaphors for mental health professionals, I was aware colleagues look askance at the psychologist who cannot manage his illness. I also knew about the gallows humor that punctuates our practice. Being overwhelmed by the troubles of our clients, some professionals might laugh them off with dark humor: "that's just a case of the nuts running the nut house." Colleagues who were out with their mental illness were often butts of these kinds of jokes.

Self-stigma occurs when some people internalize the stereotypes of mental illness, applying it to themselves. Self-stigma harms peoples' sense of self-esteem and self-efficacy leading to the "why try" effect. Why should I try to get a job; someone like me is not worth it. Why should I try to live in my own apartment; I am not able. Why should I try to be a psychologist; I can't handle it. Think of self-stigma's implication for someone who is already depressed and anxious. It deepens the sense of shame that accompanies the illness. "Why try" was THE hurdle in my life, believing I could not handle graduate school or professional jobs, dropping out precipitously, often after only a week or two. The reader needs to understand the depth of this problem. I dropped out of Creighton University medical school after a semester. Med school was a lifelong dream that was crushed under the demands of gross anatomy, biochemistry, and embryology. I dropped out of the PhD program in clinical psychology at IIT after a summer session. I dropped out of an NSF-funded PhD program in the philosophy of science at University of Chicago after one week. I dropped out of an NIMH-post doc at UCLA after a year. I almost quit my first faculty position at the University of Chicago medical school after one week. I dropped out of a faculty position at Northwestern University after a year. While my wife and friends were accomplishing their goals, I was at the curb sheepishly looking on, very doubtful about my future.

Erasing stigma is not enough. We also must promote affirming attitudes. (1) People with mental illness recover; that is the rule, not the exception. (2) People with mental illness can achieve their goals. (3) Mental health services should be dominated by hope. If there was a sad irony to my education, it was the lesson I learned about serious mental illness and expected POOR prognosis. I learned in my class on abnormal psychology that illnesses like schizophrenia were defined by "a progressive downhill course." The expectation of people with this diagnosis was to end up on the back ward of a state institution, catatonic and unable to care for one's self. The kind thing, so we were told, was to prepare people and their families for this inevitability, to help them mourn their irretrievable losses. We stole hope from them! Sometimes the logic was circular. If a person diagnosed with a serious mental illness recovered, then they were never seriously ill to begin with.

Recovery is a vision of hope and accomplishment that replaced the wrongheaded notions of poor outcome. Programs need to foster beliefs in recovery: inject hope right back where it belongs. Recovery did not emerge from the professional and research community. People with lived experience gave voice to its wisdom. I remember, as a second-year psychiatry professor in 1992 listening to Andrea Schmook tell her story of recovery and accomplishment thinking, "what a load of politically correct crap." Andrea was a person with serious mental illness having been hospitalized many times. After seeing her, however, I thought Andrea never had a serious mental illness. People with the real serious ones are unable to do more than work a few hours a day on a janitorial crew. But I also observed the infectious spread of her messages. Others with lived experience quickly embraced recovery moving it from pipedream to predominant vision of our time. Researchers, as we often do, came along later showing recovery is a factual reality. Long term follow-up studies where people with serious mental illness were tracked for 20 years or more, found a rule of thirds. A third of this group pretty much got over their mental illness like a respiratory infection, recovering and going on with life. A third managed their illness just fine when adopting the same kind of chronic disease strategies one might consider for addressing something like diabetes. Most of the last third were able to accomplish their goals when they received the kind of evidence-based treatments that comprise a competent treatment system: self-determined medication management along with supported employment, education, and housing.

Advocates need to take a step beyond affirming attitudes to promote affirmative behaviors. Most countries in the Western world now have some version of the Americans with Disabilities Act (ADA) which bans discrimination to people diagnosed with serious mental illness. Woe to the employer, landlord, or primary care provider who withhold rightful opportunities to someone because of psychiatric label. Equally important to the ADA is provisions for reasonable accommodations. Employers, for example, need to adapt work settings so people are able to complete their jobs. These are affirmative behaviors. We expect employment settings to be set up so people in wheel chairs can easily access their desk or work station.

Accommodations for people with psychiatric disabilities have been slower in coming and harder to define. In fact, the ADA was in place for five years until the US Equal Employment Opportunity Commission formally stated the law applied to people with psychiatric disabilities, not just physical disabilities. It now seems reasonable for work supervisors to consider requests for moving employees to quieter spaces, or allow them to adjust work periods to meet medication schedules. More progressive versions of reasonable accommodations might include on-site job coaches for the interested employee, coaches that help the person adapt to in-the-day stresses providing prompts or feedback to specific coping skills. I set up and evaluated this kind of program in Peoria, Illinois where, for example, job coaches dropped in on a worker at the local Walmart, providing support and meeting with the supervisor in an effort to make sure all parties were satisfied.

Affirmative behaviors and reasonable accommodations are not charity; they are the rightful expectations of people with disabilities. The Civil Rights Act was passed in 1964 to make sure that people of color have the same chance as the white majority. The ADA provides similar assurances. It is absurd, by the way, to argue that affirmative behaviors provide unfair advantage to the person with disabilities. Reasonable accommodations level the playing field.

Accommodations are not unlimited. There are caps to reasonable accommodations, requests that cause "undue hardship" on employers and their business. Many 9-to-5 offices, for example, might find it difficult for workers to come in at midnight to do their work. However, our Peoria experience suggests the ADA and reasonable accommodations are not experienced as intrusive or demanding by most employers. Bosses want their workers to be successful, in part, because employers are reasonable human beings, and in part because these kinds of accommodations are wise policy. Businesses fail when they terminate and then need to train a new batch of employees.

How Do We Erase Stigma and Promote Affirmation?

Americans, like most Western countries, believe education is the secret to changing social behaviors. Drug Abuse Resistance Education (D.A.R.E.) is a prominent example in teaching our children life behaviors and drug risks so they have the skills necessary to avoid drug abuse in later years. My children, Abe and Liz, attended D.A.R.E. at Churchill School during second and third grade. In similar vein, education programs have been established to address other social concerns. Among these are programs meant to address the stigma of mental illness by contrasting myths with facts.

Myth: People with mental illness choose to have their symptoms because they have weak character.

Fact: Most mental illnesses are medical illnesses.

People do not choose to be depressed.

The NIMH started the decade of the brain in 1990 partly to tear down the stigma that rests on this myth. Mental illness is a brain disorder. Proponents believed members of the general public exposed to this message would blame individuals for their mental illness less.

How well do education programs work? Contrary to what might be expected, findings about D.A.R.E. are consistently negative and sobering; research from Harvard, the California Department of Education, and the American Psychological Association concluded D.A.R.E. had no meaningful effects on drug behavior, such that the U.S. Surgeon General in 2001 declared D.A.R.E. to be an ineffective program, at times leading to a boomerang effect where impact on drug use may worsen. How about education against stigma: mental illness is a brain disorder. What is its impact? While research consistently shows the message decreases blame, it too yields a rebound effect. Members of the general public who learn mental illness is a brain disorder believe individuals with psychiatric illness do not get better. The latter belief is the more damning. Employers will not hire and landlords will not rent to people who are not getting better.

Contact is the alternative approach to challenging public prejudice and discrimination. Members of the general population who have contact with people in recovery show significant reductions in stigma. Recovery stories meant to tear down stigma usually have four components:

(1) on-the-way-down messages, experiences with symptoms and disabilities of a person's illness;

(2) on-the-way-up rejoinders, despite my illness I have accomplished goals;

(3) stigma experiences, despite my recovery I have been victimized by public prejudice; and

(4) call for change; we need to stop the stigma to promote full opportunity.

To determine the impact of contact versus education, my research group completed a summary of the 70+ research studies on the approaches to stigma change in 2012. Results showed contact's impact on prejudicial attitudes and discriminatory behaviors are twice those of education immediately following the intervention. In addition, analyses showed follow-up effects to contact are still obvious up to a month later while any benefits to education return to baseline at follow-up. Let us understand the take home message here. Power to change stigma lies in the hands of people with lived experience, not an expert. I have a much bigger impact on the public when I share my personal experiences of illness and recovery than when I pull out my books and talk as a professor.

Contact also seems to positively impact self-stigma. Many people who identify and interact with peers who openly discuss their illness typically show less depression, more hope, and better self-esteem. Our research showed people who are out and share their stories exhibit personal empowerment and pride. For myself: I did not ever perceive being in the closet, a sense of shame or something I needed to carefully guard. In part, the support of my wife and parents combatted this problem. But a noticeable change occurred when I did start to disclose my story. I felt fuller; like the world is seeing me now, warts and all. I liked the complete "ME" being out there.

Coming Out Proud

Coming Out hits stigma and promotes recovery with a double punch. First, it weakens self-stigma. People who come out with their mental illness have better health and well-being. Second, it erases public stigma. Contact is the tool that undermines prejudice and discrimination. This leads to what I call the atomic bomb for erasing stigma. When we realize that our co-workers, neighbors, and fellow faith-based community members have mental illness and are in recovery, prejudices will be snuffed out. Contact needs people who are out with their mental illness.

Coming out proud? Is pride a fair word here? After all; I dropped out of school (four times), got hospitalized, had side effects, and disappointed my family. Is this an accomplishment to wear on my sleeve with honor? Depression and anxiety, what's to be proud of? Let's consider these questions from lessons learned from other oppressed groups. Social justice advocates now realize people from other minority groups should embrace their identity and heritage. Earlier, in the 1950's for example, some wrongly preached a vision of color-blindness, that Americans should ignore skin color and view everyone similarly. This was mostly an attempt to promote the white majority while suppressing blacks. We learned since then that black pride is the better way to promote justice for this group. African Americans learning about their background come to cherish their history and embrace their group. Similarly, Latinos, Asians, Native Americans and Pacific Islanders are all urged to know their culture and honor its roots. Female empowerment leads to feminist studies. Proponents of gay rights recognize the need for the LGBTQ community to embrace each other with pride.

Does that hold for mental illnesses or are things fundamentally different with us? Unlike blacks, gays, or women, isn't the number one goal of being a part of the depressed group to get out of it? When I am sad, without hope, and suicidal, I will do ANYTHING to erase the pain. When I started my career in mental illness -- my sophomore year at Creighton University -- I hurried to the counseling center in the administration building seeking the magic bullet to make the pain go away. If I become symptomatic again, I will do most anything to make it stop; I've taken my share of medication cocktails over the years, some with fairly significant side effects. I remember having to slowly walk down the stairs of Union Station one evening certain that I would fall because of the jitters from lithium. I would do so again if it would make the depression end. Mental illness? No, no, that's not me.

But somewhere along the way something changed. Mental illness became part of who I am. I am Pat Corrigan, a son, husband, father, psychologist, Irishman, Chicagoan... and person with mental illness. When and how mental illness got added to the list I am not sure. But many people at some point include some aspects of mental illness and recovery in pictures of themselves. Not everyone does so; I would still expect most of the people I meet early in psychotherapy to believe their symptoms will remit and they will go on with life untouched. Most of the research suggests they are right. However, there are other people who, as a result of their illness, corresponding treatments, and reactions of others add mental illness and recovery to the self-statements that define who they are.

So I am a person with mental illness. Is this something to be proud of? Definitions of pride include two components: accomplishment and authenticity. Accomplishments are defined by external criteria as well as personal goals. I was proud when I came in first for my age group at the Morton Grove 5K race. I was also proud when I beat my personal best time at a second 5K in Glenview. Are there accomplishments related to my mental illness for which I am proud? I've earned a doctorate in psychology, authored or edited more than a dozen books, and am a distinguished faculty member at my university (one of only twelve among the 400 faculty). The victories inherent in overcoming my depression and anxiety trumps those accomplishments manifold. I remember being physically crushed and bent over when I got out of the hospital in 2005. I had two children in school and had to get back to work. A marathon seemed less daunting than the hurdles here. What happened if I could not hack it? What if the chairman of the department found I was missing meetings and appointments? I got through it though with the help of family and good care from Dr. McSay. My dad was amazing. He was struggling with emphysema at the time and had to ride a scooter hooked up to an oxygen bottle in the front basket. Every morning he picked me up at home and drove me to my office. He then sat in the room next to mine watching daytime TV and reading the Tribune; every half hour he would knock on the door and ask how I was. He took me to lunch and then home in the evening. He took me to medical appointments and to the pharmacy. He did this full time for two weeks and then slowly decreased the support. This was among the toughest times in my life. As I write this now, my heart beats fast reminding me how hard this was. Getting back on my work feet surpassed all the challenges of grad school and moving up the faculty rank.

We have to be careful with ideas of pride and accomplishment. It might suggest people with mental illness need to meet some kind of hurdle to claim accomplishment: beat their symptoms entirely to score a success. For many, symptoms and disabilities do not disappear totally. I personally must still be mindful of stressful events (usually at work) where anxiety spins out of control. Hence, we should not hang the victory of recovery on some kind of artificial criteria like three months without depression, or two years without hallucinations, or back to full-time work, or living by one's self in an apartment. Enlightened views of recovery base the experience on a renewed sense of hope and personally meaningful accomplishment. People with schizophrenia do not have to graduate college to be a success. Perhaps an associate's degree, or a certificate, or an adult education course, or a class at the local park district captures their goal. People with bipolar disorder may continue to struggle with euphoria and disinhibitions, but do so in ways that do not throw their life off kilter: no longer getting arrested or finding credit card bills well past their limit. People with depression do not have to go back to an executive position full time. Perhaps a job with fewer hours a week, less demanding work, or volunteering meets their goals. Accomplishment is meeting one's personally defined goals.

Pride is also an issue of authenticity or embracing who you are. I am fourth generation Irish American. My great grandfather came over to the Chicago suburbs about 100 years ago. I am fairly far removed from my Irish roots. But I am proud of being an Irish American, especially every March 17 when Chicago dyes the river green. It is who I am, a part of my story that stands out for me. People who know me over time hear me sing Danny Boy or share one of my trips to the ole sod. My favorite among these was two years ago when I was in Dublin for St. Patrick's Day. That is a holiday of pride for the Celts.

I share an extra personal admission about authenticity. I am a trained operant and cognitive therapist with views about good therapy based on Skinner and Beck. I once ran a training center for Illinois, visiting state hospitals to set up token economies. Words like authenticity scared me, always seeming mushy and of no real value in helping people meet real-world goals. "Authenticity" scared me until I tried to make sense of who I am; why do I need to add experiences of illness and recovery to my stories of family and professional accomplishments? Authenticity, for me, is the full picture; nothing hidden. I admit that in weak moments authenticity still seems a little flaky to me as a therapy goal, something an existentialist (my god) might pursue rather than an evidence-based clinician. But as a human, friend, and peer, authenticity -- putting who I am out there -- has immense worth.

The Coming Out Proud Program

Although coming out proud has advantages, we still need to be wise about disclosing. Coming out clearly has its risks; if not, I could have skipped the past several pages about the nasty effects of prejudice and discrimination. Although I believe coming out is a good decision for some, it might not work for others. People need to make the decision carefully. To paraphrase a U.S. Supreme Court judge; it is hard to stop the clanging bell. Once you are out, it is hard to go back in. I would like to think others would receive my story respectfully and with acceptance. But, I also know aspects of my story are juicy tidbits; excellent gossip is also likely to occur. Did you hear Professor Corrigan was once locked up in the psych unit at Evanston Hospital? For this reason, we developed the three lessons of the Coming Out Proud program.

First, program participants weigh the pros and cons of disclosing; what are the benefits and the risks in sharing one's story with others. Many of us live in a compartmentalized world: for me, what happens at work can be fairly segregated from home and church. Hence, costs and benefits need to be considered by setting. For example, program participants might be instructed to list the pros and cons of coming out at their work. My work list includes many benefits. I get to align myself with peers whose courage I admire. I share a more complete story about myself. I do not have to worry about other people discovering my secrets. I have been out publicly for about five years so few risks are now on my list. Occasionally, I am concerned a colleague will disapprove of my disclosure. I don't particularly care about their disapproval of me, only that they might discount my science. "Corrigan's research is not rigorous because he is biased." I also have a more complex concern; I don't belong in the cadre of heroes that are out. "I am not as sick as those who I admire." I never heard voices, never attempted suicide, and was only hospitalized once. I have not earned the right to step out with those who have had greater challenges.

I am also concerned about whether coming out is self-serving. Sometimes it seems that the net of mental illness and recovery includes everyone. Depression and anxiety are not rare; almost everyone has stories of overwhelming sadness, stress, and exhaustion at times in their life. They handle it quietly and with dignity, seemingly not needing to be on a platform to tell their story. I come from a stoic family where public displays are not encouraged; as a child, I recall my parents never discussing with relatives how my brother, Mike, and I were doing in school or extracurricular activities, even though we both were fairly successful. Perhaps my public disclosures are self-congratulatory pats on the back.

Lastly, I loathe pity, absolutely hate it. I therefore do not want to tell my story if people sympathize with me. I remember in a men's group at church once telling my story when Bob DuCharme clapped me on the shoulder and said, "Wow, Pat. You really deal with a lot. I'm impressed with everything you have done." I was ashamed and angry. "I didn't tell you this, Bob, so you would pity me." As I sit at my desk and write this now, I wonder from where these reactions come. Perhaps it reflects the stoic, Irish male I have learned to be, the person who does not like the limelight for its own sake. Perhaps it also reflects my need to open myself to the good wishes and support of others. I learned a bit more about myself while on the coming out journey.

Pros and cons differ over time and place. My list would vary when comparing today to ten years ago. A different profile emerged in Coming Out to my faith-based community, a very recent venture. I and my wife are Unitarian, a creedless church dedicated to the responsible search for truth in order to promote the inherent worth and dignity of all. We are a pretty hip place with Sunday services in this well-lit, nature-grounded church. Unitarian ministers take summers off at which time services are led by members. A few years back, I volunteered to lead a July service on stigma and empowerment and anchored my sermon with my own story. I had never talked publicly about my experiences in a setting outside the relatively-safe mental health community but believed a Unitarian church would be a welcoming place. My parents attended along with my wife and daughter, the first time I talked publicly about my experiences with them present. After telling my story, I highlighted the lessons of coming out and solidarity, ending with something I had not done before. "I would like everyone here with a history of mental health challenges stand with me today." Unitarians are people who joined civil rights marches and freedom buses. I thought this would be easy and I would soon be joined by a quarter of the congregation. Of the 150 in attendance, only four stood. Many people were appreciative of my message during the coffee hour after the service; I do not in any way regret my disclosure. But I was surprised about the reaction; or the absence of reaction. I once learned from an advocate friend that an especially hard response to get to one's coming out story is nothing: no reaction.

Second, program participants consider different ways of disclosing. Some people are still not prepared to tell their story because the costs of disclosure at a specific setting far outweigh the benefits. They choose to keep it a secret. Others want to come out loud and proud, believing the more people that know their story, the more stigma will be crushed and opportunities may open. They choose to shout their story from the roof tops. A third group is in between these extremes; they are cautious and selectively disclose. The Coming Out Proud program includes strategies people might use to test the waters before sharing their stories with selected people.

Third, participants learn how to craft stories that meets their goals. There are two elements to this task. (1) People who decide to come out need to consider their goals ahead of time. People might disclose at work to obtain reasonable accommodations from supervisors, identify peers at work with similar challenges, or feel relief of no longer hiding an important part of themselves. There are no right or wrong goals but there is benefit to discussing one's expectations with peers in the program, obtaining feedback so the person is not sadly disappointed by their subsequent disclosure. "I thought Sharon, my co-worker would be friendly and invite me to socialize on weekends. But she didn't."

(2) People should decide what, of the many facets of their lives, they might disclose. "What do I want my co-worker to know about me?" Once again, discussing this with program peers prior to actually disclosing at work can diminish disappointments. "Sherry wants to tell people she tried to kill herself by hanging." Bert, a program peer, wonders whether that is a bit more info than necessary. Like goals, there is no right or wrong decision here, only the wisdom of considering one's story before sharing with others.

People should not feel compelled to tell any aspect of their story. There is no first principle on what should or should not be discussed. Generally, people coming out should not report issues that are still traumatizing or stressful for them. Most of the stressors that led me to being overwhelmed with anxiety and depression are work related. I dropped out of school and jobs because I felt the demands of the situation overwhelmed my ability to cope. "How come everyone else in med school can handle the ceaseless hours of anatomy and biochemistry? What's wrong with me?" The only way I got a doctorate in psychology was to attend a professional school part-time and at nights when I could control the demands. One thing I will not discuss publicly now is current stressors at work, things that potentially might overwhelm me. They are current and raw. Admitting them will cause more harm than benefit.

Solidarity

I learned a lot about solidarity from Abe and Liz's attitudes about gays and lesbians. They do not understand my generation's hostilities and would never expect a gay or lesbian friend to hide their identity. Abe has a t-shirt that sums it up nicely: "Gay? Fine by me." This is not so in terms of mental illness. I learned in graduate school that people should not adopt a patient identity. They should overcome their symptoms, be cured, and move on. Normalcy is the goal; pass for everyone else. I believe, however, that solidarity is a vision for coming out proud.

"I stand with mental illness." The message has several parts. Clearly there is ownership and solidarity because "I" join people with mental illness. I decide to get up out of my chair and move next to those out with their mental illness. Memorable pictures from the civil rights movements show whites stepping up and joining blacks as they march across the Selma bridge or to the Woolworth's lunch counter together. Standing and marching are active. "I stand with

I stand with mental illness.

www.COPprogram.org

mental illness" has an important double meaning. The person exhibiting the message may be saying, "I have a mental illness too." I stand here publicly showing the world. I do so proudly. The coming out proud movement seeks to upset the status quo.

Going Forward

I have said it before and I will say it again. I will do just about anything with Dr. McSay to keep the depression and anxiety from overwhelming me again. I am blessed by a wife and family who have provided infinite support and have beat my symptoms accordingly. I am 58 now and have a better mastery of things and, like in the past, hope my depression and anxiety are gone. I know, however, that it could rear its ugly head despite my efforts. I also know that I have been marked by my experiences with symptoms, treatments, and recovery, a mark which has proudly influenced my identity and my story. I am privileged to live in a community which has honored my coming out of the closet. I have a hope that someday everyone else will feel similarly safe and honored.

About the author. Pat Corrigan has a 25-year career leading to distinguished professor of psychology at the Illinois Institute of Technology and Principal Investigator of the National Consortium on Stigma and Empowerment (www.ncse1.org). He is also married to Georgeen Carson for more than 30 years; they live in a Chicago suburb and have two children with whom they are immensely proud. They have a golden retriever named Cleo and like to travel together. During this time, Pat has seen more than ten psychiatrists, been hospitalized for mental illness, learned to master his symptoms, and come out proud.

Mind the Gap
Jon E. Larson

The reason why the world lacks unity, and lies broken and in heaps, is, because man is disunited with himself.

Ralph Waldo Emerson

Jon Larson ¼ Mile Drag Racing at the Great Lakes Dragway

Road trip. 1,946 miles roundtrip from Chicago to Charleston, SC. My 2012 Can Am Spyder packed with road and camping supplies. A full face helmet secured to my bald head. I pushed play on my IPod nano velcroed to my fuel tank with "Bohemian Like You" by Dandy Warhols streaming in my ear pods. I twisted my throttle and hammered the 998cc V-twin engine while riding east on Illinois county roads; 20 minutes later I merged on to I-94 heading south. Cool clean air rushed through my helmet. Open road. PTSD symptoms in check. Headache free. Senses intensified.

Numerous aspects of my life consisted of being spontaneous and going with the flow. *Gnothi Seauton* or *Know Thyself*. Even road tripping I spent little time planning for camp sites and mapping routes, but, instead, I carried an atlas to use when lost. However, I obsessed on reading safety books and shop manuals, wrenching my own maintenance and modifications, and matching riding gear with the weather.

I obtained expert gear advice from my buddy Sanchez, a pro racer at Motorider. I always wore microfiber skull cap, HJC full-face helmet, amber protective glasses, and beat up Turnpike Cruiser leather boots. For hot weather I geared up with microfiber t-shirt, light leather motorcycle cut jacket, 511 Levis, Alpinestars leather gloves, and knee high leather chaps that I crafted during a long winter without riding. Cool weather and drag racing gear included full body microfiber for wicking, armored Joe Rocket leather pants, armored Spidi thick leather jacket, Joe Rocket leather gloves, balaclava, and mesh scarf. I carried rain gear and, for freezing weather, I threw on a layer of wool between microfiber and leather. Leather provided superior wind blockage and I avoided wearing boots with laces and bell bottoms since both could become wrapped up in engine parts.

I burned 3 tanks of fuel while unsuccessfully dodging thunderstorms, eventually reaching Fort Boonesborough State Park in Kentucky late Sunday night. I pulled into the state park entrance. Campgroup closed. While contemplating my next move, I noticed headlights moving closer and hearing the distinctive engine popping of a 2-cylinder John Deere tractor. The tractor stopped next to me with a male voice asking if I needed help. I responded that I needed a place to camp. He replied that he could help and to follow him. Apprehensive, I pulled down a dirt lane and parked next to a large barn. A lanky man early 30s hopped off his idling tractor; we shook hands and introduced ourselves. Gunner said that he owned this barn and surrounding land with his farmhouse located 400 rods to the north. He offered his barn or pasture as a place to crash. I took the barn option and thanked him. He got back on his tractor and headed north. I unrolled and crawled into my sleeping bag on the dirt floor while noticing plants hanging in the rafters. I tucked my shortened Louisville Slugger bat underneath my sleeping bag.

I read a few chapters of Jim Harrison's *A Good Day to Die*. Calm sleep overtook my uneasiness.

Next morning I packed my sleeping bag and slipped my Louisville under the Can Am seat. Gunnar pulled up on his Honda 500cc ATV towing another Honda ATV. I fired up Gunnar's second ATV and helped him with morning chores. After riding trails through creeks and woods, we stopped at a section of land with rows of cannabis plants. Gunner explained that he obtained a government certification to produce and sell organic marijuana to the University of Louisville. Huge money. Current state law allowed Kentucky universities with medical schools to dispense medical marijuana and to conduct research. Gunnar scored his contract through his uncle, a board trustee at the University of Louisville. We ATVed trails to the Hickory Grill for lunch of roasted pheasant with sautéed mushrooms and cottage fries. After riding back to his barn, Gunnar offered a black plastic bag sealed with a green Kentucky tax stamp. I thanked him for everything and stuck the bag in my first aid kit and hit the road.

Third day northwest of the Great Smoky Mountains, I turned off Kodak Road and parked at the Shoals Tavern overlooking the French Broad River in Tennessee. I strolled in and sat on a barstool eventually meeting Parker, a Vietnam Veteran and retired logger. I assumed he went by his last name but didn't bother to clarify. We split a bottle of Famous Grouse and traded road tales; he dropped bits of wisdom while I revealed my early years of troublemaking. After farm chores, I fueled and kick started a blue Honda C110; I rode down our pasture lane and headed out on country roads. A toolbox and spare parts bungee strapped to the seat. I welded a bracket to the back fender to carry a spare tire. I toured 100 miles roundtrip before running out of fuel, learning this important fact the hard way. Other times I rode a sunburst Honda CB350 with a range of 200 miles. Being way too young for an Illinois motorbike license, I avoided county deputies by staying off hard roads and bypassing towns. Being sly came easy.

Parker knew area mountain roads and pulled out a map and highlighted a route used by locals to avoid tourist traffic. While swigging whisky, he meticulously explained his route through the Smokies and handed the map to me. His obscure route started in Kodak, Tennessee passing by Clingman's Dome at 6643 feet and ending up at the Eastern Cherokee Reservation in North Carolina. Empty bottle and early evening, I grabbed the walnut bar and stood up from the leather barstool. While shaking hands. I thanked him for his mountain pass. As I reached for the front door Parker reminded me to mind the gap, meaning to keep plenty of space between my fuel tank and vehicles ahead of me. I walked outside and grabbed my camping bag while leaving my Can Am parked at Shoals. I rambled half a mile down a dirt lane to set up camp on a river gravel bar, crawled into my sleeping bag, and crashed.

Fourth evening. The sun snuck behind turquoise mountains as mist rolled across the road and stalled underneath Fraser Fir trees. I estimated 10 minutes until sunset. I pulled off Newfound Gap and stopped at an observation site. I stretched while sitting on top of my V-twin humming at 1500 RPMs. Relaxing. I focused my mini flash light on Parker's prized map secured to my tank bag. I mulled my first option, thrust my throttle and focused all 106 hp on taking Newfound Gap to Cherokee and setting up camp. This move involved riding 27 miles on a twisty dark road through heavy mist while dodging road kill. Second option required hiding my Can Am and camp site deep in the woods undetectable from the road. A Parker teaching. Option two won.

After half a mile down an elk trail, I killed my engine and without delay pulled off my riding leathers and quickly set up camp. I sprawled on the pine needle ground to smoke a pipe of Latakia and Tennessee Barley blend. Unzipped my coffin-sized tent and squeezed into my ultralight cocoon sleeping bag. Closed my eyes to notice blackness behind my eyelids. Passing thoughts sped up and moved as a slide projector. *Age 19. Sports injury. Struck above left ear with blunt force. Swirling yellow lights. Knocked out. Near death coma started. Head surgery. Injury close to my left almond shaped amygdala. A mid brain structure connected to processing emotions, learning, fear, memories, and flight or fight responses. Eyes opened. Feet tucked under white sheets. Immediate thought after waking from coma, 'Oh shit I'm back.' Painless body flushed with anger moving to rage. Blank memory of past few days. Recovered and left hospital with a bucket full of meds and diagnoses of TBI and PTSD at 19 years old.* Slide projector images continued in my mind. *PTSD intertwined with near death coma and trauma. PTSD images flashed. Emotionally numb. Flashbacks. Racing heart. Sweaty palms. Avoiding people. Poor sleep. Easily startled. Tense, on edge, and irritable. Frequent night terrors. Mind filled with one new perspective still with me today. No fear of death. No rush of angst about today or tomorrow being my last day of life. No death wish, just flat empty reactions to my own death. Locked up my death mindset for years. Avoiding ways to heal. Averting triggers.* Images continued. *Disclosing personal thoughts and perspectives to family, friends, and practitioners. Intensity and frequency of PTSD symptoms, experiences, and images continue to vary in my life.* I cracked open my eyes with a strong shiver running through my bones. I felt extreme body tension and sweat. Everything seemed foggy, then I gained clarity of my current situation. I noticed moonlight sneaking through my tent and realized that I was mountain camping on my way to South Carolina. Calm breathing. Thoughts fleeted. Twilight mind shifted to sleep.

Day five. I woke and rolled out of my tent. I inhaled mountain air to clear my achy head. Took morning med, chewed beef jerky and tore down camp. I packed my tent and sleeping bag on top of road supplies, a tool kit, engine oil, spark plugs, fuel additive, light bulbs, tire repair kit, duct tape, rubber straps, Swiss army knife, first aid kit, clothes, shaving kit, cash, beef jerky, water bottle, atlas, and battery charger. After throwing on my helmet and starting my Can Am, I pushed play on my iPod Nano cranking "Squad Car Blues" by Black Cadillacs. I pulled out of the forest and headed south to a drag strip in Greer, SC. One-hundred miles later, I rolled through the front gate of Greer Dragway to pay fees and get race approval from track officials. I ran my own pre-race Can Am check, remembering to mind the gap, meaning to pull out both high performance spark plugs and use a feeler gage to set the electrode gap to 0.7 mm. Incorrect spark plug gap caused the V-twin to miss fire. To increase hp and speed, I installed a high-performance air filter system, designed and installed a cold air intake system, and replaced stock muffler with my own custom welded straight pipe.

After finishing my pre-race check, I walked around pit row and met Sunderson and Bjorn, a race team from Minnesota. Sunderson unfolded a third chair and invited me to sit in the shade of their Greyhound bus converted to haul motorbikes and accommodate living needs. I relaxed in the chair while cooling in the shade. We sipped Red Bull supplied by their sponsor; pros for sure when paid by others to race. We traded drag strategies and built a sense of unity through discussing personal aspects of racing; I shared that running ¼ mile races calmed my mind and relieved mental stressors. Bjorn mentioned his mechanical skills and thrill of speed came from service in the Air Force. I told them about my stint in the Corps. In my early 20s, I walked into a Texas Marine recruiting office and, 4 months later, I landed in San Diego for boot camp. My legal services occupation required authorized clearance leading to an extensive background check. My commanding officer bluntly informed me that clearance was denied and application discrepancies were uncovered. I lied on my initial military application withholding medical history of coma, PTSD, and medications. He explained 2 options: court martial or discharge. I picked number 2 and luckily received an honorable discharge 8 months before Operation Desert Shield, a precursor to Operation Desert Storm. Bittersweet. Sunderson and Bjorn listened and easily accepted my experiences with PTSD. When sharing my lived experiences with mental health, I experienced positive interactions with motorbike riders and racers leading to a sense of solidarity. Sunderson, Bjorn, and I traded more experiences before shaking hands; I wished them luck to place in the money and moseyed back to my pit spot. Before racing, I closed my eyes and noticed blackness and thoughts. *My personal recovery strengthened over the years. Accepting my life situations and taking ownership of my behaviors strengthened my resilience. Sharing and disclosing with others simultaneously calmed and energized me.* Slide projector switched to racing images. *Faster time by twisting the throttle on the third yellow light of the starting light tree. Leaving before the green light. Drag start strategy. Scrunched down. Helmet behind wind shield. Calm body. Eyes focused. Mind clear. 9000 rpms. Letting it all go. Soothing.* I opened my eyes and in a state for racing. After dragging 10 races, I rode 55 miles south to Sumter National Forest in SC and set up camp.

    The next afternoon I rolled into the parking lot of the Charleston Marriot Hotel location for an EEG conference. I checked into my room and showered off 6 days of road grit and napped for 2 hours. I got up and found a laundry mat to wash clothes and clean gear. Back at the hotel, I attended an evening conference reception while hanging out with friends and eventually crashing out while listening to a narration of

Richard Stark's *Butcher's Moon*. The next morning I delivered my presentation and attended workshops. Early evening, I rode to Folley Beach on the Atlantic Ocean. I walked the beach and found the Sand Dollar Social Club with live rock music. Groovy time. My daytimes consisted of workshops, and my evenings filled with shooting pool and listening to live music at the Sand Dollar Social Club.

When the conference ended, I packed and checked Can Am fluid levels and hit the road. 976 miles later I finished my road trip and headed to my nap hammock. Before dozing I noticed blackness behind eyelids while paying attention to floating thoughts. I observed images of *my mid-20s entering a jail and leaving a psychiatric hospital; busy picking up nasty habits while drifting from job to job.* More images flowed in. *Healing. Ongoing talk therapy. Psychiatrist support. Improving my life. Stability. Positive intentions. Disclosing my lived experiences and discovering solidarity. Pursuing my ambitions and life goals. Pursuing education. Facing my situations.* My thoughts shifted to current images of *minding the gap, taking care of self, maintaining my flow, finding meaningful work, protecting my calmness, chasing curiosity, learning through books, expressing gratitude, creating with my hands, and discovering zest in life.* Sleep came...

Suicidal Ideation: A Silent Esoteric Existence

Patrick J. Michaels

Patrick with 3-year old daughter (Zurielle) and 2-week old son (Oliver)

I was born in Madison, Wisconsin and raised by my parents along with my two younger sisters. My parents provided an opportunity-filled childhood with many adventures near and far. We went to the circus, Corvette car museum, Bad Lands of South Dakota, and Prince Edward Island. They sacrificed to give us grand opportunities; I took a 2-week Outward Bound trek through the Costa Rican rainforest, sleeping in tents or at farmsteads, met a medicine man with a waterfall in his backyard, and swam in the Pacific Ocean. It seemed we were only expected to be respectful, active community members. At church, I was an usher, altar boy, co-taught religious education, and participated in a 2-week mission trip in Mexico. At high school, I played tenor saxophone in the band, played right guard for the football team and was assistant stage director for Grease. On my 16th birthday, I earned my driver's license and received a gift of a 6-year old blue Buick Le Sabre. A car meant new freedoms, but also financial responsibilities, so I worked as a Walgreen's clerk 15-hours a week. My parent's 24-foot cabin cruiser was a summertime favorite, and I was allowed the privilege to use the powerboat with friends. I appreciate my middle class upbringing and consider it to be relatively normal, and yet adulthood has included bouts of major depression and debilitating anxiety with suicidal ideation. These lived experiences occurred despite studying psychology as an undergraduate and graduate student and researching mental illness stigma. This is my story of an eight-year long silent struggle enroute rock bottom, and how recovery and coming out were catalysts for emotional enlightenment ultimately bringing me peace, empowerment and social support.

College(s)

After graduating from a Catholic high school, I attended the University of South Carolina-Columbia. The palmetto trees and humid weather was my dream college ambiance. The dream began in middle school after my mom finished her Master's in Business Administration and dad received a 10-month paid severance package. My dad and I went weekly to the downtown Madison library to look through classified sections of newspapers for employment opportunities for him. I photocopied interesting human resource manager jobs for my mom in southern U.S. cities in hopes of moving near the ocean, palm trees and beach. We never moved, so studying psychology in Columbia was a dream come true.

The summer before college, I held three jobs, a Ford car dealership lot attendant, Walgreen's clerk and gas station cashier. Summer meant swimming, tubing, and skiing off of my parent's powerboat with friends. My high school girlfriend, Angie, and I broke up for the umpteenth time, normal for our on-again off-again relationship. This time, I was dedicated to quit: I avoided phone calls and refused to return messages. Avoidance gave me freedom. The last summer before college was truly memorable and carefree.

In August, my mom and sister, Claire, drove the 1,000-mile journey with me to Columbia. They helped me settle in, buy books, and decorate with an MC Escher poster of a melting clock. Before my mother hugged me in front of Preston Hall dormitory, she said, "We can make this college work [financially], but please do your best." I promised I would do my best, noticing two tiny tears in her blue eyes.

Columbia's campus was beautiful with old red brick paths and buildings, and large trees. My co-ed dorm was a haven for new friends. We attended home football games, watching Lou Holtz and his Gamecocks. I spent countless hours listening to downloaded music with my friend, Fiona. For Halloween, Fiona's friend Courtney double dog dared me to dress up as a cat in a tight gray white-spotted leotard, a tail and ears. That cat went dancing and watched a drag show. College was emancipating, and my dorm friends and I became quite close.

Mid semester, my dad visited after a meeting in southern Ohio. I told him about volunteering at a free medical clinic and my interest in psychiatry. After taking a career interest test, I upgraded my trajectory from psychologist to psychiatrist, so my goal was to go medical school to write prescriptions as well as provide therapy. He bought me a blue Raleigh mountain bike to save me travel time to the clinic, where once weekly I filed charts and organized medication in the pharmacy. Juggling extracurricular activities was a curriculum vita "must have" according to the Pre-med club; admission committees expect all medical school hopefuls to have excellent grades and a track record of involvement in clubs and organizations. No problem! I was determined to put in the effort and work hard. Except, my introductory biology grades were not good.   My first biology test grade earned me a D.   I thought, just keep trying, its first time jitters. False. The 2nd and 3rd tests were the same. My other course grades were okay. What I was doing wrong? I never skipped class and faithfully read my books. I saw an advertisement that said "stressed out?" from the counseling center. With one other student, the counseling center facilitators ran through a 90-minute PowerPoint presentation suggesting to eat balanced meals, avoid alcohol and drugs, sleep, exercise, socialize, and relax. I was doing all of the "right stuff." My mom suggested a tutor, which had helped me with high school Spanish. A tutor helped me improve my Biology grade dramatically, but short of my goal with a C+. I started thinking about transferring to a smaller college, my #2 choice: St. Norbert College. Transferring, even mid-year, to a cozier academic environment might pave the path to medical school. I went home at Thanksgiving to investigate. However, the idea of transferring was my dirty little secret from my dorm friends.

During Christmas break, my mom and I solidified the transfer. Then my dad and I returned to Columbia in early January in advance of my dorm friends. We packed and shipped my belongings to St. Norbert. I anxiously packed. What if somebody sees me? I wanted to escape; this seemed much easier weeks earlier in Wisconsin. My dad suggested I say goodbye or leave a note, but I was overwhelmed. I did not know what to do or say. I justified avoidance by saying nobody was there. As we drove away, I felt relieved but dirty for not saying anything. Irish "good-byes" are one thing, but a sober disappearance seemed disgraceful. The "goodbye" kept bothering me, festering in my mind, but I did not really talk much more about it. Other than my academic reasons for leaving, what else was there?

My dad dropped me off at St. Norbert. Soon I began living alone, an empty bunk above me. My foreign exchange student roommate departed for China within 2-weeks of my arrival. Over email and AOL instant messenger, I talked to my Columbia friends who were shocked and saddened about my actions. "WHY did you just leave?" "How come you didn't talk to us about it?" Some friends had suspicions. I had been so worried about disappointing them. I felt convinced they would try to persuade me to stay for spring semester. My AVOIDANCE of emotions and lack of communication was foolishly shortsighted. The decision was academically driven, but I had ignored the impact on the other people in my life. I later visited Columbia as a college junior, but the relationships were never the same.

School became a near obsession. Determined to conquer Biology 102 and statistics, I got tutors preemptively. I made a few dorm friends, but spent most of my free time studying. I ate "quick" lunches and dinners so as not to waste studying time. I began needing more and more sleep, using my cell phone alarm for multiple daytime naps. My eyes would flutter heavily, then I would sleep on my forearms in a study cubby or in upholstered chairs. Once I overslept an alarm missing the first 30-minutes of MY BIOLOGY TEST! I sprinted to class. At least I had a good relationship with the professor from attending office hours. He let me complete the entire test after I caught my breath. Beyond academics, I volunteered for a school fundraiser "100 men who cook" and tutored an 8th grade boy in math and English.

Within six weeks, depression and occasional suicidal ideation began. My mom referred to my occasional childhood moodiness as "feeling my oats" (akin to growing pains), but never were these 'mental health' problems. I wanted to be a psychiatrist, believing physicians did not have mental health problems. If so, how could they help people? Also, "good" Catholics never think about suicide for fear of hell. Moreover, two close high school friends were grieving recent suicides. One friend lost a father to carbon monoxide poising and another friend's brother hung himself. Those terrible, selfish, reprehensible people! Who could EVEN think of doing such a thing! Now, I was one of those people who thought about it. But, I desperately wished suicidal ideation away. Does that make me awful? I was ashamed and kept the secret buried, telling no one. Suicide is illegal and if you survived you would get locked up. Thinking about suicide was a "slippery slope into attempting," or so I believed. A few weeks later, I gathered up the courage to try a counseling session. I left ashamed and never returned only to continue self-battling my mental illness. I did not know who to talk to and counseling seemed futile, so I did what I knew- worked harder to distract myself with the golden carat of the future. I pumped all of my energy into my biology, philosophy, English and statistics. Nearly all of my free time was spent on academics. I developed a strategy of re-reading, re-writing, and re-reviewing in addition to tutoring and study groups. It seemed hard work was my panacea, but learning this way was exhausting and socially isolating. At the end of the semester, I was proud of my medical school quality grades. However, weeks earlier I had again decided to transfer to start sophomore year at the University of Wisconsin-Madison. Angie attended there and despite our stressful off-again on-again relationship, I justified another uprooting with family, opportunities, and nearby friends. My biology professor and I had become friends, but again I kept my transfer a secret. I avoided the inherent emotional turmoil I would feel about disappointing another friend.

At University of Wisconsin-Madison, I enrolled in five courses per semester. I preemptively enrolled in a group-based tutoring program in Chemistry. My regular daytime naps continued to counteract constant fatigue. Part of the pressure came from Angie who made me feel guilty about studying, which I passively endured until junior year. After watching a movie with roommates and ignoring countless calls, I finally answered. "WHY haven't you taken my calls?" She demanded. I blurted out, "I had NO intention on calling you, I was having a nice time [without you]." That finally ended my relationship with Angie. I justified my behavior with the path to med school, but emotional awareness was not my forte.

Another time constraint was that I worked 15-20 hours a week between two jobs. I worked as a Veteran's Administration Hospital phlebotomist drawing blood in the emergency room, intensive care unit, internal medicine and psychiatry wards. Also, I was a certified nursing assistant, primarily stationed in a dementia ward. My job was to provide direct care to support independent engagement in activities of daily living for patients with debilitating conditions such as knee replacements, stroke, and tetraplegia. What really struck me was seeing a 19-year old elementary school classmate, who had been paralyzed after hitting a deer with his car. His new residence was the nursing home! Work was a reality check, a time to get out of my head, but it was also yet another checklist: bathed Mrs. R, toileted Mr. S, cleaned dining room, laundered clothes. Direct patient care was something a good curriculum vita must have and wearing blue scrubs made me feel like I was closer to medical school than I actually was.

During junior year, I enrolled in Physics, a med school necessity. I spent countless hours with homework, tutoring, and help sessions. I had gotten behind in the coursework due to work and course load, and catching up was proving impossible. In late October, I left a pre-exam help session having learned nothing. "How will I get to medical school, if I can't learn physics?" I was so focused on the future that I ignored the present. Come November I had to drop out: a D in physics was worthless. I tried again but results for physics 101 and 102 were mediocre. While I studied quite a bit, as I turned 21, I began to go to the bars and house parties throughout the week and weekend. For me, a little *Southern Comfort* lived up to its name. I worked and played hard. A couple of buddies with the same philosophy are now physicians.

After college graduation, I moved with my now wife, Jackie, to Maryland for her research fellow position at the

National Institute of Mental Health. Jackie and I met through a mutual friend the summer before our senior year of college. Within a week, I found temporary employment in a downtown DC law firm, Steptoe & Johnson, in the secretarial services office as an administrative assistant. I made two friends in the office, Jon and Mary. Jon and I spent most of the day chatting and occasionally working. This was not work avoidance. Our boss, Georgia, had a habit of assigning urgent tasks in the late afternoon. Georgia's staff generally worked 60+ hour weeks. About a month into the job, Mary shared a secret. Georgia told Mary that I was, "Cute, but stupid." I was furious and devastated. I called the temp agency to request a new placement. Despite mediation by the temp agency with my boss as well as an apology, I was determined to find a new non-temp job.

I was hired a research assistant job at the Henry M. Jackson Foundation's HIV-Vaccine research clinic. My boss, MJ, was an explosive middle-aged woman, who frequently belittled me and another nurse, Yolanda. I understand now that MJ classically conditioned a fear response in me. My armpits were never dry and I worried most of the day about MJ's potential reactions to me. One might see this pattern of consequences as a variable-ratio reinforcement schedule (i.e., an unpredictable pattern) leading me to develop anticipatory anxiety. Was it just me? No, Keisha and Cassandra were clinic research assistants and both switched jobs. Cassandra was a strong black woman and had the good sense to walk out after a huge blow up with MJ and never return. Keisha transferred within the organization. I wished I had Cassandra's strength; she refused to let MJ verbally abuse her. Most days, Yolanda and I leisurely ate lunch in the conference room, telling jokes and stories. Yolanda was my savior. She told me about growing up in Belize and about black culture. One Saturday, Yolanda took me to a Caribbean festival and parade outside Howard University.

But work triggered significant anxiety and I talked about it a lot. Jackie urged me to seek counseling- obviously work was adversely impacting me. I would become "trapped in my head" worrying and dreading work. Episodic, heightened anxiety distracted me from being in the moment. These periods were akin to having a phone conversation with an obviously distracted person who is poor at multi-tasking. At times, I worried about what questions or comments to make, and about "boring" others. Maybe I was stupid after all? I still could not shake Georgia's derision. Counseling just did not seem right. Growing up, I learned that people complain a lot about work. How is my complaining not normal? Years later, I believe counseling was merited, my baseline anxiety was not at a healthy level.

Living in the Washington D.C area was a haven for new friends and adventure. Jackie and I played on a kickball team, hiked Sugar Loaf Mountain, went river tubing, shucked oysters fresh off the boat, and visited museums and monuments. We also traveled near and far to visit friends and family in Boston, Nashville, New York City, Raleigh, Seattle, and Vancouver. Outside of work, I loved my life and spent time studying for the Graduate Record Examination (GRE). My dream of medical school faded as I realized that I was interested in psychiatry only for prescription privileges; clinical psychology was far more interesting to me.

By December 2006, I submitted graduate school applications and hit the jackpot with a research fellow position at the National Institute of Diabetes, Digestion, and Kidney Disease. The protocol investigated the neuropsychological and health status impact of obesity and metabolic syndrome. This randomized controlled trial administered sleep over a 1-year period to assess health benefits. My new colleagues, Dr. Cizza, Meredith, Sara, and Priya, were warm, friendly, and hardworking folks.

In late winter, I was admitted into a clinical psychology Ph.D. program at the Illinois Institute of Technology (IIT). I was shocked to receive an offer. I had only met with the clinical training director for a 5-minute interview before she said, "What happened on the verbal GRE? Honestly, I expected you to be a foreigner." She did not rattle me. I am fond of interviewing and find it to be a pleasurable experience; it is a rare exciting opportunity for uncertainty. I nonchalantly responded as if I had nothing to lose, "If you tell me that is a deal breaker and I have to retake the GRE I'll do it. I'll just reapply next year, no problem." However, the offer a few weeks later WAS a problem! I was supposed to work for 2 years on my current contract. For weeks before decision-day, April 15th, I was anxious and slept little. Again, I avoided having an open dialogue about my "transfer." What would my boss say? How would I tell him? What if he was mad? I worried constantly and sweated profusely. In years past, I would have labeled *introspective,* this much "thinking" or "mulling things over" believing that I was "in-tune" with my thoughts and emotions. Today, I label this rumination, an unhealthy anxiety-related behavior that requires pause, acknowledgement and healthy self-care. Finally, I gathered up the courage to talk to my boss. He was VERY happy for me, but wanted me to help ensure a smooth transition. We still occasionally email. I even wrote a glowing letter for Dr. Cizza's tenure committee on his mentoring style.

Chicago, Illinois: Rock Bottom

Graduate school was hard work. I applied my time-consuming study tactics, re-reading, re-writing and re-reviewing. Academically, things went well, but the first year was exhausting with five courses, 15 hours per week of practicum (testing pre-kindergarten through 3rd graders for giftedness for the Chicago Public School system), and working as a research assistant with our lab post-doc psychiatrist. With the thousands of dollars of loans, there was no turning back. I dove into my academics as hard as I did at St. Norbert College, except I was much more socially engaged. While sometimes I joked that IIT had mistakenly admitted me, truth was I felt privileged and cherished my opportunity.

It was not until the 2nd year of graduate school that I got slammed with depression and anxiety. Near the end of fall semester, I remember telling Jackie, "I'm not sure I can do this grad school thing anymore." Trying to hold tears back, I told her I was stressed out, needed hugs, and wanted respite. Beyond coursework, my "to do" list included counseling people with serious mental health conditions at a community mental health center. I worried about my clients and felt responsible for their well-being. Weekly supervision was helpful, but I worried that it was a "test," a way to see if I was really "psychologist material" or if I should be kicked out of graduate school. Maybe my director would finally realize the school had made a mistake? Am I the most incompetent therapist ever? While we learned about cognitive distortions in coursework, awareness of my own irrational thoughts was yet to be understood as such. Young therapists have much to learn about how to do therapy. I sought knowledge to improve, buried the emotional distress, and felt terrible about the quality of my counseling services.

After reading Irvin Yalom's "The Gift of Therapy," I had an epiphany, a correction of my expectations. I only met with clients for 1 hour, at most, out of 168 weekly hours. Each client had certainly survived without me. This was not to negate my usefulness to my clients, but to recognize that my true impact was limited. Accomplishing something remarkable every 50-minute session was completely unrealistic. In fact, the client and I were supposed to work together; change ultimately resided within the client. It came as a relief that I could not control my client's well-being. The end of the semester came and my mental health improved. I felt better than when I had self-administered the depression inventory a month ago (the instrument's interpretation said "moderate depression"). I could still function at practicum, accomplish schoolwork, and maintain my relationships, so I believed I was fine. If I was not 'impaired,' how serious could my depression really be?

Rock Bottom

The summer of 2009 brought big changes. Jackie decided to attend a fully funded child clinical psychology program in Southern Illinois, 350 miles from Chicago. We began living apart in August for the first time ever and got married in September. Jackie would drive to Chicago once a month, I would visit the other weekends. Cognitively, the plan seemed sustainable and adventurous, but the emotional toll was unforeseen. On Fridays, I rode the 8:00 AM Amtrak train for 5.5 hours from Chicago to Carbondale to see my wife for the weekend. Jackie managed a psychology lab and finished work about 6:00 PM. Saturday was our only "full day" together and I dreaded returning to Chicago. On Sunday, I boarded the 5:30 PM train arriving in my studio apartment at about midnight.

I dreaded my $500 a month Uptown neighborhood studio. The 1st floor smelled like Zoo dwelling monkeys, roach pesticide permeated the stairwell from weekly spraying, the 2nd floor oozed of barnyard hay, and the 3rd floor reeked of residual lacquer paint. Centipedes were a weekly kitchen countertop and bathtub spotting. The real zenith was awakening to a dead bed partner- a poisoned roach. Should I change my sheets? It seemed like a lot of work and I felt exhausted by the thought of doing laundry, which required using the mildew smelling basement laundry machines.

A few months earlier, in July, I began a 20-hour per week practicum at a neuropsychology clinic well-known for overworking its free-labor. It was excellent training, but the work environment has historically been quite far from receiving an American Psychological Association award for being a Psychologically Healthy Workplace. Each practicum student completed one assessment report per week, while colleagues at similar sites did two reports a month. Other practicum students seemed to have much better experiences and supervisors cared more about didactics than financial productivity.

Neuropsychology practicum entails administering and scoring tests to understand client's presenting cognitive concerns (i.e., dementia and attention-deficit disorder evaluations). I habitually worked 12-hour days twice a week, working through lunch and drinking extra coffee. By mid-September, rumination and fear significantly clouded my ability to concentrate. "Oh my god, this is taking too long. I can't get enough done." Talking with the other three interns about report writing did not help, but at least they were friendly folks to be around. No matter how many hours I put in, it was never enough to produce good reports. The clinic's post-doc was becoming noticeably upset with me. I was making silly errors, which tremendously aggravated her. She provided passive-aggressive feedback regarding my errors. I could sense her irritation when she interacted so I kept my distance. My supervisors, Drs. Arrot and Schith, rarely expressed positive feedback. After six months of working for Dr. Schith, I FINALLY got a thank you for working on a report. I was a pawn in the clinic, desperate for experiences to attain ample hours for the capstone: internship.

I held it together at the clinic despite experiencing occasion suicidal ideation. "You know if you jump off the roof you don't have to stress over this report anymore." It becomes a rational-irrational argument within one's mind.

"Why would I kill myself over a report? Yeah, but you are so stressed out?" It is a distressing back-and-forth internal dialogue. Am I losing my mind? Is this my worst nightmare that I can't seem to wake up from? No, this is the life I am living. I did not know what to do. Silence seemed best because suicide talk is a real fast way to get hospitalized. I certainly cannot control this ridiculous internal thought pattern. But, who could possibly handle talking about this?

After one clinical interview Dr. Arrot said to me, "Okay, so this guy is pretty anxious. You are not anxious so just try to manage his anxiety." Did Dr. A really not know? I might be hiding my anxiety facially, but my armpits were never dry. My appetite plummeted and I dropped to a pre-middle school weight: 150 lbs. I tried a slew of antiperspirants like *Certain-Dry*. That had to be answer! I was in denial, not ready to call this a mental health problem.

By October, depressive symptoms intensified. In my apartment, I had daily crying spells. I'd yell at myself, pleading in the mirror, "SNAP OUT OF IT! Get it together!" I began to sleep as much as I could at home and on the el train on the way to practicum and school. I always felt exhausted. Suicidal ideation continued with a vengeance throughout the day. I was overwhelmed and drowning in misery. Distraction helped a little bit, but practicum agitated the situation. I was trapped in my head with wishes to end the pain.

Jackie and I had regular Skype video dinner dates. One night I could no longer hold back the streams of tears. I felt weak-minded and pathetic. For me the "what-if" internal dialogue gets triggered with high anxiety. Did Jackie marry a hot mess for a husband? How long would she put up with this? I wonder if she'll divorce me. Truth was, my wife was only kind and supportive, encouraging me to go get help. This transition was harder than we thought. But she seemed okay? She had it together, something I desperately wanted to have back. She suggested I go to the counseling center.

The counseling center? I just can't go. I just felt so much stigma about going to a counselor as a clinical psychology student. What would other people think about me? I felt so much shame and embarrassment. Here we go again, another psychology student doing "me-search," trying to figure out what is wrong with himself. I had no idea anymore why I was in clinical psychology. What became clear was that I had many self-imposed expectations of what I should and should not do.

A few more weeks elapsed before I gave in and went to the counseling center. Maybe just a quick vent is all I need. In the waiting room, tears trickled down my cheeks as I completed the depression screener. I stared at the blue carpeting and breathed deeply to control myself. A practicum student came out and invited me back to a counseling room. When he discovered I was a grad student, he informed the clinic's director. Dr. D took me to his office and I sat on his couch. He said, "Grad students cannot see other grad students." I looked down at the floor, breathing deeply. Every 10-12 minutes, I watched the green line train through the window as it stopped at the station on the elevated tracks. He asked, how I was doing and then I cried uncontrollably for 40 minutes. I emptied half of a Kleenex box as I dried my eyes and nose. I felt mortified for Dr. D. During the session, Dr. D. asked, "have you had any thoughts of hurting yourself?" I lied, "no, I have not." Truth told, I was terrified of being hospitalized and my thoughts raced with anxiety-provoking questions. What would hospitalization cost me? What will I tell people? What if I am kept in there a whole week or two or a month? What about practicum? What will my supervisors think? Will I get kicked out of grad school? And then a recent practicum memory popped into my mind, an adolescent girl strapped down to a stretcher enroute to an ambulance. When I saw her, weeks earlier, I wondered how long until I would be strapped down, locked up and forced to deal with the same thing. So I lied to Dr. D. At least if I did not admit to suicidal ideation, he could not lock me up. However, overt denial does not mean the thoughts dissipate.

Jackie asked how therapy was going. "You don't have to tell me any details you do not want to," she said. Revealing some details was useful, but I could not help but feel like a liar. The suicidal ideation was something I purposely skipped over. Why can't I just tell her? But anxiety dominated, not a chance. As the weeks went onward, I felt more comfortable. I told Dr. D about my suicidal thoughts. Much to my surprise, Dr. D did NOT send me to the hospital for confessing. He encouraged me to reach out and talk to my wife. I could not do it. I feared she would not trust me anymore. WHY would you want to kill yourself? DON'T you love me? WHY did we just get married? With the guilt and worry mixed in the same cauldron. I did not have answers to those questions! But those questions would emotionally torment me, spike my anxiety, and overwhelm me. My default decision: silence.

My mental health remained status quo with therapy and by late November the neuropsychology post-doc exploded, "WHY are you making these errors?" It was then that I realized that I was somewhat impaired. That is why I cannot concentrate and am sweating, losing weight, having suicidal ideation, and feel perpetually overwhelmed. I avoided these problems for so long and deflected the etiology, calling it anything but mental illness.

Two weeks later, I met with a psychiatrist in the counseling center immediately before my last final exam in December. She prescribed an anti-depressant. I felt giddy about the prescription. Maybe it was new hope? Within a few weeks school stressors were gone and my mood improved dramatically. Was this a placebo effect? Has my personality changed? I was skeptical about psychotropic medications of any kind. Scientifically, the mechanism of action for these medications vaguely understood. The explanation was that antidepressant's effects occur "downstream," hence the 4-6 week delayed onset. I clung to my belief that doctors were immune to mental illness. As spring semester approached, it dawned on me that I had internalized stigma, which had prevented me from seeking help. Interestingly, my graduate school research was on mental illness stigma, but I could not educate away my own stigma. I started actively focusing on self-care, and part of the process was not living in silence. As I started feeling better during spring semester, I slowly amassed courage to talk more openly about my lived experiences.

Recovery: Beyond the Dark Days

Recovery has been defined as a process and outcome. As a process, recovery is a continuous experience, a modifiable trajectory. As an outcome, recovery can be viewed as being cured of a condition, a snapshot in time. My process of recovery began after starting an antidepressant and continuing therapy. Suicidal ideation remitted, sleep returned, and mood improved. Rumination and anxiety were better controlled. A clear mind allowed me to concentrate on the details at practicum, take on more complicated cases and write good quality reports. The post-doc and supervisors were happier with my performances as well. I became more present and my relationship with my wife improved. Recovery is more than being symptom free, for me it is about self-care and having healthy and meaningful relationships.

Part of my recovery was activism-based. I founded an Active Minds Chapter at IIT. Active Minds is dedicated to mental well-being and suicide prevention. I began to see mental health as a continuum rather a dichotomy (mentally ill or mentally well). Mental health could deteriorate or improve and was not static over time. Cognitively, I understood that mental health challenges and impairments can remit;

however, such issues may not vanish forever. My goal was to network with student leaders and draw attention to mental health on campus. As chapter president, I secured funding with my team to host a movie night, relaxation training, ice cream social, anti-stigma presentations, and an anti-stigma theatre presentation. I watched presenters from a local National Alliance of Mental Illness chapter share their *In Our Own Voice* stories of lived experience. I began to see how I might tell my story. Society taboos such topics, so I never learned how to talk about my experience. Why can't we talk about mental health more openly?

None of my wild fears came true and recovery meant new resilience, more social support, and engaging in self-care activities such as exercise, cooking, socializing, gardening, traveling, and playing Nintendo Wii. One of the biggest benefits has been improved concentration and cognition. I am proud of my ability to more easily learn, retain, and manipulate information. In addition, the absence of high anxiety has allowed me to concentrate on the present moment. This part of recovery allowed me to also begin more directly communicating my preferences and thoughts without worrying so much about other's reactions.

Life changes are exciting and stressful. The birth of our 8-pound daughter, Zurielle, was both. Despite being in graduate school, she was planned. For 18-months we battled chronic sleep deprivation even after her colic remitted. The Mayo book described the situation as having "a high needs child." Yet child rearing is inherently stressful and incessant crying grated on my nerves. Nevertheless, I continued to evolve, manage stress, monitor my emotions, and communicate my needs. I say all this to point out my resilience and prioritization of my mental health.

Watching Zurielle grow, crawl, smile, giggle and talk has brought me much happiness. Life changes are inevitable and Zuri accompanied us on our busy lifestyle to visit friends

and celebrate weddings. At two years-old, Zuri had already
visited Boston, Chicago, Dallas, Detroit, St. Louis,
Milwaukee, Nashville, New Orleans, New York City,
Philadelphia, Portland, Rhode Island, and Seattle. In August
2013 we moved to Boston for Jackie's internship. My 2-year
old, Penske truck co-pilot demonstrated remarkable stamina
for the 1,200 mile move. Life challenges continue, but
resilience and self-care do too.

My resilience has been reinforced with emotional
growth, profoundly impacted by the work of Dr. Brené
Brown on emotional vulnerability. Dr. Brown's TedEx talk
showed me how to be emotionally supportive and empathic
rather than trying to immediately "solve" problems. My first
response to a person would focus on content of what a person
said, emotions were barely acknowledged. Dr. Brown got me
to re-think how to "be present with the person" by asking the
person a simple open-ended question: how are you feeling?
So simple, but not my penchant. Dr. Brown's work has
inspired me to acknowledge my emotional reactions and my
cognitions.

In 2014, I attended an emotional CPR workshop
(eCPR; http://www.emotional-cpr.org). eCPR conceptualizes
suicidal experiences as desires to escape feeling significantly
overwhelmed and emotionally vulnerable. In conjunction
with Dr. Brown's work, I conceptualized my suicidal ideation
differently. The epiphany was that intermittent suicidal
ideation was related to high, seemingly relentless stress. I
have since embraced suicidal ideation as emotional pain that
needed to be processed and worked through with social
support. Most importantly eCPR destroyed my belief that I
was emotionally fragile and taught me that social support
during such sustained stressful times was my path forward.

Mental wellness and recovery have led to
accomplishments of which I am proud. I am the Assistant
Director for Resource Development for the Center for

Dignity, Recovery, and Empowerment
(www.dignitycenter.org). I have published 16 peer-reviewed
publications, written two book chapters, presented at seven
national conferences, and am near completion of my Ph.D. in
clinical psychology. Beyond laudable professional
accomplishments, I am proud to share my personal story of
overcoming depression and debilitating anxiety.

Coming Out Proud

Telling my story of mental illness has been cathartic
and empowering. I have told my story to my wife, mother,
mother-in-law, sisters and sisters-in-law, select friends and
colleagues and peers at the 1st annual Active Minds Region
Mental Health Summit at Marquette University. I have never
felt comfortable sharing my story with my father or father-in-
law. Sharing has been purposeful and meaningful, as I have
found solidarity with people who have and have not battled
mental illness. For me, suicidal ideation has been the hardest
experience to share. Some people were shocked, "You
depressed? You don't look depressed." You are correct, in
fact I do not look like the mopey depressed person depicted in
a televised *Abilify* advertisement. Others naturally inquire
about my risk and/or penchant for suicide attempts. Ideation
and behavior, especially for suicide, seem to be interpreted as
synonymous; for a long time, I agreed. Despite graduate
school ingraining the major crux of cognitive behavior
therapy (thoughts do not equal behavior), this belief persisted
and it was eCPR that created the distinction for suicide:
thoughts do not equal behaviors. Thinking of suicide does
not mean I will act on those thoughts. I have shared my
struggles with ideation and mental illness to varying extents,
with select captive audiences, which can be categorized as
easy, wild card, and difficult.

My easier disclosures. Easy disclosures occurred
with people I trusted. Usually, I navigated by talking about

mental health and transitioned into talking about my lived experience. When I told Jackie in person at dinner about my mental health and suicidal ideation she sincerely did not know about the suicide portion of the story. It was emotionally beautiful to be completely honest, but there was some residual fear about risk for suicide attempt. She was very supportive and checks in on me occasionally; I consider this helpful and caring. When I told my mom over the telephone, she was very supportive, not verbalizing any major concerns even about the suicidal ideation. I talked about grad school hardships, medication and suicidal ideation with my sister Claire in a Cold Stone ice cream store. She responded very positively about my struggles; in the end we had a shared understanding of such challenges. I told a few grad school classmates about the struggles and sincere helpfulness of my antidepressant, not sharing as much about the suicidal ideation. I told my story to my friend Beth as a way to build social support and describe my resilience. Coming out has been positive and allowed creation of a support network to lean on.

The wild card disclosures. Some mental health disclosures are more challenging than one would think. During a webinar I provided on developing a mental health disclosure story, I provided a brief biography of myself. While the group was certainly non-threatening, sharing that I was a person with depression was anxiety provoking. The webinar was recorded and became something that anybody searching the Internet could watch. Here the benefit of shared understanding of mental health challenges was worth the risk to let my audience know that I was a person who had a story too. However, my story was limited to stating that I was a person with depression; other details were not presented because they might have been distracting to the presentation. Coming out and the number of details provided are both part of my decision-making and sharing process.

Another wild card presentation was talking to my friend Matt whose father had committed suicide. I shared my struggles with depression and how frightening suicidal ideation was for me. I confessed that I thought of Matt's father during these challenging times and feared ever disclosing such thoughts to him. Matt's response was neither overly warm nor cold. He told me, "No worries, buddy" and then we talked about something else. Nevertheless, disclosure helped me to confront something that had kept me from seeking treatment. I must admit it felt a little selfish to bring up his father's suicide especially because I had always been told, "We just don't talk about suicide," do not talk about it with Matt. Despite talking to Matt about the suicide and his father, our friendship continued.

At the Active Minds summit at Marquette University, I shared my story of suicidal ideation with a group of about 30 peers. Other people shared lived experiences and an aura of safety filled the room. However, it was the first time I had publicly come out to a group about suicidal ideation. I told the group that I was a person who had struggled with suicidal ideation and described the thoughts like a "freight train running through my mind." The group clapped and seemed grateful for my disclosure. I felt brave and relieved. The experience was powerful for me and fears about being locked up were further shattered. I also realized people with shared experience could be accepting and supportive. I have come to understand that there is strength in vulnerability and taking a risk can pay emotional dividends.

Difficult situations. At times I have decided not to disclose my mental health conditions as the cons outweighed the benefits. Recently a lady asked me what I did for a living. I told her I was a consultant for an advocacy group for people with mental illness. Her pitying response was "awwwwww!" It was like she had just seen a cute puppy kiss a kitten. While my blood boiled a bit, I did not know what to say or do.

Sometimes, disclosing a mental health condition just does not feel right. I felt a bit like a fraud for not standing up, but haphazardly disclosing in anger would be a mistake. I reframed the experience as a learning opportunity, not failure.

The first time I met my brother-in-law, Dan, his tirade about mentally altering psychotropic medications was based on public misperceptions rather than fact. Dan was a Lieutenant in the U.S. Army and survived two tours in Afghanistan. The conversation with Dan short-circuited my coming out, rendering me speechless. For years I had held similarly negative beliefs about psychotropic medications. Yet as a person taking an antidepressant, I knew my personality was unchanged and I was not a zombie. My experience was anecdotal; yes sometimes medications do leave a person zombie-like. The conversation was awkward so I relied on my graduate school training. Coming out seemed wrong in that moment and listening to my gut was easy to do. It was self-preservation, but again coming out was ultimately my choice. Despite wanting to be strong and open, ultimately I conceptualized this as another learning opportunity, something to help me understand my limits.

What guides my selective disclosure of lived experience?

My style has been to selectively share my story with a goal for disclosure. My goal might be social support, shared understanding, or to be human. Sometimes friends or colleagues ask about mental health treatment, "You know, for a friend?" I offer emotional support and sometimes share my story of depression and suicidal ideation. Most importantly, I discuss the downsides of avoiding treatment and my rock bottom. Coming out and sharing a stigmatized identity can certainly be anxiety provoking. However without risk there is no reward when disclosing private experiences. Other people's responses are unknown ahead of time, but hiding my identity makes me feel disingenuous. Nevertheless, coming out is a decision with consequences that need to be considered.

Part of my coming out has been out of frustration with the stigma within the healthcare system. A few years ago, my doctor asked me about my dissertation during a medication refill appointment. His response to my project, investigating the explicit and implicit attitudes toward medication adherence among people with serious mental illness, was "Just take your meds. There, dissertation, done." I was irritated, but not surprised. A systematic review by Beate Schulze (2007) in the *International Review of Psychiatry* showed that health care providers held attitudes equivalent to the general public, despite specialized training. Mental illness stigma cannot be educated into extinction by contrasting myths and facts. In fact, a meta-analyses conducted by Corrigan, Morris, Michaels, Rafacz, & Rüsch (2012) published in *Psychiatric Services* demonstrated that meeting a person with lived experience had three times greater impact than education alone.

Why do I come out? Well, I know that people with lived experience are powerful messengers of resilience and hope. As a person with lived experience, I choose to be a messenger. I am not damaged nor ruined by mental illness. I tell my story so other people might not struggle in silence. My silent struggle only prevented higher functional capacity. By sharing my story, I actively confront past fears and silence. I am proud of being in recovery from mental illness and continued self-care efforts, and I believe speaking out about my experiences will help others hear and see the living, breathing truth. I am being the change I want to see in the world.

Biography
Patrick Michaels is Assistant Research Director for Resource Development for the Center for Dignity, Recovery,

and Empowerment. The Center provides technical assistance and program evaluation services to existing and developing California-based stigma and discrimination reduction programs. In this role, Mr. Michaels coordinates a research study evaluating the Coming Out Proud program's impact on self-stigma and mental health disclosure. Mr. Michaels also manages the Coming Out Proud program website and social media efforts on Facebook and Twitter. Mr. Michaels has presented at seven conferences and published 16 peer reviewed journal articles including a meta-analysis of public stigma interventions. In 2012, Mr. Michaels received an Active Minds Emerging Scholars Fellowship to qualitatively evaluate the impact of the Active Minds Speakers Bureau. In 2014, he received an American Psychological Association Student Travel Award. Mr. Michaels plans to complete his clinical psychology Ph.D. from the Illinois Institute of Technology in 2015 after completion of a 1-year internship at the Louis Stokes Cleveland Veterans Administration Medical Center.

References

Corrigan, P. W., Morris, S. B., Michaels, P. J., Rafacz, J. D., & Rüsch, N. (2012). Challenging the public stigma of mental illness: A meta-analysis of outcome studies. *Psychiatric Services 63*(10), 963-973. doi: 10.1176/appi.ps.201100529

Schulze, B. (2007). Stigma and mental health professionals: A review of the evidence on an intricate relationship. *International Review of Psychiatry, 19*(2), 137-155. doi:10.1080/09540260701278929

Saved by Imagination: A Memoir of Depression and Recovery by the Book
Carl Blumenthal

For Susan and my other angels

2012 NYC Peer Conference
(credit: Elizabeth Saenger)

Memoirs of mental illness often seem long on dis-ease and short on recovery. For every step forward the author usually slides back two. Lessons may only sink in after repeated failures. During five years of depression and anxiety I, too, often stumbled backwards when not paralyzed.

Why did my condition last so long? It was difficult to overcome the shock of being strangled by my psychological innards. Then I succumbed to a hopelessness, which enabled me to avoid all efforts at (self-) help. I felt as immobilized as prey in the jaws of a predator.

Rather than fighting or fleeing when threatened, animals may freeze, either to play dead or reduce the pain of being eaten alive. During the battle against depression, I feigned "rigor mortis" without expecting to survive.

Contrary to conventional wisdom, misery lacks company. It's an unwanted addiction to solitude, a stage in life without applause. Only after you've outlived it, do you want to tell the world that trying to break your fall hurts as much as hitting bottom.

Putting this story into words is more than therapeutic; it's an exorcism of years of inertia. Reading about the struggles of others was often the extent of my resistance. Yet this activity sustained me until I was able to support myself by writing. In fact, I now read and write more easily because I broke through the barrier of perfectionism by tapping into the well of my (creative) unconscious, which was replenished rather than depleted by years of inaction.

Based on his survival of the Auschwitz concentration camp, Victor Frankel in *Man's Search for Meaning* outlined what he called "logotherapy," a way of helping troubled people discover purpose in their lives. Because I found meaning in books I define my form of self-help as "bibliotherapy."

This memoir would not be possible if I hadn't learned from other people who have written about their disease and recovery. Fifty years ago the stigma of mental illness meant *The Bell Jar* and *I Never Promised You a Rose Garden* were published as fictionalized chapters of Sylvia Plath's and Joanne Greenberg's lives. Authors of such autobiographies are no longer figuratively locked in closets.

Thus during the past 20 years the literary doors have been blown open on once hidden psychiatric conditions. Susana Kaysen and Elizabeth Wurtzel initiated this trend with their respective bestsellers *Girl, Interrupted* (1993) and *Prozac Nation* (1994). Mine is a small contribution to a growing bibliography.

***

I've compiled this record three years into my recovery— three years of doing what I failed to do during my self-imposed exile from living:

- relying on writing and other passions as if my life depended on them;
- appreciating nature for being the source of creativity;
- seeking help from peers who understand my struggles;
- finding love in the advice of family and friends;
- pursuing therapy's never-ending search for self-knowledge;
- accepting that how well I do at work isn't a test of manhood;
- engaging in politics as a form of community responsibility;
- counting my blessings by donating time and money to social causes;
- integrating care of mind, body, and soul; and generally
- putting one step in front of the other as Elizabeth Swados recommends in
  My Depression: A Picture Book.

As with the TV program "Scared Straight" to keep teenagers out of jail, I now must remind myself how bad things were to prevent them from happening again. This fear keeps me running in the right direction.

***

"I think we should keep on nodding terms with the people we used to be. Otherwise they turn up unannounced and surprise us, come hammering on the mind's door at 4 AM of a bad night and demand to know who deserted them, who betrayed them, who is going to make amends."

Joan Didion, "On Keeping a Notebook"

"I inhabited a territory of loneliness which I think resembles that place where the dying spend their time before death, and

from where those who do return living to the world bring inevitably a unique point of view that is a nightmare,

a treasure, and a lifelong possession."

Janet Frame, *An Angel at My Table*

"*Depression is a double whammy. Negative thoughts and feelings flood in. The positive dissolves in a sea of self-doubt.*"

Carl Blumenthal, "Six Angels at My Writing Table"

***

Briefing for a Descent into Hell, Abridged

During my long depression I tried to cope by withdrawing from the world: quitting my job and school, ceasing hobbies and volunteer work, neglecting physical as well as mental health, avoiding friends, and limiting contact with family, except my wife, Susan Palm.

Most painful of all, I suspended my part-time career as an arts critic. Penning hundreds of articles about writers, painters, dancers, musicians, photographers, and film-makers, I earned respect because unlike most critics I didn't suck the life out of my subjects. Now writer's block prevented me from living—vicariously.

My world shrank to the living room couch where lying down was the most comfortable and comforting position, both during the day while I listened to the radio and at night when I retreated farther—into sleep and dreams. It was like clinging to a raft of calm on an ocean of bad thoughts and feelings. (I'm indebted to Doris Lessing, who in *Briefing for a Descent into Hell* employed a similar metaphor for her hero's defense against psychosis.)

I maintained this fetal-like pose by avoiding as much stress as possible because undertaking the simplest task made me feel as if I had a permanent case of indecision. Thus hygiene went down the drain even though I didn't shower. Determining what to eat and how to prepare it required an appetite I lacked. And household chores seemed like opportunities to malfunction.

If my living room couch resembled a raft in a storm, I also tried to batten down all hatches to the outside world. I only left our apartment to get the mail before other tenants arose in the morning. Then I would throw away letters from family and friends yet save bills. (Unpaid debts scared me more than social disconnections!) I dreaded checking my e-mail and browsing the Internet for fear I would have to respond to those demands on my attention as well.

I let my wife Susan answer the phone so she could say I wasn't available. I responded anxiously to her return from work every night because it meant I had to face her recitation of the day's events. My only other knowledge of the world came through the radio. As I listened my mood rose and fell with the stock market, in which our retirement funds were invested, and with the fortunes of the Democrats, defenders of the Social Security Disability Insurance on which I depended.

Susan shopped, cleaned the apartment, washed our clothes, did the banking, paid bills, and generally interceded on my behalf whenever the world seemed too oppressive. She took everything in stride just as she had raised her three younger siblings when their parents weren't around, became the first member of her extended family to finish college, and successfully ran her own commercial art business, in spite of chronic depression, regular migraines, and two forms of arthritis.

From Mountain Climbing to Freefall

That oppression peaked the last week of spring 2006. For a year, I had excelled at a new, more stressful job while pursuing what seemed like the last-chance dreams of a 55-year-old.

I rode the subway three hours roundtrip each day from central Brooklyn to the heart of Queens to serve as a peer counselor at Venture House, a psycho-social clubhouse, modeled after the original Fountain House in Manhattan. Recognized as the best recent employee I attracted the largest number of members, who picked me as their case manager due to my empathy and support of their ambitions.

During the 1970's I attended college in Massachusetts. After a stint in Manhattan for graduate school, I lived in New Jersey from 1983 to 1995. Then I joined my wife in her Brooklyn home once we married.

I represented the fourth generation on my mother's side to live in the borough where I worked three jobs in succession. Perhaps the change of venue to a foreign land like Jamaica (Queens) entailed bad karma, although at the time the excess energy I possessed seemed like a natural extension—of the F train which brought me there.

So why not also turn my life inside out by:

- overseeing installation of a new roof as president of our 54-unit co-op building;
- swearing off the realism of reporting for the fantasy of becoming an artist;
- trying dance, drawing, sculpture, poetry, plays, and short stories;
- hedging my bets as a freelancer for a Brooklyn newspaper;

- facilitating in off hours Mood Disorders Support Groups;
- helping my wife establish a new gardening business; and
- preparing for employment and social work school, each full-time;

Finally I thought God, in whom I had lost faith, after a fairly religious Jewish upbringing, had inspired me to join the Religious Society of Friends (also known as Quakers).

The number of academic, literary, professional, and civic awards I had earned over the years suddenly weighed as heavily on me as the medals pinned to a four-star general's chest. I was supposed to be a role model for people down on their luck, but never admitted the privileges I enjoyed as a white, middle-class male. Still I ignored the warning signs that all these accomplishments were dragging me down. Being a peer counselor also intensified my mood swings. Despite my presumed distance from clients I identified with their ups and downs.

Then one day when I thought I was ready to lead a workshop on peer counseling, I had a panic attack which felt as if I had fallen through the ice on a lake and gotten tangled in the weeds at the bottom. I completed the seminar through sheer will, but was consumed by an anxiety so pervasive I couldn't think straight or decide what to do next.

In the past I'd used Ativan and therapy to prevent or relieve anxiety attacks; sometimes I talked myself out of them. But this time a feeling of hopelessness overwhelmed my words. Although I felt terrified, what I said lacked emotion, because how could I articulate being so out of control!

In *Depression and the Body*, psychiatrist Alexander Lowen insists depression is not a feeling; rather it's a divorce from feeling. Without emotion as its ground, language makes no sense, giving new meaning to the term "talking head." I feared mine would explode at any moment, filled as it was with so many ugly thoughts.

Not seeking help from my support network of peers, family, and friends tripped me up further. Like Alice who quickly plunged down the rabbit hole, I swallowed 40 Ativan pills and awoke two days later at Maimonides, a nearby medical center. By my side were my wife and a hospital aide whose sole purpose was to prevent me from trying suicide again. In an effort to console me, my psychiatrist explained, "An overdose of that drug won't kill you."

Treading Water in a Pool of Waste

From there I transferred to Brookdale, another Brooklyn hospital where my doctor, Maria Paz, served as chief of the inpatient psychiatric staff. I became obsessed with old symptoms of depression and anxiety: urinary retention so great I required a catheter for relief, and constipation so deep-seated—a pun which at the time I didn't appreciate—that I drank cup after cup of coffee for its laxative effect.

I could barely dress, shave, brush my teeth, or take care of other activities of daily living (so-called ADL's, one of those hard-to-swallow acronyms).

Like during a prior hospitalization when the Love Canal pollution scandal flashed on TV screens, this time Israel and Hezbollah tried to bomb each other back to the Stone Age in Lebanon. Once again outside disaster reinforced the disaster within.

As each new patient arrived on the unit—I identified most with the women who tried suicide, often to escape abusive boyfriends—my attempts at communication failed because words stuck in my throat. In art therapy we watched several of Tyler Perry's Madea movies during which he cross-dresses as the fierce matriarch of a large family. I didn't find them funny; the jails in which many of the characters ended up resembled our locked ward.

Meanwhile a resident psychiatrist with a knack for charcoal sketches insisted on drawing my portrait for the gallery of inmates posted on his office walls. Whether for his edification or amusement, he listened to me recite my short story about a homeless man who slams a social worker's head into the floor of a subway car by yanking the emergency cord, perhaps as a silent cry for help or in anger at his lot in life. (Written shortly before my manic crash, this tale was a premonition of disaster.)

The hospital discharged me after three weeks not because I had made progress—in fact, I spent most of the time on suicide watch—but due to my insurance company's insistence that I had overstayed my welcome. I had only gained admission by pleading for someone to save me from myself. Confronted with this fiscal hurdle my treatment team declared me "a winner" of its
inpatient trials.

Unfortunately the depression and anxiety followed me back to work at Venture House. A large salary bonus didn't compensate for the mental torture which became so agonizing that clients had to console me as each day I discovered more reasons for not helping them. In a fit of false conscience I quit two months later.

All I wanted was to lie down on that living room couch and suffer in peace. However, I couldn't escape the forewarning of being clutched in a downward spiral like helpless prey.

Taking the Plunge Again

Even the Democrats' victories in the November election didn't cheer me up. With the darkest days of the year ahead, I left Susan a note saying I was going to the nearest subway stop to kill myself. I taped it to a folder inside which I had collected all the financial documents she would need to survive because I assumed she would be too upset to search for them.

After arriving at the station, I climbed down to the tracks amidst the scurrying rats and placed my right hand on top of the third rail, expecting the shock of my life. When nothing happened—I hadn't actually touched the inner, electrified groove—I left the station and returned home despairing that, like some over-the-hill pitcher, I had failed to throw away my life again.

There the police greeted me. In panic my wife had called one of her friends, a psychologist who was calm enough to dial 911. They gave me the "option" of going to the hospital voluntarily or against my will. Feeling hopeless I didn't resist. An ambulance arrived and whisked me to Maimonides Medical Center. The emergency room staff declared me hazardous to my health although the only mark on my body was the grease on my hand from clutching at the train track.

Breathing Stale Air

My inability to function intensified during the two months I spent on the psych floor. How this hospital gained reimbursement of $86,000 for my care from private insurance and Medicaid, when the prior one had apparently exhausted my benefits, was a huge stroke of luck, if not a complete mystery!

Rather than delving into the details of my suspended animation, here's one example of my dilapidated state: I buttoned my shirts with the dexterity of an arthritis patient. In addition, my constipation became so severe I begged the attending physician for enemas, which I self-administered in the bathroom while my roommate tried to rile me by banging on the door.

Susan visited daily. I played Scrabble with her as if I could discover a vocabulary to define my bare existence. My inability to construct more than four-letter words was not what I had in mind.

Finally I passed a psychologist's reality test on the second try. In my eyes I had done no better than when I flunked the first time. I felt as incapable of caring for myself outside the hospital's walls as inside them.

Maybe this stamp of approval occurred because the medical center could no longer afford me after I had racked up such a large bill and refused possibly lucrative electroconvulsive therapy (ECT). I feared mental confusion following such treatment would render me more vulnerable to the bullies on the ward. Meanwhile South Beach, the state hospital on Staten Island, wouldn't accept me for long-term treatment, either because I lived too far away in Brooklyn or my insurance was about to expire (again).

As a result, on January 8, 2007 I was released with a paper bag of meds and instructions to return for day treatment. This satisfied the doctors as well as my family; I no longer was an endangered species. (In retrospect, I admit the staffs at both Maimonides and Brookdale hospitals saved my life when I least valued it.)

***

Thus my recovery began. However the days blended into weeks, months, and ultimately years. Today it's hard to describe the course of that improvement because so little happened for so long. Yet it seems to fit into four stages:

Stage One: Gathering Moss as When a Stone Stops Rolling

First I frittered away two years in the continuing day treatment service, during which I avoided as much as possible the available classes, from not-so-creative arts therapy to men's and other support groups.

To maintain good standing as a client, I participated in group therapy but said little or nothing. The problem was I could only describe how dead I felt inside, and no one, least of all me, wanted to hear those words. I also feared such a confession would land me back on the inpatient unit.

In weekly individual therapy I talked mostly about the politics and books discussed on the radio—another way of avoiding the real issues. The main reason I came to the program was to eat the free breakfast and lunch offered and watch TV in the community room.

I didn't try to make friends with other clients. As a peer counselor, I should have regarded them as sisters and brothers in suffering. Yet after an entire life of managing my ups and downs, I was so ashamed of losing control that identifying with other dis-abled folks seemed like an admission of defeat.

At best this was an inconvenient truth. At worse I felt terribly alone. Even conversations with Susan, who had lived with depression since childhood, could not bridge this gap. Nor did my parents' history of propping up their children during mental breakdowns console me. True, I'd lived with a diagnosis of manic-depression (bipolar disorder) since college, but never had I felt so down.

No Future and No Going Back

As a child in Derby, Connecticut, outside New Haven, I had been a small-town over-achiever and a small-time juvenile delinquent. On the one hand, I attained Eagle Scout the same year I became valedictorian of all six eighth-grade classes and learned how to chant a portion of the Torah (Old Testament) for my Bar Mitzvah. On the other hand, I ran away from sleep-over camp, burned the upholstery in my family's car, vandalized cemeteries, stole money from neighbors, and shoplifted.

Instead of turning me in to the police, my enlightened parents, David and Rhoda, sent me at age 11 to Yale-New Haven Hospital's prestigious Child Study Center, where my younger brother, Hank, another sick offender, had done time.

Over the years we would "compete" for the most and longest treatments. He won easily with several more hospitalizations, including one which lasted a year and a half when he was in his early 20's. I still feel Hank is my mirror image. Because my brother's condition is more complicated than mine, he deserves greater credit for surviving on his own.

At the clinic I purposely lost Chinese checkers to a doctor every week for a year because I felt sorry for him—an important man having to play with a naughty kid. Later in Psych 101 I learned this behavior was called "repetition compulsion," a defense mechanism discovered by Freud, summarized by the cliché, "doing the same thing over and over while expecting a different result."

The diagnosis—I was my father's son. Despite earning degrees from Yale and Columbia universities by the age of 19, my dad joined his father's business of recycling scrap metal instead of becoming a lawyer. He unconsciously handed down to me his conflict between dream and reality, between a desire to employ his intellectual talents and the fear he couldn't measure up professionally. Hence he instilled in me ambition on top of an inferiority complex.

Prior to the latest mishaps I had survived two other suicide attempts (crashing a car and cutting my throat) and two hospitalizations in Massachusetts and New Jersey. Fortunately lithium and therapy enabled me to adjust to dropping out of schools, being fired from jobs, breaking up with girlfriends, and other temporary setbacks.

As an urban planner in the fields of public health, affordable housing, environmental protection, economic development, culture and the arts, I changed jobs often—the grass, if not the money, always appeared greener on the other side. I also wrote articles on a variety of subjects demonstrating either my versatility or a short attention span.

For years I had blended into a "chronically normal" society. Thus in spite of a family history of mental illness, I ignored appeals for membership by the National Alliance on Mental Illness (NAMI), sent to me at the request of my mother, who was a teacher, social worker, and president of the local mental health center for many years.

Eventually I signed on the dotted line and began speaking at NAMI NYC-Metro meetings about my experiences with manic-depression. In 2002 I changed careers, becoming a peer job counselor at Brooklyn's Baltic Street Mental Health Board (now Baltic Street Advocacy, Employment & Housing) because I wanted to give back, from a position of strength, to the community I finally admitted was truly mine.

Continuing to Go Nowhere Fast

When not blaming my psyche for lying on the couch, I used the excuse of an old running injury to my left foot and ankle, which was painful enough to require an air cast whenever I ventured out. Sometimes I believed I was just lazy—difficult to admit for someone who had worked hard his whole life.

With the help of one of my sisters, Robin, a successful single mom and social worker at Manhattan's Beth Israel Hospital, as well as my Maimonides' case manager, Jack Beacher, I obtained disability benefits on the first try, probably because of my dire circumstances. In April 2007 without lifting a finger I began helping Susan pay the bills again. Occasionally I consoled myself that 30 years of full-time employment merited such assistance.

Playing Musical Chairs Leaves Me Sitting on My Ass

Later that year Susan decided my desk in our small bedroom was too bulky and therefore expendable. My base of operations and writing post for 20 years had changed into a useless repository of the newspaper clippings and mementos proving I once mattered. Given how insufficient I felt, I reluctantly helped her remove the desk for pickup by the sanitation department.

To set up a makeshift office in the alcove by the front door, my wife, a one-time fashion designer, had to move her drawing table from there to the dining room because it wouldn't fit in the bedroom where she wanted it. I couldn't tell whether she was just unlucky or this oversight was payback for what she did to my writing table—the only time during my illness she acted on her own in what she thought was "my best interest."

Although we had the presence of mind to dismantle my desk we didn't realize hers could be taken apart too. So for a year we piled junk on the table until one day I had the bright idea to take it apart, move the pieces into the bedroom, and reassemble them. The process took four hours. I was elated and Susan was pleasantly surprised. We celebrated this new development. Yet the feeling I could do something for someone else faded after a few days. It was a kind of artistic flash in the pan.

These two episodes symbolized momentary inspiration and activity followed by inevitable decline. Maybe Sisyphus was just dumb for rolling that boulder up the hill again and again as the Greek gods commanded him. If so I could have benefited from a little of his bullheadedness.

Stage Two: Books, Books, and Nothing but the Books

At the end of 2008 New York State's Health Department drastically cut Medicaid reimbursement for day treatment. While the medical center kept the program open for the most disabled clients, I was shifted into weekly outpatient treatment.

Over the prior two years I had reduced my participation in the day program from four or five days a week to one or two, hoping no one was keeping track. Perhaps my treatment team regarded this as progress, which is why they didn't demand I come more often. As much as I feared leaving a disliked but familiar program for an unfamiliar one, I looked forward to more free time on the couch even if hiding from reality also meant negative thoughts and useless flights of fancy.

Still too depressed to reveal much of my inner life, I wasn't thrilled about continuing with weekly sessions of individual therapy. However during the next two years I discovered that pleasing my wife and therapist reduced the pressure on me.

I vacated the couch long enough to:

- take care of our four cats and dozen goldfish;
- water plants in the co-op's lobby and backyard;
- shop for necessities, especially food;
- cook for myself, an oh-so-finicky eater;
- wash our clothes, vacuum the apartment;
- pay creditors, balance the check book; and even
- argue with our upstairs neighbors when they got too noisy.

Life Writ Large in Imagination Only

During my second hospitalization, at Maimonides, I read to escape the emotional chaos confronting me in the form of other patients. I preferred reading especially because watching TV brought me into contact with people I believed were from another planet.

How I finished a half dozen mystery novels was a function less of my ability to concentrate and more of my desire to withdraw. The ingenious, often gruesome murders were appealing because they allowed me to secretly vent my anger at the world. However when I began a memoir by the humorist David Sedaris about his real-life, dysfunctional family, the story hit me so hard I couldn't finish it.

After I returned home my meds were increased to make sure I didn't do anything "foolish," beginning a vicious cycle of symptoms and side effects. One of the results was an inability to concentrate on reading. Such activity also would have required sitting up and I just wanted to flop on the couch.

Listening to the radio was the extent of my work ethic: WCBS for news, WNYC for culture, and WWRL for politics. Previously sweet songs grated on my ears as if playing them reminded me of long lost lovers. Thus I avoided listening to music stations while my collection of jazz, folk, rock, and pop cassettes lay neglected in cardboard boxes.

If Lyra Ward, my personal psychologist at day treatment hadn't been a book lover, I might never have started reading again. She overcame my resistance to the written word by lending me the novel, *What You Owe Me*, written by Bebe Moore Campbell, about the relationship of an African-American woman and a Holocaust survivor. (Her children's book, *Sometimes My Mommy Gets Angry*, won an award from the National Alliance on Mental Illness in 2003.) However Moore's story was an example of how fiction proved too real, too raw, but non-fiction books on nature and history represented safe ground at first and room for growth later.

After finishing the unread volumes I owned, I began borrowing literature from the Windsor Terrace branch of the

Brooklyn Public Library. Although the branch was only a block away I agonized for days before making the trek there. Yet when I withdrew movies, which had weekly due dates like my outpatient appointments, the library became another social outlet and a measure of what I craved but couldn't acknowledge; namely a reaffirmation of my intellectual prowess.

I was drawn to murder mysteries again, preferring suspenseful plots which distracted me from my problems rather than identification with characters who reminded me how troubled I was. Histories and biographies from the 1930's through the 1960's also garnered my attention; in other words, from the low point of the Depression my parents had survived to the high of the 1960's I had "inhaled." Compared to the present the past may have been more turbulent, but it seemed more caring.

Soup by the Book Leads to Spoiling the Broth
Susan always baked apple, pumpkin, and pecan pies for our Thanksgiving celebrations at my other sister Toby's home near Boston, Massachusetts. A wife and mother of two sons, she had been a corporate lawyer before suffering a brain injury from a skiing accident, and had picked herself up as a reference librarian.

For the 2009 holiday I contributed one of my family-friendly soups which I had learned to cook at kosher summer camps during college. I chose lentil with a stock made from leftover chicken to which I added cabbage, carrots, onions, and brown rice.

If I l couldn't dazzle my outpatient therapist, Yelena Repka, with my life's story, here was a potboiler bound to please her. Gradually I changed the base to healthier garlic and Dijon mustard supplemented by beans, potatoes, tomatoes, and collard greens. The taste of the soup varied with my mood depending on whether it took 1½ hours to prepare on bad days or the usual 45 minutes when I felt OK.

On New Year's Day 2010 I enjoyed a holiday meal with Susan and her sister, Rosemary. Although we share families with depression and other emotional challenges, on this occasion we exchanged toasts to a brighter future. High on two glasses of wine, I immersed myself in a book by a self-made genealogist who wrote about the many surprises in her family's history.

Susan and Rosemary's stock is French Canadian and Scandinavian. Their great grandparents had immigrated to upper Wisconsin in the middle-to-late 19th century. In the late 1800's and early 1900's, mine had voyaged from Belarus, between Poland and Russia, to the Lower East Side of Manhattan. Perhaps those origins in northern climes account for our normally gloomy personalities.

The author's curiosity about her past inspired the following resolution regarding my future: I would compose an article on the naturalist Terry Tempest Williams, who taught me in 1993 at the Bread Loaf Writers' Conference, near the poet Robert Frost's farm in Vermont. For two weeks, when not absorbing her instruction, I tramped through the surrounding Green Mountains. Seeking inspiration along Frost's "roads less traveled," I tried to wrap my mind around the too-thick-to-hug trees.

I chose Williams, who like me came of age in the 1960's, because her most celebrated work, *Refuge*, chronicled the death of her mother from ovarian cancer while the Great Salt Lake flooded their favorite bird sanctuary. Helpless as nature ran riot Williams was nevertheless determined to find meaning in her deathwatch. The book was a breakthrough in nature writing because she so sensitively balanced love of people and places.

I also wanted to make amends for a critical article I wrote after the conference about her essays in *An Unspoken*

Hunger. Instead of understanding her desire to be free of the patriarchal Mormon religion in which she was raised, I berated her for preaching feminism. In addition, I forgot what we had in common as childless authors. In *Refuge* her mother quipped, "You can't hug a book."

For background I read *Leap*, her unusual meditation on the fantastic plants, animals, and people in the 15th-century Dutch painter Hieronymus Bosch's "Garden of Earthly Delights"—she studied it in Madrid's Prado museum—and *Finding Beauty in a Broken World* about her attempts to save endangered prairie dogs in Utah and provide hope through an arts project created with survivors of the 1994 Rwandan genocide.

In *When Women Were Birds,* Williams revealed why she suppressed the knowledge that her mother left behind numerous diaries with nothing in them: "It showed how terrified I had been of my own blank mind." (Quoted from an interview in *The Daily Beast,* May 22, 2012.)

Combined with the discovery of a brain tumor, for which she refused surgery because the procedure might impair her thinking and silence her writer's voice, it's no wonder she imagined, "Once upon a time when women were birds, there was the simple understanding that to sing at dawn and to sing at dusk was to heal the world through joy." Williams may not have been traumatized, but her fears and hopes resembled mine.

Unfortunately I couldn't sustain the elation induced by Terry Tempest Williams' shimmering prose. The thought of all the work necessary to interpret her writing exhausted me; I was more stuck on my couch than on her.

Other Artistic Infatuations

Williams was one of five incomparable women, who were like the animas supporting my animus, Jungian archetypes in the collective unconscious. "Because a man's sensitivity must often be repressed, the anima is one of the most significant autonomous complexes of all... [influencing] a man's interaction with women... [and manifesting] itself by appearing in dreams... Jung viewed the anima process as being one of the sources of creative ability." (Wikipedia)

Called the "Dark Lady of Letters" because she upset the male world of cultural criticism in the 1960's with her pioneering *Against Interpretation,* Susan Sontag led me to comparative literature in college with her manifesto for passion in the arts—from Holocaust memoir and French New Wave cinema to science fiction and gay male style.

I began corresponding with Sontag in 1977 after defending her controversial *On Photography* in a letter to a Boston newspaper. For her, taking photos robbed rather than reproduced reality.

No doubt to indulge a young fan she agreed to let me write her biography. Yet instead of gaining her attention when we met at a posh women's club, I stuttered like a supplicant in awe of the queen. Before I knew it a bunch of well-wishers crowded me out. That was the end of my fairy tale. However when I read Sontag's journals after her death, I discovered that like me (and my father) she had grave misgivings about her ability to succeed.

A journalist from the same generation as Susan Sontag, Joan Didion inspired my application to journalism school. Rather than outperforming her subjects with acrobatic prose like her male counterparts, she explored in *Slouching Towards Bethlehem* and *The White Album* the chaos of the 1960's and 1970's, including her own nervous breakdown, with a fearlessness needing no advertising.

Yet for all her ability to find the meaning of the American way of life in a journalistic grain of sand—her homage to the Hoover Dam's construction reads like Stanley Kubrick's film *2001: A Space Odyssey*—in a recent memoir, *Blue Nights,* she admits ignoring the ways in which she might have worsened her gifted daughter's mental illness. Given Quintana's premature death Didion felt she had a lot of explaining to do.

Deborah Hay was another 1960's iconoclast, who made a mark by including amateurs in her modern dances. During 1993 I wrote a column, "Whole Earth Dreams," for a New Jersey shore weekly, about the intersection of nature and the arts. To practice what I preached I traveled to the Omega Institute, in New York's Hudson River valley, for her workshop "Playing Awake," an exercise in how adults could recapture the joy of childhood movement.

How Hay encouraged a bookworm like me to "invite being seen 50 trillion cells at a time" in Zen-like fashion was a testament to her charisma. Looking to integrate dance and life, she had practiced for six years alone in her studio every day with the goal of never repeating a step. From this version of Christ's temptation in the desert, she gained a new faith, a combination of discipline and spontaneity on which she based her gospel that rehearsals are just as important as performances.

She acted like a ringmaster in a clown's suit, her big features alternating between grins and pouts. Long before Cirque du Soleil (Circus of the Sun), originally from Quebec, made popular its choreographic style throughout the U.S., Deborah Hay created a one-ring show which anyone could join. As I wrote in my article, "What were the odds I would be the last one dancing after breaking my glasses, scratching my legs, cracking two toes, skinning both knees and bruising every vertebrae from my sacrum to my iliac?"

By the end of the week-long course, cavorting eight hours per day, I was ready to follow her anywhere and did. Every few years I've seen Hay perform in Greenwich Village. Her greatest desire: "to dance when I'm 90, in a stillness so attractive the audience will remain engaged."

Another contemporary of mine, Elizabeth Swados, breathed new life into the form of musical theater in 1973 with *Nightclub Cantata*, a blend of poetry and world music like the aroma of Turkish coffee mixed with the sound of a ram's horn (the Jewish shofar blown on the High Holidays).

Over the years Swados has proved to be an avant-gardist with a bent for such comic-strip-like Broadway productions as *Runaways* and *Doonsebury*. As a director she harnesses the mania in her admitted manic-depression to the energy of teenage actors without letting them run amok.

Her *Four Lives: A Family Autobiography* detailing the suicides of her mother and brother is a cautionary tale like no other. Plus *My Depression: A Picture Book* is achingly funny and informative, a self-help *Depression for Dummies*. Another example of this cutting-edge humor is her casting of Job as a clown in one multi-media production.

These mothers of invention not only doubled and tripled up as playwrights, poets, novelists, short story writers, children's book authors, song lyricists, and film-makers—a versatility to which I aspired in my arts criticism—we also shared ethnicity and geography.

Sontag, Hay, and Swados were of Jewish descent. Whereas Hay grew up in Flatbush, a few blocks from where I live, Sontag, Didion, and Swados relocated from elsewhere in the U.S. to Manhattan. Including Terry Tempest Williams, they were all born outsiders, who stood up for themselves by challenging the intellectual and artistic norms of the day. They certainly made me squirm in and out of my seat. Sadly even recalling their inspiring examples couldn't rouse me from my stupor.

Reading about Bodies, Dead and Barely Alive
However, during the next few months I managed to write a couple of short pieces at my therapist's urging: one on the horticulture therapy/job-training program Susan runs at

Brooklyn's state psychiatric hospital, Kingsboro, and a second describing my treatment by a dermatologist for skin cancer of the "schnozzola" (as the Brooklyn-born comedian Jimmy Durante called his enormous nose).

I also consumed a heavy dose of biographies about other heroes. These included the Algerian-French existential novelist Albert Camus; the U.S. Depression-era photographer Dorothea Lange; Beat poet Allen Ginsburg and radical folksinger Woody Guthrie, who both lived in Brooklyn for many years; Thomas Paine, pamphleteer of the American Revolution; and the lyrical Belle of Amherst, Massachusetts, Emily Dickinson.

Why was reading about exemplary people uplifting? Perhaps I was trying mentally to prove my father had not died in vain; he claimed to have read every work of fiction in the Yale Library. Because I never won an argument with him, thinking for myself became the hallmark of an existence to which I was clinging like Sisyphus to his rolling rock. Regrettably I still wasn't ready to put thought into action by getting off the couch.

***

I also still limited socializing to occasional visits with my sister-in-law in South Brooklyn and holiday trips to my side of the family in Manhattan, Connecticut, and Massachusetts. I usually refused my wife's invitations to attend a party, museum exhibit, or night out at a restaurant. Trying to have a good time seemed like more trouble than it was worth.

Although I had more to discuss with Yelena, my social worker, I struggled to fill the 50-minute sessions with words. Yet I began to assemble bits and pieces of my story for our examinations, in particular how the desire for success and fear of failure mixed with my mood swings.

Given Susan's approaching retirement I anticipated financial distress because I depended on her health insurance and salary. There were also Susan's physical problems. Due to arthritis in her knees and hips she needed crutches at one point, and we were alarmed by spots on her lungs which luckily turned out to be the scars of childhood tuberculosis.

I possessed a long list of physical woes caused or worsened by my mental condition. These included:

- anorexia (down from 135 to 105 pounds);
- angina as a result of coronary artery disease;
- high cholesterol and blood pressure;
- dislocated foot bones/strained ankle ligaments;
- broken and decayed teeth;
- skin cancer, psoriasis, and acne;
- a leaky bladder alternating with urinary retention;
- rectal bleeding, diarrhea, or constipation;
- poor thyroid and kidney function.

Wishing to deny these signs of decline, I seldom complained and hardly ever took care of them. (If only my garden-variety depression had been exotic enough to merit an episode on the TV show *Grey's Anatomy*, I might have paid my symptoms more attention.)

At the end of my first hospital stay I had told Dr. Paz, the head psychiatrist, that my cholesterol level increased 100 points. Was it something I ate? "No," she said matter-of-factly, "Mental illness will do that to you." Feeling down was bad enough, but psychosomatic symptoms increased my self-pity.

Stage Three: An Angel to the Rescue

In March of 2011 I watched in awe Jane Campion's film, "An Angel at My Table." It is based on the three-volume autobiography of Campion's countrywoman Janet

Frame, who survived years at mental institutions in the 1950's, enduring more than 200 electroshock treatments. From a poor, working-class family, she became New Zealand's most acclaimed author of the 20th century.

Yelena challenged me to write about the movie. Despite my low expectations, I returned to her the following week with 40 pages of an incomplete essay, "Saved by Imagination."

How I got carried away was as much of a miracle as Janet Frame's recovery. Even when not pinned to a stretcher for ECT's, Frame, like me, spent most of her time prone to despair. Cowering in bed on the verge of being carted away for a lobotomy, she is greeted by the asylum's director with the news of her release because she has won a literary prize. As if escaping a firing squad she's bundled into a taxi for the ride home. What a relief! Later her first novel is accepted by a publisher on the first try. Another miracle! Both times I cried with joy.

I reviewed the film for every nuance of imagery, dialogue, and sound. *An Angel at My Table* is composed of episodes from Janet Frame's tumultuous life strung together like jewels on a necklace. I believed the parts added up to a whole I could absorb by osmosis. This was the trick of a critic who rather than trying to outsmart the artists (both Frame and Campion) channeled their deepest desires and mine.

The experience was like unlocking in college the secrets of Virginia Woolf's masterful novel, *The Waves*. During three sleepless days of reading fueled by lots of coffee, I so identified with the hero Perceval's search for immortality that I wrote my best paper, defying the English instructor who believed I couldn't think for myself.

In fact, my first suicide attempt (senior year of college) followed a depression when I couldn't organize my thoughts at all. This established a pattern of writing inducing highs and writer's block triggering lows. Luckily I rebounded in time to achieve highest honors and head to Paris for graduate school with the goal of becoming a professor. Janet Frame went to London on a fellowship after her release from the hospital, saying, "There would be no second chance for survival if I stayed in New Zealand."

From Breakdown to Breakthrough

Frame too had her first breakdown and failed suicide at university. She cracked because while hoping to become a scholar she was forced as a woman into teaching.

Harking back to childhood when a school marm stood her in front of the blackboard for lying, Frame abandons her class while a state inspector sits in judgment. Running in tears outside she can no longer pretend to be a teacher. In a desperate attempt to reconnect with her own nature (symbolized by the trees and flowers around her) she discards responsibility along with her prim shoes.

It may be a panic attack like the one I had but it's not a shock. Since childhood practically her only friends were the characters in books and her own poetry. She often reads and writes in cemeteries as if to defy death with her efforts. In one scene she and her sisters wander in the woods at night dressed as fairies. In another she almost swoons as her teacher recites from memory how the Lady of the Lake retrieved the sword Excalibur from King Arthur.

In a secret candlelight ceremony at age 15 Janet swears on her favorite collection of stories to become a writer. Nevertheless she prepares for teacher's college by burning her poems. As the flames crackle in an ashcan and birds fill the air with song, I wondered whether higher education would suppress her true self or renew literary inspiration.

Why was she so shy and introspective? Her narration "frames" the film as if the action reflects her thoughts alone.

A pudgy, bristle-haired redhead, she is also marked from birth by the death of her twin. Two other sisters, both trouble-makers, die by drowning and when he's not bullied because of his epilepsy her brother is treated by their parents with cold baths. What seems like a triviality—her need for dentures at age 20—represents her embarrassment at being identified as crazy. These events may explain her alienation.

This is reinforced when Frame is betrayed to the psychiatric authorities by a beloved psychology professor who, while praising her writing, is alarmed by her confession that she swallowed a bottle-full of aspirins. She is punished as when she and one of her sisters secretly gorged on their aunt's prized chocolates. For this new sin against her body she gets eight years in hospitals and the label of "schizophrenic."

Finally she writes a novel which is a thinly veiled account of her mental illness (and a more impressive literary effort than Sylvia Plath's better-known *The Bell Jar*, produced at the same time). Frame entitles it *Faces in the Water* and plops the manuscript on her London psychiatrist's desk like a big fish she's caught. To her relief and terror (because independence is scary) he concludes she was never really ill; all the years in hospitals made her so.

In other words, by trying to save her life, doctors (and the society which shuns her) almost take it away. Fighting back at one point she scratches a poem on the wall of an isolation cell.

Perhaps this is why the movie ends on a different and triumphant note: Janet returns to New Zealand and types in a cozy trailer these words from her novel *A State of Siege*: "Hush, hush, hush, the grass and the wind and the fir and the sea are saying; hush, hush, hush..." At last she is content with (her own) nature and so was I.

We come from different countries, backgrounds, and times. Frame (and Susan Sontag) died from leukemia in 2004. Yet I felt like her lost twin grown up. Thanks to Janet Frame, who bequeathed a record of unprecedented struggle and success, I had cracked a five-year writer's block. She was the medium for the message to me that "recovery is possible."

With this weight lifted I wrote humorous essays during the next few weeks about our cats, old lovers, my bodily ills, and cockroaches raining down from the apartment above. I hadn't regained enough confidence to submit them for publication, but drafting the articles was good practice.

Keeping High Ain't So Easy

I also took on more work in the apartment, such as patching leaky pipes, discarding broken appliances, shopping more often for food, and preparing new dishes, including, for Susan's birthday, recipes from MFK Fisher's *How to Cook a Wolf* (written during the austerity of World War II).

Encouraged by these achievements I proceeded to buy a used car for my wife because her arthritis made use of mass transit so difficult. I obsessed over the paperwork for registering the vehicle and underestimated the pitfalls of dealing with slick salesmen and dishonest mechanics. The car was a lemon and it cost a lot to make lemonade out of oil leaking from a damaged engine valve.

Along with Susan's cancer scare, threats of layoffs at her job, other family members' troubles, and a snafu with our telephone service, I plunged back into the previous funk. After reluctantly celebrating my 60th birthday with immediate family, I refused to attend a cousin's wedding. Exposure to a wider group of relatives still felt unbearable.

Stage Four: Waking Up to Smell the Roses

By the beginning of September an old obsession returned—underlying my physical symptoms was serious disease and ultimate death. What legacy did I want to leave behind? The last five empty, irresponsible years? If so I could at least put my affairs in order again so Susan would suffer as little as possible.

I started by filing all the financial papers scattered about the apartment. Then I cleaned our rooms from top to bottom and convinced Susan to throw away clothes she had hoarded since the Age of Aquarius dawned. Next I uprooted an unruly viburnum shrub from the garden and trimmed a multi-flora rose bush, which had grown six feet wide and as high as the backyard telephone wires.

As I stood on a step ladder pruning the normally beautiful roses, I associated them with a life out of control— my life. Not only did I climb up and down carefully, I also fit the thorny branches into garbage bags by cutting them into small pieces. This seemed a symbolic way of gently laying to rest the last five years, a period during which I had earned what amounted to a PhD in suffering.

I wanted to sculpt a work of art out of the lilacs which had also reached telephone-line proportions. My wife insisted I wait until after they flowered the following spring. I accepted her advice while muttering, "OK, I'll stick around."

With the bloom back on the rose, so to speak (even though the trees were beginning to blush with autumn's colors), I received an invitation to an exhibit by Elizabeth O'Reilly, one of my favorite Brooklyn artists, whose Irish brogue is as thick as the oil paint on her canvasses of Red Hook and Gowanus' decrepit waterfronts. Ten years ago I had written two articles about her. Why not a retrospective review of her works!

So I called my former newspaper editor, Raanan Geberer, at the Brooklyn Daily Eagle, as if five years had passed in a day and convinced him I could handle the task. After I met with the painter in her studio and drafted the article within two weeks, the paper published it. I also interviewed Brooklyn novelist Siri Hustvedt, a Norwegian from Minnesota, about her brushes with mental illness, as described in *The Shaking Woman or a History of My Nerves*.

These newly creative juices overflowed into other arenas: a tearful reunion with my family during the Jewish New Year; a trip to historic sites in Connecticut (including Mark Twain's Hartford homestead); going out to restaurants when not cooking at home; and worshipping at Brooklyn Quaker Meeting where the resident pacifists welcomed me back like a veteran of foreign wars.

Then I took care of my neglected body with visits to the primary care physician, cardiologist, gastroenterologist, urologist, ophthalmologist, and dentist. After getting my teeth fixed I could hardly believe stomach gastritis was my only remaining problem. A year before I had stopped wearing the ankle brace; walking without it strengthened my muscles and reduced pain—good aerobic exercise too. Helping Susan with her part-time gardening business also lifted my spirits.

Epilogue: Keeping the Pieces Together Requires Strong Glue

I always counseled clients and other peers to do something they loved when feeling ill. For five years I ignored this advice because doing less than my best seemed like a waste of time. Hence I wasted away to spite myself. Now I realize how feeling, thinking, and doing connect like the circuits of a thermostat which requires monitoring. It's a form of self-awareness. Yet even after 63 years I appreciate that resting on my laurels is a great risk. I need to grow, but not too fast; I don't want to come undone again.

That means:

- writing for mental health websites;
- attending arts exhibits/performances;
- reading inspirational memoirs;

- working as a peer job counselor again;
- advocating behavioral health care reform;
- serving on the housing co-op board;
- adopting/fostering homeless cats;
- cooking for Quaker Meeting;
- keeping my social worker informed;
- exercising in local parks and eating properly; and
- taking medications regularly.

Although my "life sentence" of manic-depression has not been lifted, the five years I put mind, body, and soul through a form of house arrest has earned me time off to practice loving-kindness towards myself and others. I may not be a victim but I am my worst enemy, which means it's up to me to prevent psychological distress by regulating the temperature of that inner thermostat.

***

In olden days the arts were woven into everyday existence. Creativity suffused life even when it was a struggle. With the help of Janet Frame, Terry Tempest Williams, and other angels, especially my wife Susan, I've compiled a Wellness Recovery Artistic Plan or WRAP for protection against the elements. (Apologies to Mary Ellen Copeland: My WRAP is an imaginary take-off on her Wellness Recovery Action Plan; see my www.brooklynsgotculture.blogspot.com for what I mean.) Whether "beauty in a broken world" is enough to sustain me depends on how well I create new bonds with people, places, and things I find here and now. Earth is for living—unlike heaven and hell.

***

"It is perfectly true, as philosophers say, that life must be understood backwards. But they forget the other proposition, that it must be lived forwards [too]."

Soren Kierkegaard (the mid-19th-century, dark-minded Danish philosopher),
Journals and Papers

Recovering from Depression as a Young Mother in Staffordshire in the 1950s

Rhoda Thornicroft and Graham Thornicroft

Introduction

This chapter relates the stories of a mother and a son about events that took place over 50 years ago. We start in central England, in Birmingham, and the force of these changes, for a time, separates our family and takes some of us to Scotland, in search of recovery. Some of the themes we touch upon refer to issues very much of their time: views about the best treatments for depression, or about how long treatment should take. But other aspects of these experiences have a more enduring nature, for example, on the nature of stigma affecting people with depression, and in particular on the impact for health care staff of having a mental illness.

Rhonda's Story

I had a 'nervous breakdown' when I was about 28 years of age. I had 2 children, a boy aged 3 ½ and a daughter aged about 2. I didn't really realise when I was becoming unwell…you don't really. It was a nervous breakdown, that's what they call it then. For perhaps several weeks prior to my 'breakdown' I began to feel that I couldn't cope with the day to day looking after the children and our home. I had a very good husband who helped me in every way and was very good to the children. I know he didn't realise I wasn't myself at that time, and I wasn't able

Rhonda Thornicroft

to tell him. I gradually lost weight and I started thinking that I might gas the children in the gas oven, when I wasn't in 'my right mind' and able to think coherently. One day I realised I desperately needed help, and as my husband was at work, I asked my son Graham to run to get a help from Violet, our neighbour. There was snow on the ground and he fell and came running home. I asked him to go again and he came back with her. She saw the state I was in and immediately rang for my husband to come straight home.

As I was so unwell, and my husband was not able to take time off work, I went with my children to Oban in Scotland to stay with my parents for 6 months and the GP (family physician) put me on anti-depressants, but I didn't really do anything. I was there for about 6 months and I'd lost quite bit of weight, from 8 ½ to 7 stones as I recall. I didn't really feel any enjoyment and I didn't have much of an appetite and I was not sleeping well. I always felt worse in the mornings and gradually felt somewhat better as the day wore on (see Figure 1). It was felt that I wasn't improving, and so I went with the children to stay with my husband's parents (in Staffordshire in central England) for another 6 months.

Figure 1. The Thornicroft family at Oban in 1956

I was taken by ambulance to the St. Matthew's Asylum as a day patient for electro convulsive therapy (ECT) every week for 3 weeks. They told me I would likely lose my short-term memory temporarily, which I did. I don't really remember much about it. I now know what it entailed as I subsequently saw a TV programme about it. They would give me a sedative and then afterwards I would wake up and the ambulance would take me home. And gradually I just started to feel better. The doctor said that it would take about 2 years to get back to normal and that I would never have another period of depression again. My weight picked up again and I felt more able to cope. I was still on anti-depressants and as I began to feel better I very gradually decreased the tablets over a period of time, on my own initiative. I went home with the children after being away from home for 1 year altogether, and was able to cope again.

I had been District Nursing previously, and a couple of years later, when my daughter started school, I applied to go back to my job. I had to fill in various forms and some of the questions were regarding my health. I didn't mention that I'd had a 'nervous breakdown', you didn't in those days, as I know I wouldn't be re-employed if I had mentioned that. People had peculiar ideas about mental illness in those days. Sometimes the medical profession is worse than anyone else.

Most of the family were very kind, but a sister-in-law told me to 'pull myself together', and I told her that I was annoyed that she was not more understanding. No doubt thinking she was being helpful. I tried to explain to her that when you have a mental illness you have nothing to fight with, and can't help yourself.

It is now over 50 years since I was ill and I have never had any re-occurrence and I have been in good health all my life since. I never became depressed again. I would never wish depression on my worst enemy. If I met someone with depression now, I would be very understanding, more so possibly now as I've had it myself, and advise them to see the GP and get help as soon as possible, that's the point. I hope that people are more understanding these days.

Graham's Story

When I was 4 years old, living normally with my parents and my sister at home in Birmingham, things changed. While my Dad carried on working as a policeman in Birmingham, I moved with my Mum and sister to go and live with Mum's parents in Oban, a small town on the west coast of Scotland immediately overlooking the Inner Hebrides. I don't think that I was told why we moved, but for me this was an adventure as our new home was near a beach, had a playground nearby! Although I don't remember much about that time, one very specific memory stays with me. My grandfather was a

Graham Thornicroft

lighthouse keeper, and had worked all around the Scottish coast and islands. Near his house was a small brick building which as special radio station he used to keep in touch with his central office in Edinburgh and his colleagues in distant lighthouses. The critical issue was the weather forecast, and from time to time I would go with him to the radio station and listen to the very detailed shipping weather forecast. The sectors of the sea around Scotland are named, and have lilting and highly evocative titles, often based on ancient Norse traditions. So in this small, dark, musty smelling room, with radio diode lights glowing in gentle orange tones, I would have a special thrill to listen with my Grandfather to the weather reports for: Viking, North Utsire, South Utsire, Forties, Cromarty, Forth, Rockall, Malin, Hebrides, Bailey, Fair Isle, Faeroes, and Southeast Iceland.

Several months later, life changed. My Mum moved, with my sister and me, to my Dad's parents in a small village in Staffordshire in central England, while he carried on working in Birmingham. This was an important time in my life as I started school in that village. The other children seemed to know each other, and I was the new comer. I recall a very traditional classroom with old wooden ink-stained desks covered in the inscribed names of generations of young children beginning their education. Every evening I would walk from our temporary home with Mum and my sister to the middle of the village to the pay phone, an old red traditional kiosk next to the village store. We would phone my Dad to keep in touch tell each other the day's news. I recall, but vaguely, how important that contact was for me. After one term (semester), as Mum got better, we moved back to our own home in Birmingham, and not long later Mum went back to work. It was only years later that I learned why we had left home for a year.

Commentary (By Graham)

In many ways the whole mental health landscape in England in the 1950s was almost unrecognisably different from today. The language used referred to 'mental breakdowns', and the legal framework used the Lunacy, Mental Treatment and Mental Deficiency Acts (Berry, 1951). In 1950 54,890 'defectives' (people which we would now refer to as having intellectual disability) were in hospital. Nevertheless depression was recognised as a syndrome well before this time. The 1924 edition of the Handbook for Mental Nurses, for example (Medical Psychological Association, 1924) states 'Depression is an extremely common and very important symptoms among the insane; and it is imperative to remember the intense mental suffering which it causes ...All degrees of depression may exist, down to the most profound melancholy and despair' (p 419).

The provision of psychiatric treatment at that time was largely based in institutions, of which 140 were built across

England at the end of the preceding century, the largest ever programme of civic construction (1). Indeed it was during the 1950s that the number of psychiatric beds in England reached its peak at 154,000, since then the number fell to about 40,000. My mother was treated at St. Matthew's Hospital (formerly called the Country Lunatic Asylum at Burntwood) which in many ways was typical of its type. Opened in 1864, it was designed to be almost self-supporting. It had its own gas works, electricity plant, bakery, church, laundry, fire department, mortuary and a farm and gardens which provided the majority of the vegetables used for meals. It had a boiler man, carpenters and gardeners, and it even had its own orchestra. Initially male patients would work on the farm, as shoemakers, tailors and ward cleaners. Women would work in the laundry, kitchen or in needlework and as ward cleaners. Those inmates who were violent or may harm themselves were locked up in padded cells (http://www.bfhg.org.uk). Over the decades, 3103 patients were buried in the grounds, many with unmarked headstones. The governmental policy of providing more psychiatric care in the community led to the closure of the hospital in 1995, and in 1999 a new housing estate was built on the site. As the central administration block was of some architectural merit, it was preserved and converted to apartments (see Figures 2-5)

Figure 2. Burntwood Asylum

Figure 3. Nursing Staff at Burntwood Asylum in 1925

Figure 4. Communal dining
room at Burntwood Asylum

Figure 5. Unmarked headstones at
St. Matthew's Hospital

What were the consequences for our family of this year when we were so much affected by Mum's depression? For her, the prediction of her psychiatrist that she would never become depressed again proved to be correct, and perhaps was a therapeutic intervention in its own right. She made a full recovery, returned to work as a District Nurse working in the community with patients with long-term psychical conditions, and later retired after a career of service to others (see Figure 6). Our family was reconstituted and our separation healed over. Perhaps this episode played a part in my decision years later to become a psychiatrist.

Some aspects of this story have a contemporary resonance. I now often give talks about stigma and discrimination (2) and mention my mother's experiences of mental illness. Often when I speak to audiences of nurses and doctors, and I mention that Mum decided not to disclose the reason for being unwell when she return to work, many staff nod in agreement. There remain strong elements of stigmatisation among health care professionals (Henderson et al, 2014) and indeed in countries where there have been reductions in stigma among the general population, less progress has been made for health staff (3). The central message of this story, however, is that with the strong support of many family members, Mum fully recovered from her episode of depression.

References

Berry H. (1951) The law relating to mental treatment and the health service. Churchill, London.

Henderson C, Thornicroft G. Evaluation of the Time to Change programme in England 2008-2011. Br J Psychiatry Suppl. 2013;55:s45-8.

Henderson C., Noblett J., Parke H., Clement S. Caffrey A., Gale-Grant O., Schulze B., Druss B. & Thornicroft G. (2014) Mental health related stigma in health care and mental health care settings. Lancet Psychiatry (in press).

Medical Psychological Association (1924) Handbook for Mental Nurses. Balliere Tindall and Cox, London.

Thornicroft G, Bebbington P. Deinstitutionalization - from Hospital Closure to Service Development. British Journal of Psychiatry. 1989;155:739-53.

Thornicroft G. Shunned: Discrimination against People with Mental Illness. Oxford: Oxford University Press; 2006.

To Come Out, Not to Come Out, To Come Out, Not to Come Out, To Come Out….. Not to Come Out

Ingrid Ozols

Ingrid Ozols

*"I will be a free fish in the sea
teaching the young ones to swim,
I will be a tree in a forest leading
you to the right path
I will be a lamppost lighting your
way in the dark"*
© 2007 Amber Ozols

To Come Out, not to come out…
that is the question. My answer was
spontaneous and very quickly
"absolutely, of course". In the back
of my mind I knew that some people
wouldn't understand or want to know. I wasn't always very
selective with who I shared my vulnerability….. But now it
was time to stand up and be counted.

Then once I started sharing, I didn't give it a second
thought. I did "tell" some people I was seeing a "shrink".
Initially no one said anything positive or negative. What did
the silence say? They did ask a little while down the track if I
was "popping a happy pill?" For many years I didn't take any
medication, but eventually with reoccurring bipolar
depression we had to try something. So we did. It was like
someone had given me a new pair of glasses, I could see
colours that I had not seen before. The outside was no longer
black and white with shades of grey. The sky was a beautiful
clear blue, the grass a wonderful bright green.

The catalyst for my "coming out" was being tired of
secrecy, and pretending all was fine. Family, culture, society

had engrained in me that the only way to live was being stoic. Showing emotionality and vulnerability of any nature was weakness, weakness of character and that others would perceive you as negative and a burden. Yet to be confident and happy was viewed as arrogance and self-love. There was no middle ground! I opted for the later. I would be a chameleon or the happy but sad clown.

More than 16 years ago as a Human Resources executive, a manager in my previous life, I saw mental illness poorly dealt with by every organisation and industry. I was overwhelmed with employees coming to me about personal issues. My instincts told me such employees work performance was hindered by more than work, personal and life issues. In too many instances I sensed there where mental health problems. Many people shared their thinking about suicide with me. I was referring a lot of people to my general practitioner until he told me to stop because he couldn't keep up with demand.

This is also where I had to be careful. There were confidentiality landmines to navigate. If I dared say anything to someone else in the organisation this could be a CLM (career limiting move) for the individual. Stigma and discrimination was very alive. I was all too often directed to "deal" with employees who were viewed as "heavy maintenance." If their "personal issues kept interfering with work" then it was time to call in the "redundance or managing them out" process. I felt totally out of my comfort zone. I was not equipped or skilled to deal with these complex human issues. Managing the stigma was an added burden. People's livelihoods were potentially at stake. They shouldn't have been, as many were great employees, but had hit a stumbling life block. Yet this played in the back of my mind that a person could be, would be punitively treated rather than helped.

I started wondering why there where rehabilitation return-to-work programmes if one had a heart attack, but when it came to emotional and psychological ills no one wanted to know. There were whispers in the kitchen or behind closed doors, no flowers or cards were sent. It was far easier to work out ways to "eliminate the person" from the workplace, which felt horrid and wrong.

One situation changed everything for me. A director of one of my clients wanted to talk to me about an employee. This employee had been with the company for 6 months. She was one of the few souls who had been honest at her appointment interview where she shared briefly a history of mental illness adding that she was well treated and controlled. I thought nothing of it. During her tenure she did have the odd tough day, she was a little tearful and on those occasions, but kept to herself. Once or twice she came to me to talk about her issues. Her performance was always of a high standard. For each infrequent low, she would make up for it by working later evenings or on the weekend when appropriate.

I enquired about the content of the meeting and was given little information. I checked her records, absenteeism and noted she had only taken a few days off for the flu. Vaguely it struck me that perhaps her mental health vulnerabilities could be the reason for the meeting. In my thinking I hadn't seen anything untoward as she was a team-player and people enjoyed her company.

In the meeting the director was very serious and asked the employee directly "if she could write a report outlining how many sick days she would need for this depression thing?" We were both taken aback. Not knowing what to say.

He went further on "we all experience depression, but we *have to get over it*". At this point the now distressed employee walked out and stated she would get that report into the director the next morning. Wouldn't it be wonderful if we could know beforehand when we would get sick or injured so as we can plan ahead and around it?

The director looked at me and said, "This is not a charity, we are a business." By this stage I could feel my cheeks were getting very hot. My anxiety was climbing. He had no idea what he was saying. He looked at me and asked, "What is wrong? You look unhappy." I indicated I was and he asked me why. My reply was with another question, "how long had he known me professionally?" He thought about it and said at least a decade. In that time I asked him if he thought that there was anything untoward about myself and the work I had been doing for the organisation. He said, "no of course not." I replied "I have a psychiatric history as long as my arm." He didn't believe me, especially as I didn't really wear this on my forehead. I was always dressed most professionally, wore bright makeup and a smile...somehow I managed to work. I have no idea how at times when I was in a dark space or hypomanic. I did however do some things, and during my recovery I was getting help and care, to improve my functioning enormously.

At this moment I felt really sick of the secrets. I was tired of hiding. I know when I am well that I am articulate and I contribute positively to work and community. Sometimes it is easier than others.

I felt that as I was in a good space and that I was able to pull a few words together and make some sense that I could and should help somehow. I knew that I could not be the only person in a workplace or community dealing with such seemingly big problem(s).

I went looking for workplace training in this space. There was nothing available 16 years ago in Australia. From approaching educational institutions and business associations I received the response; "Go back to university and study to be a doctor or a psychologist." I didn't fancy that option. Yet this was the catalyst for becoming a consumer advocate/lobbyist and mental health educator, initially in the mental health sector and more general community and then into workplaces.

There was no real time for thinking specifically about "coming out" per se. Rather I was asked to do a few events and activities for a mental health organisation. Before I realised, I was speaking to community groups about recovery through mental illness and appearing on the media, television, and radio.

Then stigma and self-stigma really hit. I was ashamed and second guessing myself. My anxiety was overwhelming. I did not feel genuine. Something was wrong with me for doing this. Maybe the motivation for doing this was "the 15 seconds of fame" – but there had to be easier ways then getting in front of a television camera and saying to 400,000 Australian's "Hi, I have a mental illness!"

I recall a television crew arriving at my home requesting to take a picture of me in my car. I declined, believing that if appeared on camera many people, including family members would say the typical line I was most tired of hearing, *"She has an expensive car and a lovely home, what does she have to be depressed about? She is just seeking fame and attention."* I could hear their voices saying this over and over again. It didn't help my constantly climbing anxiety increased feelings of shame, paranoia and guilt. I tried to make this look easy and pretend I could handle this and do it well. However, I felt physically ill before and after presentations done in front of a group of people. This occurred every time, several times a week, for several years. I was terrified, doubting and questioning my motives. I had done public speaking for years, from school with formal training as a youngster. I wasn't afraid of public speaking – it was the subject matter, undressing myself emotionally, bleeding publicly. What was I thinking? Who would really benefit from this? What would/did I gain? This was all voluntary – which I didn't mind in the slightest. I couldn't ask for a fee. I did receive some remuneration along the way, but mostly over the years I have done this for other more selfish motives than money – pain, fear, and an obsession to try to make a difference has become the driving motivator. Even if the difference wasn't for a family member (the opposite is true), I was a trigger for other vulnerable members. If I can help just one person then I believe I can reduce stigma for our next generation. A society better equipped to embrace and tolerate vulnerability.

When I commenced doing this work 16 years ago showing vulnerability so publicly wasn't commonplace. Seldom was it done in front of large or small groups of people. When I appeared in the media, the response was mixed. I was deliberately honest and emotional. This is and has been my lifelong reality in some most painful form. Mental illness and suicidality is emotional and uncomfortable to live with let alone talk about. My late mother had spent most of my childhood in psychiatric care receiving ECT treatment for manic depression (now known as bipolar disorder). More recently, my teenager has been navigating adolescence with her own mental health vulnerabilities and hospitalisations. We are all vulnerable. All afraid of rejection, being seen to be *"weak or negative, self-pitying..."*

So far I haven't seen much improvement by keeping secrets, so we may as well talk about this openly. Knowledge is power after all. Attitudes, behaviours, services, systems can't be made worse by talking about this issue. When I took a plunge, I had no idea what drove or motivated me to do this. There certainly weren't many willing people to "Come Out so publicly" to say, "Hey I have a mental health vulnerability!" On one occasion my husband joked with me saying, "What have you got to worry about – it's my surname out there!" I had been asked if I wanted to be anonymous when I appeared in media or print. Why would I do that if I wanted to scream on the top of every building "treat us carefully, respectfully and sensitively, we are human"? Without question my name, and my face and voice has to be out there with this or what's the point? I may never work again, be ostracised or not be treated the same – but for me to be authentic and to move people toward change. I was proud despite feelings of insignificance and overwhelming anxiety that renders me voiceless, speechless and cognitively impaired. Something drove me to not look back. I keep the mantra in my head, *"believe, believe, believe...Hope is always there for each of us."* Otherwise the negative, self-deprecating voices in my head putting me down and being most self – critical would win.

The feedback about my first person stories from audience participants has been most humbling. I received hugs and thank you's in so many different yet rewarding and affirmative ways. One of my Key Performance Indicators is the number of hugs I get at the end of each presentation! Emails, letters, cards, phone calls after every presentation or session are still the norm. When I have requested feedback from audience members, I have been told that my simple storytelling intertwining my reality and life experience is highly engaging, relevant, striking cords with audience members that they themselves can relate to. I so believe the more people that share what mental illness is like will then give others permission to talk about what has been hidden for too long and ultimately reduce stigma. Increasing awareness and knowledge is critical for education to take place and confidence to replace fear.

Some family members were horrified I was "so negative and telling unpleasant personal things, being too honest and "shouldn't be sharing the family linen on the clothes wash." They saw nothing positive, inspiring or hopeful in these messages. I always tried to be respectful and careful of family, avoiding mentioning anyone except my husband and daughter in positive ways. I wouldn't be here if it wasn't for their love. Some relatives ignored my work or laughed. Some assume my media work has made me wealthy and money was the motivator. No one comes into this highly stigmatised, unsexy, traumatic sector for remuneration. Especially since many advocates and lobbyists give their time and effort voluntarily. I, too, volunteer most of my time and am able to keep activities afloat. My motivator is pain. I can't seem to help those nearest and dearest, but perhaps I can reach-out to better the lives of others.

The ultimate price for "Coming Out Proud" would however strike hard, like a handful of machetes through my heart. It was nearly 10 years ago that my father and I last met and shared a short morning together. I haven't seen him or his second family since. I had just had a major story appear in Australia's broadsheet on a Saturday morning. One couldn't miss this half page spread! As usual in my media appearances, I talked about my life's journey, my late mother's bipolar disorder and hospital visits, my parents bitter divorce, my dysfunctional family, my depression and bipolar and the work I was doing as an advocate. I received an email months later telling me how appalled they were that I could have allowed my/their story in such a horrible public way. I hadn't mentioned anyone by name. What I did share in my "safe box" was similar each time. This was my reality and no one was to blame. Being human means we will all experience a range of events and emotions, including love, joy, adversity, loss, vulnerability, injury and illness to name a few. My parents divorced when I was young. I had not grown up with my father or his second family, I had been estranged from them for a decade. Instead I lived with my mother and alcoholic stepfather and spent a lot of time being raised by my grandparents, uncle and aunt. In my presentation, I reflect on the many potential contributing factors that may have influenced my identity and mental health vulnerabilities.

I tried to apologise to my father. I rattled his emotions and suspect he felt deep pain reading the words in the article. I don't doubt that we both felt great pain and grief at what we had lost years before. The written word hurts more in the absence of facial expressions, tone and body language, which soften our perceptions. I kept the proverbial olive branch out for so long but I wasn't sorry for my words, or my reality. Should I give this work I love up for family peace and acceptance? At 40 years of age, stigma from within my loved ranks revolved around what was I doing was made me think. I had invested my very self in this space, finally owning something and being true to myself. I was contributing to things that were making a difference in Australia's mental health policy reform. Would I change my parent's view about my participation, which they disapproved of and eventually gain their or receive their approval? What if I stopped doing work I loved? Giving a little of myself to help give permission to others that this was ok to talk about, how would I feel then having to start another career? Now I had a choice to make. I decided to take the power back and stood up to stigma in the most excruciatingly painful ways such as having more family members avoiding me. I survived the daily brick in my chest, the mood swings, the grief and loss. I walked through the mountain and have unexpectedly become healthier along the way. I learned that my relationships with my father and the family where a major trigger for my lows and unwellness. I was forever retraumatising myself when in their presence. It's not that they or I are "bad" people, but rather our psychopathologies were incompatible.

So I love my father from a distance. I don't regret choosing "what I live breathe and do" instead of approval and peace. I couldn't have lived with my wings clipped, locked in a cage to keep others happy by not speaking up of the injustices that those of us who are vulnerable, experience.

The movement I represent was most political – just as the whole mental health sector in Australia is. Service users and their carers where the toughest critics of us and our work. I was often told by the old guard; "I *was too functional, part of the chardonnay set, the worried well and had no idea what it was like to experience or manage life with a mental health vulnerability."* Weren't we on the same side? Clearly not!

Since my journey into advocacy commenced I have had the privilege to meet inspirational people. Many of these gifted souls and peers have become my rocks, friends, colleagues and confidantes who have helped me to stay standing in the darkest of times over the 16 years working in this arena. The experiences have been a privilege. The more I give of myself the more gifts I have received. Doing this is more about passion and love. Even now, years later, I am still constantly standing up to stigma - but it is losing its power over me. I am and have turned vulnerability into strength.

Invitations to speak around Australia and globally have taken me to unexpected places, from New York City, USA to Paris, France, London, Scotland to name a few. In Australia, I have been invited to many committees and am involved in local, state and national government lobbying and advocacy groups and boards. I have helped general practitioners to receive the highest level of quality mental health training and education. In one of many national committees and government advisory groups I was a member of The General Practitioner's Mental Health Standards Collaboration. With a colleague, we set mandatory training standards for general practitioners in mental health on include lived experience and carer perspective to be a part of design, development, workshop delivery, implementation and evaluation. Given the diversity of members representing the major professional services and academia this was a ground breaking achievement that many years later is now accepted as the norm.

Being a proud member of the Mental Health Council of Australia in the early to mid-2000's it was an honour to serve on the Commonwealth Advisory Group of Leaders, Prime Minister and Cabinet for the first major provision of $1.9billion (AUD). Through this board position I contributed to many senate inquiries and human rights and mental health injustices. In one senate enquiry I was able to table in Australian parliament my personal work with workplaces and the outcomes of those relationships and the impact of the lived experience in corporate Australia educating employers about mental health, reducing stigma and improving these environments to be more conducive to mental illness, resilience and wellbeing. This was later tabled in Victoria's enquiry into workplace participation and mental illness. The many years work was provided to the members of these committees – books, video's, dvd's, workshop materials, that we had an evidence-based peer support approach. All these opportunities served me also. A much needed dose of empowerment, encouragement, and achievement. Indeed I was capable and intelligent contrary to stereotypes of incompetence or stupidity. Yet there were times I felt incompetent, foolish, inadequate, and incapable. This would soon include worthlessness.

As a former board member of The Royal Australian and New Zealand College of Psychiatrists Community Board, I influenced the organising of the World Psychiatric Association's Conference in Melbourne in 2007. We ensured that lived experience was present in every event to bring awareness and reduce stigma that pervades very much within health services – particularly mental health services. It is counterintuitive, but the worst stigma occurs from the very sector we occupy and seek help from. These experiences have given me the ability to shed my self-stigma and shame for managing life with a mental health vulnerability. They have served as potent doses of Prozac for my recovery journey. I exchanged fear and shame for confidence and pride.

What Has Been My Message and Why?

I tried to die on many occasions since I was young. Bipolar...is me, a label yes, a diagnosis yes, but in essence it is a part of who I am. During an episode of hypermania, hyper anxiety, hyper-arousal, the nervous energy, excitability, everything racing, my talking, my doing anything, intensity, high levels of agitation, aggression, paranoia, obsessive thinking, hypo-sensitivity to criticism, impulsivity, low ability to manage or control emotions is all there. Everything, words, emotions spill out without thinking....see what I mean?

Family, friendships, relationships, suffer during an episode. It takes a huge load of love, support and incredibly patient people to withstand the ups and downs, the intensity. Now with internet, emails, texts. It is so easy to go full on, pressing the one button that I shouldn't but do nonetheless. Then the "fix it" obsession starts. Many letters, emails, texts later. The more I try to apologise endlessly for something, anything, everything I perceive as my fault and didn't you know I am to blame for everything that goes wrong in the world? The guilt, shame, hyper-anxiety all come together and I am crippled by pain. I can't write, work or even talk. I can't even breathe.

There are times when this monkey stops swinging from tree to tree, the crash into the neighbouring tree hurts too much. The mice in my head come out to exercise, running frantically around a wheel in opposite directions! These clever pesky creatures don't help and play tricks when one is stuck ruminating endlessly. The noise isn't silenced easily. The psych ache just builds and builds and builds and the world seems smaller as the disconnect widens not only between loved ones, but everyone, especially oneself, I disconnect, wanting to desperately flee my skin. It is on these occasions I wish I could run from myself. Looking at that person I am starting to feel more resilient and less vulnerable, the rawness of the painful psychological prison I have been locked in for too long and the many different experiences this has ignited, isn't forgotten or lost. Pain is pain, we all cope and show it differently. I am so blessed to be rich with many wonderful family, friends, clients and colleagues who do reach out when they recognise my triggers and signs and symptoms that not all is well. This is a paradox from feeling disconnected. Every friend has a different role to play, a different understanding or ability, or inability to know what to say or do. I don't do "less is more" easily at this point and my listening skills are taken over by the urgency and intensity of everything else. Sometimes I wonder if they want to shake me or hang me on the washing line upside down. I know that some people want to step back, they do. Some have even walked away.

The impulsivity is a part of my personality, but when hypomania hits towards the end of the Richter scale my excitability comes through in my language. I can't keep up with my own racing dialogue. I know this puts me at risk with relationships – personally and professionally. Somehow I have been able to leverage the differences between these two worlds as it has been a necessity to try to hide vulnerability in the professional arena. Then when the gushing waterfall stops, I go to the other extreme and am known to be the turtle who pulls her head in neglecting those near and dear, who I tried to drive away with my intensity and constant neediness. It's on those occasions it's like I come down with an emotional psychological laryngitis - I can't talk, there is no voice. If I dare speak a word my world will collapse. I will collapse into a thousand broken pieces.

Then when depression hits...I become a butterfly.

"Imagine a butterfly caught in a spider's web frantically trying to escape. The more the brightly coloured creature flutters and panics, the more enmeshed it becomes. Terror and paralysis sets in. The butterfly is unable to move or fly awaiting impending doom."
-Ingrid Ozols beyondblue annual report 2002-2003

All I want to know is that I am connected to a few people, in the simplest of ways. When the head goes to this surreal place it's like life is moving in slow motion until I am frozen. Then the pace picks up and I know that life does go on. I can either sit back and watch or get up and join in. Joining in takes such effort, and every ounce of energy and work, every morning, every minute, every word...but believing in self, writing and saying self-nurturing affirmations and most importantly knowing that things will get better and episodes will stabilise takes time to stick. I am also impatient. Let me be at the other end, the stable, steady as she goes, calm waters.....it doesn't happen fast enough. Patience, impatience isn't helped with this.

There is a positive in all this that I wouldn't give up for anything though...."getting it", vulnerability, managing life with a mental illness from this side helps my antennae to connect with others who are in similar place and I can empathise and relate. The connectedness helps me to support someone vulnerable. I have spent many years learning how to negotiate the landmines of life with bipolar disorder. Recovery, though painful and slow, is doable. It is a process, a journey of self-discovery, learning and managing new, different life skills. This isn't linear or easy, but set in an environment of hope and optimism, connectedness and social inclusion are key to the journey.

Having also been touched directly and indirectly by mental illness and suicide since childhood and over the years professionally, this is a part of who I am. My journey of caring, living with vulnerability and recovery over several generations of immediate family members and relatives is the fuel that drives a personal crusade to decrease stigma, share hopeful messages and insights to others. Recovery takes work, support, patience, compassion and trust from family, health professionals, community, workplaces, and educational institutions.

The meaning of recovery has an underlying philosophy that encompasses the ability to live well with and beyond illness in terms of enhanced connectedness, social inclusion, activities taken up and control over one's life. What is needed is all of community coming together. We need to know what we can do to help ourselves and each other be proactive about health and not just reactive. We don't need to be medically qualified to reach out and help support people with mental illnesses (or any illness). We need to fight stigma by "Coming out' to share.

Giving a little of self to others creates an atmosphere that gives permission to others to talk about this highly stigmatised subject. It is ok to be vulnerable. Role-modelling hope, resilience, recovery and capability provides others who are touched by this that there is always hope, that they are not totally alone, that they too have possibilities and potential for recovery and to uncover their true potential. If I can give individuals comfort and community confidence and a sense that they are not alone. There are many people working tirelessly and passionately to make a difference to stigma, services and systems. Fundamentally we should be able to receive quality care when and where we may need.

Mental illnesses are complex. Self-stigma, vulnerability, and fear of rejection are overlooked burdens to the individual. The more people with mental illnesses who are willing to disclose publicly on a large scale is a strong way to send positive messages to improve society. The need to help others has become a critical element of my own recovery.

"We who seek to serve are taught by those who need our serving. They tell and teach us how to be a servant." We connect because we are human, the human touch, heart to heart, soul to soul. Ultimately this is about our humanness.

Footprints

One night I had a dream....
I dreamt I was walking along the beach with God
and across the sky flashed scenes from my life.
For each scene I noticed
two sets of footprints in the sand,
one belonged to me and the other to God.
When the last scene of my life flashed before us,
I looked back at the footprints in the sand.
I noticed that at times along the path of life
There was only one set of footprints.
I also noticed that it happened
at the very lowest and saddest times of my life
This really bothered me
and I questioned God about it.
"God, You said that one I decided to follow You,
You would walk with me all the way,
But I noticed that during
the most troublesome times in my life
there is only one set of footprints.
I don't understand why in times
when I needed You most, You would leave me."
God replied, "My precious, precious child,
I love you and I would never, never leave you.
During your times of trials and suffering
when you see only one set of footprints,
It was then that I carried you."

One Person's Story
Jacqui Chaplin

I spent nine weeks lying face-down on the lounge room floor at the beginning of 2013. It was not by choice. My brain chemistry literally took control of my body and laid me out. The metaphorical black dog was heavily seated on my back and was determined not to move or let me move. And that dog was doing a good job of hiding what else was really going on. It was the harbinger of a change for me that I would simultaneously want to sustain and reverse. It was the beginning of a loss that I am still mourning.

Jacqui Chaplin

There is also cause for hope and celebration based on my experiences. I am dedicated to the importance of moving beyond awareness and into understanding, compassion and acceptance for people living with mood disorders and other mental illnesses. This piece is one of my contributions, as is the radio show I host on the topic, But I Feel Good: talking about pink elephants (positive resilience strategies) and black dogs (the down sides and challenges associated with low moods and mood

Sitting by Jacqui Chaplin
©2013

disorders).You can find out more and listen to on demand episodes at www.jacquichaplin.com/bifgondemand   The Radio Show also has a Facebook page at https://www.facebook.com/butifeelgood. I'd love you to be part of the community working towards a speedy dissolution of the stigma that people living with mental illness experience.

Let's go back 20 years. I was diagnosed with clinical depression after the end of my first marriage in 1993. Despite prolific evidence to the contrary about marriage and divorce rates I thought I could make it work. Discovering I was wrong about that coupled with the loss of my 'married status' and a marked sense of personal failure saw me slide inexorably in to my first black hole of despair.

In my first clinically depressive state, I remembered my inability to sleep between 2am and 4am, lying in my bed alone, staring at the ceiling. It was characterised by a life draining lethargy and a desire to not have to move more than going between the bed and the couch. Previously a lover of food and wine I could not be bothered, what was the point anyway? I lost 24kg in the three months of this episode. I socially isolated myself. I did not want to be me. How could anyone want to talk to me? I would save them the trouble. My saving grace was that at some level I knew that my experience was not normal for me and that I had to do something about it. Off to the GP I went. After a long, teary consultation I walked away with a script for one of the best known antidepressants on the market at the time and a referral to see a psychiatrist.

I can't recall the time between my GP appointment and getting my first appointment with the psychiatrist. Very little of the content and detail of my conversations remain with me after two decades. On reflection I suspect that not being able to recall the specifics was simultaneously a wonderful safety mechanism and a dangerous trick of my subconscious mind to suppress the mess that needed to be surfaced and dealt with.

The most impactful part of that experience was the recommendation by my then psychiatrist that I tell my employer that I had glandular fever, of which the symptoms and side effects were similar to depression so that no one would have to know the difference. I am pretty sure that the psychiatrist made that recommendation with my best interests at heart, understanding that in the field of education not only might my employer be reticent about having a staff member with depression but imagine what the parents would think. The other implication was one of insurance, twenty years ago depression was a dirty word when it came to every kind of insurance from travel to income protection, to life insurance and home loan insurance. So what was not openly declared could not be held against me.

From my perspective the stigma attached to depression twenty years ago is different to the stigma that still exists today. Back then depression was not an everyday term. I didn't hear about very many people, except in the most abstract of terms, who had depression. The general level of awareness and understanding were infantile. All of this seemed to make the lie about my illness and absence from work understandable and excusable. The reasons I chose not to disclose generally, and at work, felt solid.

The skerrick of public knowledge that existed was miniscule. Little did I realise, that twenty years later, the familiarity with the language of depression and mental health would have increased exponentially yet genuine understanding, knowledge, compassion and acceptance would still be lagging behind like a tortoise starting after a hare.

Several cycles on the standard offering of anti-depressants worked to lift me from my recurrent minor slumps and recover enough to feel normal again. Thinking I was cured I would go off the medication, plateau, and slide magma-like back into the maw of depression. During this time many well-meaning people in my life shared their opinions on whether or not the anti-depressants were worthwhile, safe, or effective. The list goes on. Then there were those who thought that it was "all in my head" and those who thought I should just drink a cup of cement and toughen up! I am not sure whose interests were always at the heart of those suggestions and opinions. It often felt more about them and their stories and their expectations than any genuine care understanding or concern about me.

What I learnt from a decade of cycling on and off medication was that I was better staying on the medication than I was being off it. However there was something else at play and it had yet to make itself evident. No-one, myself included, had been able to connect the dots between my depression and some rather erratic, aggressive and risk loving behaviour.

As the summer of 2003 arrived I was feeling on top of the world. I was invincible. I was working full time, volunteering in an Asia Pacific Leadership role. I had made it a full time adventure. I would finish my day job and then do another eight hours on the volunteer job. My energy was boundless. I was on the right track, the fast track, I was heading off to meet with Oprah. When the summer holidays arrived I decided for one last time that I was feeling so good I could halve the dose of my anti-depressant and be fine! The holidays were a disaster. By the end of summer I was an unpleasant piece of work who did not want to be around anyone else and who no one else wanted to be around.

And then that feral, stinky huge mongrel of a black dog reappeared. Approaching slowly, leaving me with a sense of impending dread that I could do nothing to stop. Crap! Here I go again!

Interestingly, I initially couldn't recall much of anything to do with my second major episode. And then bits and pieces started to come back.

There was another teary visit to the same GP. I recall an inability to access a psychiatrist for at least 3 weeks. I knew I could not wait that long. And bless the cotton socks of my compassionate GP she did not just send me off but rang around until she found me an appointment that day. I went to one of the crisis mental health clinics and not only found an empathetic ear, but one that was aware of all the latest research that pointed to the on and off medication behaviour that I had been doing as a contributor to the severity of my current clinically depressive episode. I gave the clinic my history as I deemed relevant and they asked questions only associated with my depression. New medication was prescribed. It relieved some of the depressive symptoms but had me sleeping 18 hours a day and made me barely functional enough to walk around the block, as long as I didn't have to cross any roads.

When my three week wait was up I went to the next psychiatrist, as the crisis clinic is exactly that, a once off experience. Seeing the new guy at the end of each week, I would then head down to a caravan in Ocean Grove to escape the expectation of a speedy recovery. It just doesn't happen like that. After about 6 weeks I started to feel a little better; enough to realise that the psychiatrist I was seeing was NOT the one for me. He spent our sessions asking questions, and then proceeding to stare down at his pad and take copious notes that looked like a spider was crawling across the page. He would sit with his back to his window, his face in deep shadows. On the second appointment after I noticed all these things I decided it was time to find a new psychiatrist. Upon asking whether his notes on me could be forwarded to a new psychiatrist he said, and I quote, "Aside from the fact that your hour is up, the short answer is no!" I really wasn't sure that he said that initially, I was in shock. How could someone who is supposed to have your best interests at heart say that to a patient? Yes, I found a new guy and he was great. A couple of things from my conversations with the new guy have stayed with me and I continue to use the strategies today.

The swap to a psychiatrist that had more compassion in his little finger nail than the one I waited three weeks to see had in his whole body was an important one. I seem to recall some exploration of my more elevated moods and a brief discussion about bipolar but I don't think my intellectual capacity was really in the place it needed to be for me to fully process the implications of a potential bipolar diagnosis. Consequently it got left behind.

New medication took me from 18 in 24 hours sleep to 6 in 24 hours within a week and then settled back to 8 hours sleep a night over three weeks or so. That was a tremendous boon. Sleep issues significantly impact my state of mind; thinking I am sleeping too much to not being able to get to sleep for hours, despite being exhausted. Life seemed to eventually slip back into a regular groove. I stayed on the medication, happy to abide by the research coupled with my personal experience. I knew I could not go without it. Another ten years cruised by with a life filled with all the things I enjoyed. I had a career I loved, a great partner, I travelled, I jumped off the Auckland Sky Tower twice. I was having a ball. Through 2012, I started to notice that people wanted to 'pop my balloons', 'let the air out of my tyres' and 'rain on my parade'. The more energy and enthusiasm I had the more push back I seemed to get. At the beginning of 2013 something happened which created an immediate and euphoric release for me. For two weeks I was invincible, electrified and free. It did not last. I started the well-recognised slide down the slippery emotional slope and came to a thudding stop, face down on my lounge room floor.

This time the psychiatrist spotted the pattern that preceded my clinically depressive episodes. The feelings of euphoria and invincibility, the constant talk, not needing much sleep, to name a few, were the hypomanic (low level) symptoms of Bipolar Disorder Type II. I finally had an explanation for my particular way of being. With hindsight I could clearly see the long ten year cycles where the hypomanic symptoms started out being subtle enough not to cause undue concern or notice in myself or from others. Then over a couple of years they would gradually escalate and I could see the greater risk taking behaviours occurring in all areas of my life. My energy and enthusiasm would intensify, I would come up with all sorts of new activities and ideas to engage myself in activities that would match the unbounding energy I felt coursing through me.

For those of you that don't know much about Bipolar, generally speaking Bipolar 1 has extreme manic episodes and a person may even experience hallucinations, psychosis or delusions. Bipolar 2 has lower manic episodes. Both experience devastating episodes of depression. And wretchedly so, every mania ends with a depressive episode.

I read as much material on first hand experiences as I could get my hands on when I was first diagnosed. It was such a relief to have people willing to share their experiences so that others who are at the beginning of the journey could feel like they are not alone and that their experiences are shared by many others. Most importantly it allowed me the hope and recognition that my mood disorder diagnosis was something that I could get "in order" and continue to live a productive life. So that piece was written when I was in order. Let's take a look at what it can take to get in order.

There are lots of parts to the bipolar puzzle from managing the manias and riding out and recovering from depressive episodes. And then there's the multiple puzzle pieces associated with disclosure. Should I? When and where should I? How do I go about it? The puzzles are not the same for different people. They are not even the same for any one individual.

I think the trickiest part of my bipolar diagnosis came about a year after I started on appropriate medication. Upon reading the first hand manic experiences people had written about I could not fathom why people would not want to stay on their medication, especially knowing that the fall would follow the mania. So many people noted that they hated what the medication did to their creativity, spark and enthusiasm for life. Having finally sorted out which medication didn't make me itch, twitch and feel positively disgusting I hit a plateau. It is on this plateau that my daily experience feels muted and diminished; all the things that were once possible seem unattainable. The logical me knows the importance of staying mediated and is working on ways around the feelings of limited possibilities and opportunities. In this space I understand why people with bipolar would choose to be un-medicated. I will not be one of them.

My disclosure journey has been one of extremes. Partly a sign of the times and partly a more recent decision to be open with people about my mood disorder as part of a commitment to be part of the movement to see the dissolution of stigma associated with mental illness and mood disorders. I have gone from telling all but a very few that my depression was glandular fever through to telling everyone who asks "What's new?" about my Bipolar II diagnosis. I saw every conversation as an opportunity to be open and comfortable about it to educating others about mood disorders and being able to live with "Bipolar in order". Although everyone I told seemed initially to be fine with my disclosure on reflection I wonder what has happened when they've gone home and back to life. Whether there has been a conscious or a sub conscious decision to stay away because they're not comfortable with potential mental health conversations or that they think it might be catching or whether it suddenly means I might be unstable when I am far more stable medicated appropriately than I had been over the last two decades. These questions and thoughts whether about them and their stories or me and my stories have me in the question about whether my whole sale disclosure was the best thing for me or not.

It can be a long winding path out of each depressive episode, the path varies each time for me. And that's the path in as well as the path out. The signs I became aware of earlier in my second and third episode as a result of each previous episode help keep my head up and seeking help much sooner than I did the first time around. And the more I educated myself about the importance of recovery plans, the range of resilience strategies and the more I read about other people's experiences the more I have been able to read the signs and more effectively ride the whopping waves that hit me when having a major depressive episode to recovery.

The experts say that bipolar is usually a genetically inherited disorder. Being adopted it took me a long time to build the relationships in order to be able to have the conversation with my biological mother about where my bipolar may have sprung from. It became evident over the course of time that it was likely to be my biological father. In his heyday he was a rodeo rider. The first picture he ever showed me was him standing up, barefoot on two galloping horses, holding the reins in one hand and waving his cowboy hat in the air with his other. People have talked to me about a number of other characteristics he exhibited that seem to fit the bill. Suffice to say horse riding is not a genetically inherited gene but bipolar is.

One of the most productive and self-affirming strategies that I have used when riding the whopping depression wave is creativity. During my most recent episode it was art, putting ink to paper, that allowed me to maintain some sense of self and keep the festering darkness at bay. I couldn't do anything but draw and sleep and the drawing made the waking hours vaguely tolerable. I invite you, if you are faced with depression, to find something creative and self-defined to keep your mind as far from the destructive self-thoughts that can plague a depressed mind. (See Picture Below.)

My Sweet Desire (Triptych) by Jacqui Chaplin © 2013

One of the seemingly insurmountable challenges of experiencing any mood disorder can be accessing primary health care from someone who is expert and you can trust.

I don't profess to be highly educated in relation to Medicare's Mental Health Care Plan (MHCP) and its process. I write this to share my experiences as a result of the apparent differences and disconnect between the knowledge that I would assume the professionals working in the mental health field would have. Sometimes even when you find good primary health care givers things can still go wildly wrong.

I recognise that being in the midst of the final step of withdrawal from an anti-depressant will have played a role in the severity of my response to the situation I am about to describe. Having said that, most people who need a MHCP and access to a psychologist will have one or more factors influencing their ability to effectively cope with the circumstances I encountered.

In March 2013, I had a MHCP written by my then long time GP in Brighton and went on to access six sessions with a local psychologist as well as being under the care of a nearby psychiatrist. I moved to the eastern suburbs in July 2013 and had to find new medical and mental health practitioners. Knowing about the Better Outcomes in Mental Health Program that includes training GPs through my involvement as a community volunteer presenter with the Black Dog Institute, I checked with my local clinic and found an appropriately trained GP.

The new psychiatrist after an appropriate settling in period recommended that I come off the anti-depressants I had been on for a decade as the more recently added bipolar medication was expected to be able to hold my manias and depressions in check. And the particular anti-depressants I was on were known to potentially trigger maniac episodes. This is not something I wanted as I had learned that depression follows a mania like night follows day.

Suffice to say this withdrawal, in its final stages, did not go well. A messy, teary state prevailed and there was no appointment scheduled. I called my psychiatrist's office and asked for her to call me as things were not going well. She did and discussed two options both related to my need for an anti-depressant to bolster my bipolar medication. One option was to go back on the anti-depressants I had been on because I had historically responded to them well. Given I was getting off them because of their potential to trigger manias this suggestion was something I was not interested in doing. It would mean going through this whole withdrawal process again should they start triggering manias. So option two, a different type of anti-depressant was floated and selected. She said she would fax a prescription to my chemist. It's a curious thing to me that the less capable I am of managing unexpected events the more likely they seem to be to occur. Anyone else had that experience? The prescription went missing in action. Tears in the chemist, tears on the phone, tears in the supermarket all ensued. Interestingly, there are people who cope well with people in distress and there are some people, who work in the caring professions, that you would hope knew better and were more compassionate and yet don't and aren't.

While all this was going on I knew I needed some help dealing with this, and at the same time recognised that there are still some long term mind health issues that I would benefit from addressing.

My GP recognising my current state worked to find the easiest solution to get access to the rebates for the MHCP. She advised that plans only need to be written every two years and that with a referral from her I would be able to access service with the rebate in play based on my 2013 MHCP. My GP and I agreed we would draft a new plan in a few months.

I called the psychologists and the intake person advised my 2013 MHCP was required to be addressed to the new psychologist before moving forward. All I wanted was an appointment as soon as possible. I think the missing part in this interaction is that getting help was more important than getting a rebate. By this point I was a raging mess of emotions and couldn't believe it was this difficult to get an appointment.

So believing that the psychologists had to have the current MHCP I went back into the clinic and a receptionist checked with Medicare and reaffirmed the 2 year requirement. If memory serves me it was at this point that my Grandma Cranky Pants showed up and I started to get unpleasant.

I rang my old GP's clinic and asked them to readdress the plan, based on intake instructions, to my new psychologist. The upshot of this is that "it couldn't be done".

In the end I just asked them to fax the document with a cover page to the new psychologist.

That done I thought it would be resolved. Later that day I got a call saying my plan was more than a year old and I would need another one. Head explosion occurred as my amygdala went into full flood and completely overwhelmed my ability to think. Hadn't I just been told by my new GP that a plan written within two years was enough?

Several calls with the psychologist later, everything had become quiet blurry as tears from the Sumerian flood story the Epic of Gilgamesh were flooding out of my eyes. There was some news. If my psychiatrist writes a referral I don't need a Mental Health Care Plan! Simple!

Given I had indicated to my psychiatrist on my last visit that this was my intention, I am surprised it was not offered! That didn't help my emotional equilibrium. And the other option was that the new GP could do something else, it got lost in the ridiculous simplicity of the psychiatrist writing the referral and all of this distress would not have occurred.

I appreciate that the psychologist I am currently seeing offered to personally follow up on the psychiatric referral. She did ask why, after all my distress would I still agree to see her organisation and her. The answer was simple. There was NO WAY I was going through that whole process again.

It was distressing, escalated my unhelpful emotions to the point where for only the second time in 18 months I actually wanted to be dead. That is not being melodramatic. I know when I am doing that. I was seeking an escape from the inordinate distress. I am grateful for a husband who knows how to deal with people in distress and that he was home when I arrived. I was in a state of inner torment, crying and thinking hospital admission was my only option. The outcome could've been very different for others who either don't have home support, the logic to know that *"this too shall pass"* and the ability to use 15 years of executive and corporate coaching experience and personal development to avoid a final end.

Challenges abound. They don't necessarily ever go away. Too many tears sting. Hope floats. A mental illness does not always equate to poor mind health. And I believe you can experience eviscerating mind health without a mental illness.

When it comes to mental illness and mind health matters, awareness does not equate to understanding. Understanding comes with openness and education. The issue of disclosure is still a big one. Awareness is so much better than it used to be and there are so many more services and resources than there used to be. There is still a massive gap between services required and services available and the stigma that is dumped at the feet of those of us living with mood disorders. There is something that all of us with mood disorders can do to be a part of a speedier dissolution of stigma. It does not have to be personal disclosure, yet there is so much opportunity for us to speak openly and comfortably about mental health, mental illness, and resilience. There is always another person with their mental illness or mind health story. Just waiting to be told. Waiting to support the broader community to have greater awareness, better understanding, more compassion and to be more accepting of those of us who live with mood disorders. Will you be part of the dissolution of the stigma we still live with? I am so excited to move towards better understanding, greater compassion and ultimately to be accepted as any other person with a physical illness is in our society.

It's past time to say farewell, good bye, adieu and so long to the stigma of mental illness. One person's story at a time.

From Silence to Advocacy: Overcoming a Family Legacy of Mental Illness
Stephen P. Hinshaw

The main "sound" I recall from growing up, back in Ohio, is silence.

All those things not said, all those words not spoken: the silence was overwhelming, even at times deafening. Somewhere underneath it all lay an abyss of shame. But where it was or what it was, I couldn't fathom.

How could I have known, all those years ago, that my father's doctors had ordered this stonewalling? I simply had no idea that they had told Dad, during and after his episodes of paranoia, agitation, and subsequent depression, that if his two children (my sister and I) were ever to learn of his behavior and hospitalizations—

Stephen P. Hinshaw

misdiagnosed since he was a teen as schizophrenia—it would permanently destroy the family.

Dad and Mom did everything possible to hide the erratic, psychotic behavior patterns and deny anything and everything about his disappearances. For two, four, or even twelve months at a time, nothing could be said while he was away, as though he'd seen airlifted out during the middle of the night. Life went on for the three of us as if nothing were different. No questions were allowed. I retreated into schoolwork and sports. The routine was numbing and vaguely comforting.

Once Dad returned, as though transported back via a magic carrier without notice or ceremony, the pretending continued but it was now even more extreme: no one could raise the fact that he'd been gone.

What was underneath such mystery? I couldn't know, but it had to be almost lethal.

This kind of acting was exhausting, the costumes confining. I put one foot in front of the other, trying not to see beyond next task—the next homework assignment, the next practice, the next game.

The whole thing gave me the chilling sense that I hadn't done enough as a boy, son, or family member to prevent his vanishing acts. If I paused to think about it, the guilt and fear were crushing.

One of the most devastating outcomes of enforced silence for children—when they know that something is amiss but are simultaneously denied any grounding or reality checks—is that they tend to internalize blame. If only I'd done a better job of things, the child begins to think, I could have prevented the absences (or, in other cases, the abuse, the parental fights, or the parental separation). This kind of belief in personal control is, of course, devastating to the child's sense of self-worth, but it's probably far better than a young child's sense that the world is just a random, cruel place.

A huge legacy of the stigmatization of mental illness is what Erving Goffman called, over half a century ago, "courtesy stigma." In other words, when people are identified as members of a castigated "outgroup," it's only common courtesy that members of society begin to stigmatize and blame those people surrounding the individual. The penumbra of stigma, Goffman was asserting, is large and impenetrable.

Little wonder that those in the mental health fields are held in lower regard than those in "mainstream" medicine or that those in clinical psychology are viewed as "softer" than those in the basic psychological sciences. After all, in these professions one works directly with individuals experiencing mental illness. Courtesy stigma is pernicious.

Regarding family members, added to the mix is the painful reality that the main theoretical models in psychology and psychiatry during much of the 20th century explicitly blamed parents for having caused the offspring's disturbance. Autism was believed to have its origins in being raised by "refrigerator parents," with schizophrenia caused by "schizophrenogenic" mothers. Family members couldn't win.

Perniciously, the blame tends to seep inward, especially for children in the family. The resultant internalization exacerbates whatever genetic tendencies may exist for intergenerational transmission of mental disorder. The all-too-common result is a vicious cycle of shame, self-blame, and feeling utterly stuck.

When Dad was around during my childhood, life could be pretty great. He was a philosopher, a professor at Ohio State, having studied with Bertrand Russell and having interviewed and written about Albert Einstein while a graduate student, at Princeton, years earlier. My mother went back into academia herself, teaching English at OSU and participating in the rarefied life of scholarship and Ohio State athletic events that were the mainstay of our community. Little did I know, then, how much Mom had sacrificed just to keep the family together—or just to endure the comments of Dad's doctors who utterly discounted a spouse's potential addition to the assessment picture or treatment plan.

Cracks in the surface sometimes appeared when Dad was back. Strange behavior might leak out, like his snarling at Walter Cronkite's report over the rise of gasoline prices and insisting that class warfare would not be far behind, or when he similarly transformed into an angry tyrant on outings with our grandmother, mom's mom. When I experienced such outbursts, I felt wiser and more mature than Dad, of whom I was usually in awe. Yet I was also deeply fearful.

Who was this man, who seemed to carry different personas inside his skin, which showed through when the mask slipped off ever so slightly? Why was nothing ever said in our family about what was happening?

The family code of silence largely prevailed until I headed off to college, back East, and then returned home for my first spring break. Dad shyly pulled me into his study and began describing his lifetime of 'breakdowns' and hospitalizations, intermixed with his other struggles and accomplishments. At the time, I didn't realize that he'd waited until I was no longer a child before he dared disobey the doctors' orders to keep silent. Finally, the truth was revealed; some forms had begun to emerge from the empty vault of silence in which I'd lived my first 18 years.

I was initially entranced: THIS is what all the silence had been about! Finally, I had a mission in life, to solve the mystery of Dad's periodic mental illness and perhaps of mental disorder altogether. I soon became part of an interdisciplinary social sciences major at Harvard and intensified my volunteer work with children and other marginalized members of society (for example, teaching in prisons). Maybe, eventually, I could give something back, given that I still sensed I was sane.

At the same time, though, I was terrified. What little I knew assured me that severe mental illnesses like schizophrenia were transmitted genetically across generations—and that, unless I led an extremely controlled life, I would certainly be next, joining not only my Dad but many other relatives who experienced serious mental disorders, high achievement, or both. There was no one to

tell, not even roommates or girlfriends: the risk was too great
to reveal our family's curse. The rituals I put myself through
to get enough sleep each night—in order to prevent the
madness from entering my body and mind—were tortuous.

Once out of college and then working in summer camp
and school programs for children with special needs, I came
to understand, by frantically reading everything I could, that
Dad had actually experienced manic-depression (bipolar
disorder) for forty years. I intervened, helping him get the
right diagnosis and evidence-based treatments, as we
continued our deep talks several times per year. Once on
lithium, after two decades of antipsychotic medications and
electroconvulsive therapy (ECT), he experienced an absence
of episodes for a period of some years.

I subsequently pursued a doctorate in clinical
psychology, more determined than ever to solve the crushing
issue of mental disorder and to transcend the "all
psychosocial" vs. "all biological" models that had never
succeeded in getting Dad, or so many others like him, the
right kinds of diagnosis and treatment and needed support. I
could never understand the arrogance of those professionals
who seemed to think that their particular theoretical and
clinical orientation was all that was needed. The battle felt
uphill, all the way: where was the integration needed to make
real progress?

Each experience I had in graduate school, then as a
post-doc, and later as a young professor reinforced my
perspective that a viable science could and should underlie
our approach to serious mental illness. I wanted to learn all I
could about biology and experience, genes and peer groups,
families and school environments. I became entranced by the
emerging field of developmental psychopathology, with its
emphasis on transactional models and multiple levels of
analysis. At last, a framework for understanding the origins
of mental illness. Gradually, however, I came to realize the

slow nature of the field's progress, despite the new discoveries appearing in the scientific and clinical literatures.

Most important, I learned that I had to communicate about Dad's experiences, my family's, and my own if the scientific methods I was learning could ever begin to humanize the whole topic of mental disorder. At first haltingly, I began to speak and write and teach about our family's utter silence and about the openness needed to break through the shame and despair.

Clearly, science needs to be objective, if causal models are to be realized or treatments evaluated impartially. But the motivation to pursue such science may well have its roots in deep personal and family experience.

Looking inward, I realized that I had largely escaped the kinds of severe episodes Dad experienced. Still, I became paralyzed, from time to time, by anger and by immobility. I had inherited, it was becoming clear, a partial load of the genetic liability of my family's legacy. Even more than the underlying biology, though, the burden of trying to protect everyone in my family…or of worrying about whether every emotion I experienced was the signal of a slide into despair or a rise into irrationality…or of witnessing too many other family members experience depressions, bipolar episodes, psychosis, and unfulfilled lives…the cumulative burden took a toll. Mental illness exerts a steep price on those who experience it, but for family members—who must bear up, bear witness, cope, and long for a better understanding on the part of all society—too often suffer in silence. My mother, who kept us together against the odds for all those years, ended up with a severe case of rheumatoid arthritis that she coped with for 40 years, the undoubted consequence of so much silence and pain.

Many years transpired before I expanded my interests in the origins of childhood disorders—and their treatment with both medication and intensive behavioral/psychosocial intervention—into the realm of stigma per se. I looked inward to the ways in which I had internalized our family's silence and shame, and outward to models in social and evolutionary psychology that considered stigma as a core process in human interchange. I ended up with a deep and abiding interest in both understanding and preventing, particularly in young people, the stigmatization and discrimination that still comprise the #1 problem encountering the entire mental health field.

At this point, I feel more inspired than ever to be able to teach and advise, conduct programs of research, consult with others, and perform advocacy related to children, adolescents, and adults who are at risk for and who experience mental illness. My life as a parent, scholar, advisor, and advocate is more integrated than ever before. As I continue to experience the aftermath of my family legacy, I feel energized by the quest to blend the best of objective research with the best of experience. Narrative accounts must convey the realities of mental disorder to the world, which can no longer be in denial.

Beyond the pain, what an honor it is to have experienced mental disorder in both my family and myself and to attempt transcending it, each and every day. The journey ahead is long, as brain science and personal experience have only recently begun to link together. The complexities are indeed daunting in each domain. Yet with renewed energy and, I hope, wisdom, it's the quest of a lifetime to bear witness and pursue an evidence-based set of practices and procedures. We need the best minds and spirits of future generations to join the journey.

Recovery as Reality
Bill McKnight

I'm a service user with a 30 year history of mental illness.

Mental illness knows no borders and crosses all divides. Mental illness is no respecter of persons. Mental illness affects the crude and the cultured; the employed and the unemployed; the educated and the uneducated. Mental illness affects young and old; rich and poor; the religious and the irreligious.

Bill McKnight

Mental illness is torment – as every sufferer knows. Mental illness is a cruel form of pain that not only disables the sufferer but puts great strain on family, friends, careers, loved ones, resources, etc.

And mental illness isolates. Loneliness can be an unwelcome effect of suffering from mental ill health. Also, individuals, communities and society can stigmatise those who are mentally unwell – and stigma is like 'being off the guest list'.

I invite you to come with me on a poetic journey – to view mental illness, stigma and recovery from a service-user perspective…

I was first admitted to Psychiatric hospital in Belfast in 1983 at the age of 24. A young female nurse told me to undress and put my clothes in a black bin bag. She also told me to put on my pajamas. It was mid-day. I was frightened, confused, embarrassed and humiliated by this situation. The point I'm making is that staff perceptions, indeed, staff training can be at odds with the perceptions and experiences of service-users. The nurse didn't want me to run away from the ward; I didn't want to put on my pajamas at lunch time! And I was told what to do – I wasn't asked. Thus, mental illness and stigma were bed-fellows from the outset.

On another occasion whilst attending a Psychiatric Day Hospital (hospital by day and at home in the evenings), I learned that even friends can stigmatise the service-user...

Friends
They don't call me sad.
They don't call me bad.
They don't call me mad.
They don't call me.

Powerlessness, isolation and feelings of helplessness often accompany mental illness and those who are mentally ill.

Loud Silence
Withdrawn from society.
There's stigma.
There's secrecy.
There's shame.
And the service-user's pain.
Loud silence is often the voice
of the voiceless 'insane'.

Service-users are often frustrated by the doctor/patient relationship. A ten minute appointment with a psychiatrist can *seem* to lack warmth or any sense of the personal 'touch'. After all, we are not mentally ill people. We are *people* who have mental illness. And mental illness is not just a medical problem. Though doctors have to make clinical judgments, a service-user may be looking for a friend.

Dr. Who?
I disclose to you. You don't disclose to me.
In this power imbalance lies an inequality.
Dr. Who, if such a relationship is to your credit
I simply don't get it. Unfairapeutic!

Psychiatric Admission
Dread.
Bed.
Meds.

Coke.
Smoke.
Joke.

Ill.
Pill.
Through the mill.

CD.
T.V.
ECT.

TLC?

Professionals treat patients?
But people need people.

And service-users are dab hands at spotting the sincere from
the insincere – the caring from the uncaring.

Mentally ill (But Not Stupid)
Squirrel Nutkin's schizophrenic.
Some people say she's bonkers.
But Squirrel Nutkin differentiates
'tween hazelnuts and conkers!

(NB: 'conker'= horse chestnut fruit)

To be listened to is to be valued. However, there are those
who simply want to 'fix' people – rather, fix a problem! Such
'fixers' are like the proverbial Job's comforters…

Mr. Fix It!
Face up to your ghosts.
yes, but…

Put the past behind you.
yes, but…

Be strong.
yes, but…

Be in control.
yes, but…

You need to manage your feelings.
yes, but…

Time is a great healer.
yes, but…

Pull yourself together.
yes, but…

You'll get over it.
yes, but you're not listening.

For some, caring for people who are mentally ill can be foremost a profession – and not necessarily a healthy one!

Mental health professional
Does she really care?
With one eye on me
and one eye on her career.

Many are the obstacles on the road to recovery. Secrecy and shame still exist because today there is STIGMA! The following poems are about this hydra called stigma and how it raises its ugly head in many different ways.

Stigma
"You are mentally ill. What a shame."

Labelled by you
I wear a subtle tattoo.
Its name is 'taboo'.
Worried you'll be branded too?

World Mental Health Day
"Mental illness – raising awareness. Do you get it?"

"I'm afraid I'll get it from you!"

Comfort zone
I don't want to get involved with you –
you who are weak and upset.
Because you might upset me.

NB: Can I suggest that if service-users and professionals are
to engage in more meaningful ways both parties need to come
out from comfort zones.

The media also plays its part in promoting stigma…

The Daily Gob
The tabloid heading reads:
"Schizo kills pensioner,"
and makes no mention of the 99.9%
of *normal* murderers.

The following poem is based on a real incident I experienced
at my local hairdresser's…

At the hairdresser's
"How are you, Bill?" she asked.
"I'm a bit depressed," I replied.

"My sister gets depressed –
I must be *the strong one"*, she said.

Her razor cut my hair.

Her tongue cut my feelings.

Often families and carers bear the strain caused by stigma...

Rather dead than Fred?
He lives
in a very frightening world –
it's mostly inside his head.
Some people call him 'a nutter' –
family call him, "our Fred."

Developments
Pooh sticks.
Chop sticks.
But nothing sticks
like stigma.

My own mental health is being worked out like the untangling of a ball of knotted string or like trying to complete a Rubik's cube! Recovery requires listening; thinking; expression; time; effort; relationships; medication; learning new skills – to name but a few. Having a full-time job, socialising, studying, enjoying new friendships, having holidays, hobbies, etc. were once far-off goals for me. Now these things are present realities. **Stigma need not be the end of the story!!!**

Stigmafraid
Stigmafraid?
'Struth!

Who's afraid
of the big bad wolf?

Stigmattack
I refuse to wear
this so-called 'disgrace'
shame-faced.
My stance is plain –
no longer will you shame me
with an name.

Be encouraged! There is hope!

Hope
It is said that the darkest hour
is just before dawn.
In a similar vein
growth and change
can be gained
at the moment of greatest pain.

   Service-user do not despair. A crisis need not be an
end. A crisis can be a beginning. Growth and change can be
gained at the *moments* of greatest pain. Life is a series of
crises. Recovery is not a straw to be clutched at but a reality
for those who enter into the risky business of life. I never
thought I could drive a car, enjoy friendships or do many of
the things others (might) take for granted. My hope for you is
that you might stop and think and reflect on your own
personal situation. Talk to someone you can trust. Asking

for help may be a good place to start. Make of today an
opportunity for change. The road ahead will most certainly
be challenging but with the right help you can meet each
difficulty and move on. Let me suggest that those who
stigmatise have but *insight that is skin-deep.* I wish you well
in your ongoing recovery and for a wellness that is 'living
with illness'.

One final poem entitled, 'Friends'

Friends
They don't call me sad.
They don't call me bad.
They don't call me mad.
They don't call me.
I know! I'll be a friend.
I'll call them!

Fall Down Seven Times, Get Up Eight
Deborah Serani

I have depression.

Dysthymic Disorder to be exact.

It's a mental illness that I've successfully managed with medication and psychotherapy for 20 years. Along the way, I've written about my personal and professional experiences living with depression and became a go-to media expert psychologist and advocate on the subject of mental health.

I know I'm lucky, *genetically lucky* I suspect, that my antidepressant has completely alleviated my chronic, crippling depression. I've also taken the skills I learned in my own psychotherapy to help me stay afloat, and feel confident that I can attend to what life throws my way.

Except for one thing.

Stigma.

It knocks me down. Every. Single. Time.

Of course, I wish the hurtful remarks would just roll off my back, like rainwater to a duck. Other times, I wish I had a thicker skin, an impenetrable and unshakable armor that could withstand stigma altogether. But I don't.

Despite the fact that I'm symptom free, my status as someone with mental illness colors a great deal of my life. I find that my words, thoughts and feelings are frequently "measured" by others – especially if I'm feeling sad, angry or irritated. The experience is a well-worn one. And I can see it happening . . . the microscopic analysis from those who don't live with mental illness nor truly understand anything about it, feeling the need to check my mental status.

"Did you take your medicine today?

An impossible, unwinnable question.

When it's asked by my spouse, family or friends, it's painful. It wounds me deeply to my core that people I love would summarily criticize the range of my human experience and mince it into such a stupid question. And it's really not a question at all, is it? It's really an accusation. A pointed reminder that somehow, forever and always, my emotional reactions are held to a different standard. Once the sting of stigma passes, I take the painful moment and make it a teachable moment.

"You know, it's okay for me to be sad sometimes," I say, both protecting that fragile part of myself and educating others.

I've also bristled at the stigmatizing remarks from health professionals I've met over the years for various illnesses.

"Your depression is making your physical symptoms worse."

Or

"The problem here is stress."

Statements like these hurt emotionally and are diagnostically damaging. Not because the question is asked, but because the timing of the question comes all too soon. Before a thorough evaluation of my physical needs has been done. I call this *lazy medicine*, when doctors know your mental illness status and sweep all other possibilities under the diagnostic rug.

"I think you're wrong about this, Doc," I say, taking back control of the situation. *"How about we run some tests to see what's doing?"*

Sometimes I hear stigma echoing in the hallways of places, like counseling centers, pharmacies, hospitals or universities, where mental illness should be respected, and this hurts me the most. These moments have showed me that humanity cannot be taught to some and that sensitivity isn't a given if you work in the mental health field. Sometimes I'm so shocked by what I hear that I can't say anything more than, *"You shouldn't be working here with that attitude."* Other times, I clear the air with a sharp, smart comeback, like *"Your parents must be so proud."*

In the beginning, stigma about my mental illness made me feel very ashamed. I hid my prescriptions in the back of my dresser, out of sight, as if anyone stumbling upon it would deem me "undesirable" or "dangerous." By hiding my "going to therapy," it was as if I agreed with the rest of the uninformed world that my mental illness qualified me as "crazy." Like many who struggle with mental illness, I was afraid of being ostracized, seen as weak or impaired. It was better to keep things secret. But, in truth, I suffered quietly and alone in ways that actually made my depression worse. Hiding my illness in the corners of my home and in the margins of my life was inauthentic. It further withered my mind, body and soul, filling me with guilt and self-loathing on top of the already enormous despair that was swirling within me. I felt as if I was living a lie, betraying a part of myself that truly needed support.

As I trained to be a psychologist, I learned more about mental health and shook off the bitter brine of stigma with more ease. Being someone who had a mental illness no longer made me feel embarrassed. I became more open about my antidepressant medication and my psychotherapy personally with family and friends. I slowly began sharing my story with those who were closest to me – my parents and my sisters. Their support was extremely helpful, teaching me to feel less ashamed of my mental illness. As my confidence grew, I began telling trusted friends of my struggles with depression and was pleased to find their reactions weren't insensitive or judgmental. Each found a way to make me feel loved, supported and thoroughly understood. My disclosure of living with depression added another level of healing for me. It afforded me solidarity – a shared space where I felt safe and understood.

But it would be different outside of my close circle of loved ones. Writing about my experiences with mental illness for academic journals was not initially a welcomed subject. A decade ago, several of my papers were summarily rejected from psychological journals, with one editor telling me that I'd ruin my career if I ever had it published. It was as if showing the fact that therapists also struggled with mental illness was unacceptable. But as I continued presenting my work, I received phone calls and emails from colleagues praising my efforts. But this was done in private, after my workshop or paper presentation was over.

"Why aren't they telling me this in real time?" I often thought. Are they fearful of supporting me in public?

The answer was yes. For every colleague that praised my work, there seemed to be more that didn't find it meaningful at all – and their voice was hard to vanquish. The notion of self-disclosure about living with mental illness was deemed *controversial. Ineffective.* Even *irresponsible.* I would slink away from the academic conferences feeling defeated. But those moments didn't stop me.

About three years ago, I was presenting one of my academic papers at a national conference where a heated debate ensued. Some in the audience described my self-disclosure as *"unhelpful for the patient."* Others deemed my sharing of my personal narrative with depression *"selfish"* and *"narcissistic."* Just when I thought I was going to have to counter these opinions all on my own, something amazing happened. Other voices from the audience piped in. I was happy to finally see other therapists recognizing the data from stigma studies – how one of the most powerful ways to eradicate stigma is to show others living well with mental illness. I was moved to hear several therapists call my work *"vital"* and *"profound"* in public.

I continue to present papers about being a clinician who lives with depression, and have come to expect that my workshops will lead to lively and important discussions. I'm always up for the challenge of it, but in truth, I wanted to reach a wider audience to share my life's struggles and message of hope.

This is when I decided to start writing books about my personal and professional experiences with mental illness. And doing so opened tremendous doors. My books were well received, and enabled me to talk about mental illness on a larger scale than ever before. I found the telling of my life in books to be both healing for me and helpful for others. When a story about struggle and triumph is shared, it sets into a motion a domino effect that inspires others. *My* story gets you to think about *your* story. And if I share my narrative, you can share yours. And it's through this process that stigma gets diluted, that insecurities fade, that shame evaporates and hope grows. As I traveled nationally and internationally, I learned that as we each share our narratives, we feel less alone. We forge bonds. And together we can reach and teach others about the stigma and help dispel the myths that surround mental illness.

In the last few years, I've found more strength and joy in my life the more I shared my personal narrative. As I look back over my life, I went from a young girl who was frightened and ashamed of her mood disorder, to an empowered woman who feels comfortable in her own skin. When ignorant or cruel remarks are now said to me, I become defensive. Protective. I counter inaccurate statements about mental illness with correct ones. I scold those who joke and put those who say disparaging things about mental illness back in their place.

I realized I moved into this protective stance to defend a part of myself that needed a vocal, active and fierce advocate. It was reflexive, like a mother's outstretched arm protecting her child from harm. When you live with mental illness that illness becomes a part of you. It becomes part of your identity. For me, my mental illness and my experiences when it was at its worst were fragile, trying times. I am fiercely protective of that historical piece in my life. It's a part of who I am, and largely responsible for shaping the person I am today.

The Japanese proverb *"Fall Down Seven Times, Get Up Eight"* is all about resiliency – and it's my motto. In the thirty years of managing my mental illness and dealing with the fallout of stigma, I've not just come out proud, I've come out loud as well. I know that stigma is something that will continue to present itself in my life. I wish it didn't, but until there's greater acceptance and understanding of mental illness, it'll be there. And though it knocks me down every time, it never keeps me down for long. I get up each time.

And each time, you'll find me teaching someone something somewhere.

Coming Out Proud in Georgia
Lynn S. Garson

Coming out proud happened by accident in my life. It happened not too long after I checked myself into a mental

Lynn Garson

health facility in February 2010 because I was sinking under the weight of depression and, to a lesser extent, anxiety. My choice of facilities was based solely on the advice of a new psychiatrist who didn't know me very well. That's my excuse for her recommendation, anyway. I landed in a bottom of the barrel joint that shocked my middle class sensibilities no end. I learned some great lessons there about the commonality of mental illness/substance abuse and came away with the understanding that they are the most democratic of afflictions. I had more in common than I knew with the guy wearing the pirate's patch who talked about scoring crack at 3:00 a.m. in an Atlanta back alley where he coincidentally found Jesus at the end of a loaded shotgun pointed at his midsection.

Nevertheless, I was uncomfortable at the facility and began blogging about my experiences and feelings of hopelessness in an attempt to connect with others. Untutored in social media as I was, I got 3 followers on my blog, two of them loyal friends who would have supported anything I did anyway. Then, out of the blue, a writer friend took a look at my posts and encouraged me to turn the blog into a book. That struck a chord and I went at it with gusto, staying up all hours of the night and working through the days on some weekends. By the fall of 2010 I had a part time job as a lawyer (my profession since 1981) and by June of 2011 I had a full time job at a new firm. That didn't stop me – I kept writing and writing and editing and editing. Finally, it came time to publish the book in July 2012.

Southern Vapors is a memoir, fictional only where I changed names and descriptions to protect anonymity. Where

LYNN GARSON

my history is concerned, and to a great degree that of my family, I am scrupulously honest, and certainly every detail of my three (yes, three) voluntary inpatient visits is included. I describe my six month decline in the winter of 2007 that featured moments such as lying under my desk just to breathe, then getting up to close two deals simultaneously. I describe the unlovely details of my eating disorder (binge eating) that I have carried with me since I can remember. I talk about what it feels like to have friends with challenges similar to mine die by suicide, and what it feels like to stand two steps away from a similar decision to take my own life. Not the stuff the typical partner in a law firm wants to hear about his or her associate, or so I thought.

When I started at my new job in 2011, I didn't tell anyone about my mental health struggles and certainly not about my stay at a mental health facility. I was so terrified that my employers would find out about my background and figure out a way to fire me that I almost didn't apply for health insurance, thinking that I would have to reveal previous mental health history (I didn't). As a lawyer, I am aware of the Americans with Disabilities Act and the idea that you cannot discriminate against someone with mental health issues. I am also aware that there is supposed to be a privacy barrier between the Human Resources/Benefits side of a business and the business side itself. I was advised by colleagues not to rely on either for a minute, and to keep my mouth shut if I thought there was any possibility of the information getting out to the partners in my firm. I was ready and willing to follow their advice, and in fact did so to an extent, giving up the unlimited care option of long term care insurance in favor of a term policy that didn't require the disclosures.

I went to work in June and kept my head down for a year. By the time I was ready to publish my book a year later, my life had changed dramatically. I had a solid twelve months under my belt of friendly relations with my colleagues and a record of good performance. The clients liked my work and I had proved myself to be reliable, efficient and reasonably talented in my law practice. I had just had a review and come out rose-smelling. I had a decision to make.

Wild horses were not going to keep me from publishing my book. I had worked exceedingly hard on it for two years, was proud of it and felt that I said some important things that I wanted to be heard publicly. On the other hand, I had absolutely no idea how the partners for whom I worked would react, and I was pretty sure that if they wanted to fire me, they could figure out a way to do it. My job was not a hobby, it was the way I put bread on the table and paid half of my children's support as a divorced mother. I have three children, two of them in college at the time and one in a private high school. I was paying our expenses almost exclusively out of my salary and in no way could afford to lose it. What to do?

I did what comes naturally to me, which is to be open. I am not a secret-keeper, loathe secrets in fact. I had too many over the course of the years when my depression and anxiety was glossed over by my family, swept under the rug in a way peculiar to the South or perhaps to people who feel themselves to be elite wherever they are, making the visible invisible with a shrug of the shoulders and a wave of the hand. No more secrets for me.

One day in July of 2012, a couple of weeks before a book launch event that I had set up with an independent book store, I got up from my desk, picked up a copy of *Southern Vapors* and started down the hall. My group in the law firm, the health care department, is on the 48th floor of a lovely office building in downtown Atlanta. There were fifteen of

us at the time, six partners and nine associates. I started with the Department leader, a man slightly older than my then 58 years, with whom I had a cordial but not close relationship. I asked if he had a minute, which he did, and I sat down across from him, nervous as hell. I knew that this could go south in a big way and that there was a good chance that my life would self-destruct if it did. I held up the book, which has a blinding yellow cover that is impossible to miss, and I said, "Do you see this book?" Yes. "Do you see the name of the author on the cover?" Yes. "That's my name and it is the same name that goes out with every email from me to our clients. I want to tell you about this so you don't get blindsided if I am lucky enough that anyone who works for a client happens to read the book and recognizes my name." OK. "This book is about me being in three different mental health facilities, most recently in 2010. It is about my struggles and my recovery, including taking the job here at the firm. I want you to know this now because the book is coming out in two weeks."

George (fictional name) handled it like a trooper. He asked a couple of questions along the lines of whether I had any issues presently that I wanted to share with him, and when I shook my head, he wished me luck. I made the same presentation fourteen more times that afternoon. Not one single person was ugly or condescending or withdrawn. Fully two-thirds of my department came to my book launch event.

They are proud of me and I am proud of them. That is the point of "coming out proud" to me - to engage with those who neither suffer nor completely understand the suffering of those with mental health/substance abuse challenges. To demonstrate to them and to secure their understanding in return that I am little different from them and that there is nothing in me to fear.

The process reminds me of my experience with a partner in the first firm I went to work for out of law school, another large firm, this one known for its expertise in tax matters. Sometime during my second year, I became aware that he was secluding himself in his office and that people were talking about him. His wife had just left him and he was in the middle of a divorce that he did not want. Divorces were not common in those days and were treated by some the way mental health issues are treat now – ignored, whispered about and feared, as if they were contagious. The soon to be divorced partner was often tearful and troubled, and to the best of my recollection, people gave him a lot of space and just let him be for quite a long time. I don't remember hearing anything about his work product or output, but I imagine it suffered, if only marginally, the same way mine suffers when I am in a downturn, which still happens to me though not as intensely as previously.

I came out proud in 2012 and will continue to come out proud so that those who are uncomfortable with the idea of people who struggle with mental health issues can see that I am no different from the partner who anguished over his divorce, nor the colleague who is preoccupied with the long term impact of an aging parent, nor the one who is overtaken by concern for a chronically ill child. As a culture we have confronted stigma about a particular group or attribute more than once and prevailed, or at least made sure progress – civil rights, women's rights, gay rights and autism, to name a few. It is time to make the same progress in the mental health arena. Recently I sat in Rosalynn Carter's office and conversed with her about her role in mental health and combatting stigma. In the almost forty years that she has been engaged as an advocate, she has seen changes that have brought us out of the Dark Ages, when people with mental illness were viewed as subhuman and thrown away to rot. We stand on the cusp of changes that can be equally breathtaking. The fact that the country, even the world, had a visceral reaction in August 2014 to Robin Williams' suicide tells me that we are getting closer all the time.

I am proud to tell my story and proud of the fact that I am standing tall and strong as I tell it. I said it best in *Southern Vapors*:

> One of my oldest friends gave me the highest compliment when I told her about the new job: "You have true grit," she said. Of all the reactions to the news of my job, all of the excitement from other friends and family, that was the one that lit me up. Yes, I had gotten a

great job in the face of a bad economy, and at an age when it can be hard to find work (I was then fifty-seven years old). That was something to be proud of, without a doubt. But that didn't come close to the satisfaction of knowing that I had clawed my way out of the muck, struggled to my knees and finally stood up on my own two feet, solidly planted on the ground, unwavering. Maybe people who haven't been through a decline of the magnitude that mine achieved can't begin to understand, and there is probably a desire on the part of some to pretend that the implosions of my past hadn't occurred, that they were just a little glitch, that's all, and now look at her, why she's just fine, isn't she? For my part, I don't want to sweep any part of that journey under the rug: I want to celebrate it like I've never celebrated anything in my life. It is my crowning achievement; I can't imagine surpassing it and wouldn't want to if the opportunity presented itself. (Let's see, should I collapse again to see if I can drag myself upright one more time?)

The human spirit is more resilient that we know, it just needs a little help along the way. Be proud, too, and support those of us who are coming out proud. It will help us and you may be surprised at how much it helps you.

My Life: From A Wheelchair to the Books (Passing Through Anxiety, Phobias and Much More!)

Rita Coruzzi, Luca Pingani, Ludovica Spattini, Gaia Sampogna, and Andrea Fiorillo

The Beginning

In my life, I have suffered the pain of stigmatization, as well as the experience of self-stigmatization. Since I was born, I have been affected by motor problems and an illness that is medically referred to as "quadriplegia". This illness has made me feel different from other individuals, especially during social interactions. When I was 10 years old, this problem exponentially after a surgical operation. Something went wrong with the surgery and from that moment on, I was confined to a wheelchair. This was my first contact with stigmatization. Before this moment, I was an individual with ambulation problems. Afterwards, I became a disabled individual. An individual who was a foreigner in the able-body's world. My elementary school teachers were not ready to address a student with motor problems; however, after the surgery, they were terrified of the idea of dealing with a disabled student. For this

Rita Coruzzi and her mother the day she defended her thesis in journalism.

reason, they attempted to limit the problem by keeping me apart from the rest of my classmates, particularly during breaks. They would put my wheel chair under the shadow of a tree, where I could watch my able-bodied classmates playing, running, and laughing. Nobody looked for me or asked me to play.

My Psychiatric Story

My experience with stigma became increasingly cruel and real year by year, and in turn I felt increasingly insecure and inadequate. Whenever the teacher assigned a homework immediately I thought of not being able to do it because I considered myself not smart enough: I was inept and so I would have got it all wrong. Defense mechanisms developed in my mind, which made me feel isolated: my mind created a new world, my own world! Nobody except me was allowed to go inside it. In this world, I felt protected from all sufferings, humiliations and external stigmatizations.

This surreal world helped me to bear what I was living: in my mind, I was able to escape from reality. No one has ever asked me where my mind or soul went while I was under the tree. My mind and soul were in a tailored world that further isolated me. The idea that there were two worlds, one for disabled and one for able-bodied individuals, started to develop in my mind. Everything was possible in my world, but the only problem was that this world was not real. I was always in my universe trying to escape from reality. The reality that did not leave any space for me. This world was tailor made for me: everyone understood me, everyone wanted to spend time with me and all consoled me for what I endured and I suffered. In my world, my peers were not afraid of me, nor I of them.

As my condition as a disabled individual became permanent my passing discomfort increased, which included anxiety and phobias. I did not tell anyone, including my parents, because my anxiety was devouring me. I understood that it was something irrational and I attempted to face it by myself. I was suffering from severe anxiety and phobia attacks. It was impossible to control or hide the attacks. They typically initiated with a strong pain in my chest; so painful that I thought my heart was going to explode. These experiences triggered crying spells. I feared that I could not return back home and was frightened by the idea of rebuilding myself far from my habits and family. One example of overwhelming anxiety was the day before my last surgical operation. The surgeons had to remove metal plates from my femur. This surgery was highly recommended by physicians because I was still in the age of the development and the plaques could create problems in the future and would be more difficult to remove. The hospital stay, convalescence, infections, doctors, and nurses, provoked tremendous anxiety in me. At one point after a long crying spell, I vomited. I did not want to go to the hospital. I could have kept the metal plates inside of me for all my life, but I wanted my anxiety and fear to resolve. My mind was blocked. It appeared as if the things done prior to the surgery had blocked my mind. What I remember about the second surgical operation was the long admission and rehabilitation period, as well as the emotional consequences of my long absence from the school. These issues made me a stranger in "my" world, without any suffering and without all the bad familiar situations.

Consequences of My Psychiatric Experience

I became obsessive and followed specific rigid routines. I was aware that these habits could be changed without losing control. However, my mind needed protection to provide an appearance of serenity. I do not understand the mechanisms of my mind. My routine subsisted in habits, such as spending the same hours doing the same things every day, eating the same dishes every week, and going to the toilet at certain times of the day, and exceptions are not allowed.

Each time I have to change my routine, for example, when I had to leave for a journey for several days, the anxiety increases inside me and my old fears reappear. I fear new places, new towns, and a new routine, and have difficulty tolerating new situations.

Part of my fear is in socializing with other individuals with the same mental or communication problems. For example, after my orthopedic surgery, I remember very well that the physician suggested I move into a specialized rehabilitation center. When it was time to go there, my anxiety strongly and insistently increased. During the journey, I started to cry and vomited. I feared not returning home.

This new fear was about facing reality, in particular what I would see in the rehabilitative center. Several types of disabilities (physical as well as mental) were treated in this rehabilitation center. Some patients could not even eat without intravenous infusion, whereas other patients needed help eating; what I was saw was horrible. They chewed their food with effort. Many patients had problems with swallowing, and they would burp without embarrassment. It was disgusting. I realized that I did not want to have contact with them, and I felt different from these individuals. Yet I was also a disabled individual.

I had become a stigmatizing and discriminatory individual: I felt guilty and had a strong sense of discomfort towards myself.

I saw myself as a "more normal disable", even if I was not normal. In these moments, I wondered about my identity. I knew that I was closer to normality than insanity; nevertheless, I was different. Who am I? This question caused anxiety and phobias and worsened my isolation. I felt out of place with healthy individuals and other patients. This condition had an impact on emotional and physical levels; for example, it increased my anxiety, obsessive thinking and the fear of not reaching my goals.

With the help of my psychiatrist and family, I started treatment to attempt to solve the problem; however, the first step was to acknowledge that I was also a patient. I was aware that I created stigma (against myself and other individuals), and for this reason, I can get rid of it. I was aware that it would be a long struggle; there would be tears, chest pain, isolation, hopelessness, and antidepressant drugs to reduce anxiety and fears. I would have to be very determined to overcome my stigmatizing situation through my moral strength to confront the stigma I created to delete it.

What Happens Today?

I have accepted my wheelchair as well as my anxiety and phobias. Now, each time I visit a new place, the first question is regarding the availability of structure tailored for individuals with handicaps. I now recognize that my fear of moving to places that are inadequately equipped causes severe anxiety. During these circumstances, as suggested by my secondary school teacher, I write down my thoughts and feelings. The teacher who gave me this advice was my Italian teacher, the first one with which I felt comfortable and I could confide. Sharing this experience with her was undoubtedly a crucial point of my existence: I found the encouragement and availability I needed. My teacher was the first to show me that I could become someone even though I was a disabled person.

Every time I face a difficult situation, I start writing. This strategy does not solve the problem; however, it helps distract me from my problems, at least temporarily. When the problem comes back to my mind because I have written it down, I can analyze it more clearly, and sometimes I can even reduce it. This suggestion, which was provided to me by my secondary school teacher, has been very useful for my wellbeing and happiness; it is also a self-care therapy resource. For example, when I had a severe panic attack, I did not take a drug; instead, I started writing. This strategy was substantially better and more effective than any drug I could take: when I stopped writing, my anxiety disappeared.

My story, *A fly of butterfly,* was published in a book in which I describe the complete process of illness acceptance and the obstacles I have encountered and overcome. With the publication of the book, the process of de-stigmatization started. I continue my stigma elimination quest and have written nine books, which are available at my webpage (http://www.ritacoruzzi.it/libri.html). As of this writing, I finished writing my tenth book. This story is about a girl's trip in the US on two wheels.

The first individual who helped me to overcome stigma was my secondary school teacher, who suggested that I write down my anxiety symptoms and phobias. In doing so, I started to eliminate barriers between me and schoolmates; they started to understand my situation by reading my biography. I rapidly perceived social support from my classmates, which I never did before. They wanted to take care of me, to help me somehow and to provide me with any support I needed.

I simultaneously experienced success in gym class. The teacher developed a personalized physical program tailored to my needs, which was focused on strengthening my arms. Given the improved support from my classmates, I could enjoy the gym program even more. I remember that when I went to the locker room with them, it was normal to be there with someone in a wheelchair. We started laughing and from that moment, the process of development and de-stigmatization was initiated.

At the end of secondary school, I decided to attend high school on humanities. It was a big challenge as I was the first disabled individual to enter the school. The high school teachers had negative opinions on my decision. They most likely believed that I go through the easiest way, without risks and disappointments. However, such protective behavior focused on my wheelchair was in contrast with my dreams: I dreamed of being able to spend my life writing and trying to reach people with my books. I dreamed that disabled people would be treated better by the people who understood that elimination of physical barriers and prejudices. I dreamed that the disabled were valued for their immense potential and ability to be productive members of society.

This experience has influenced my future.

If someone had to bet on my possibilities to obtain a diploma, they would have most likely said 10 against 1. I attended school regularly and completed all school activities and homework. I followed the regular education program just like my classmates.

My internalized stigma had disappeared. The high school teachers were no longer interested in my wheelchair or phobias; they were concerned with my school results, skills and intelligence. They have done their best to help me improve my self-esteem by demonstrating that the wheelchair was only one aspect of my life. I am sincerely grateful to them!

When I finished high school, I started University with my closest friend, my mother. Attending the University, I raised my eyes and looked at the magnificence and perfection of the stars. Year by year, I improved my knowledge, opened my mind, and believed in myself. On March 29, 2012, I defended my thesis, and I received a Bachelor's degree with honors in journalism. I can now dedicate myself to what I know best and what makes me feel better: writing. During my university years, I was so lucky to publish with renowned editors. These publications led me to professional writers and their world. I continue to write essays, as well as novels, which I hope can be published. Every day, I try to demonstrate that individuals with disabilities can live their lives and realize their dreams.

According to my experience, the driving force to continue is the belief that it is possible to struggle with the cycle of self-stigmatization. Through my life and personal contributions, I hope that disabled and able-bodied individuals can be closer and the prejudices and social barriers can be broken down. I will never stop saying that the world needs both disable and able-bodied individuals. Everyone can contribute, including individuals who have a different perspective on the world.

I think it is extremely useful to share experiences and compare ideas and diversities. When we will acknowledge the importance of doing this, self-stigma will disappear and no one will be scared by diversity. In all situations of physical or mental disabilities, there will be no need to send the problem away.

A Mental Illness Story
William Vasquez

To have a mental illness is no game and it's no fun having all the issues that come with it. I can say I have a mental illness which comes from my mind and my thinking. I think I was like any other kid when I was younger. I have been struggling to be normal or to be like any other person you see on the street. This is a story of how to come out saying I'm a person and I can do normal stuff like any other person. I have been struggling with schizophrenia for a while and it's no game. I don't like saying I have schizophrenia, I'd rather just keep it to myself and have someone else say I have schizophrenia.

When I was younger I would get really paranoid, nervous, suspicious and other things that would make me seem like a person with mental problems. I would hide and keep myself in the dark which can be depressing. Those types of symptoms can make you a depressed person. I would sometimes see persons stand in front of my house and I would hide in silence thinking they would talk about me. I would do all types of weird or strange stuff that would make my mom say, ''I'm worried about you, that something's wrong with you.'' She would keep saying this in a worried, scared voice that would make me even more paranoid and nervous.

When I was younger I had friends or kids I would hang out with when we saw each other. I would go out to the local corner store where we saw each other. We would start saying, "What's up?" to each other and then we would hang out. I liked the kids I used to hang out with. After a while I started acting strange and stopped talking to the kids I would hang out with. Now I live in a neighborhood where persons talk and gossip, which I don't like. I might see kids outside that I hung out with. They might giggle or laugh when they see me. I just laugh back. The neighborhood I live in is dark, and sometimes I see persons having fun, driving around with loud music, not caring what others think about them. Then I tell myself, "Look at them. I should go outside at least for a walk to help myself get better physically and mentally." I have been eating a lot which I can tell because I am gaining weight. I want to play basketball with others that have similar problems as me. I think I can get along with others. Other persons might have different mental illnesses.

One day my mom took me to a psychiatrist to check out what I was feeling. After a long talk, the psychiatrist told my mom I had schizophrenia and that I had to take medicine for my mind. That's when I started taking medicine. That's when my mom started putting all these statements on me that would make me feel kind of angry like, "It's time for your medicine," or "Are you taking your medicine?" At first I would feel really slow and strange. I learned that those were side effects. After noticing the side effects, I stopped taking the medicine. When my mom gave me the medicine I would fake taking it. Once she found out, she told the psychiatrist that I was acting strange and that I wasn't taking the medicine. That's when the psychiatrist started changing the medicine.

After struggling for a while I seem to be able to keep myself active, meaning that I think I'm getting better in a lot of ways. I don't act as strange. I try to be more aware of myself. Then I ask myself, "What's the problem with me?" or "Who am I worried about?" Then I start to think about a lot of happy and fearful thoughts.

I have been trying to think clearly. I have been taking my medicine every day. I'm in a day program called CRP ("Community Reintegration Program"). I have been getting better every day going there. The persons there listen to what my issues are and it makes me feel good that someone understands what I'm going through. There, we have groups like symptom management, group therapy, CBT and some other ones. I think all the groups help me find ways to cope with whatever I'm thinking, may it be negative or positive thoughts. I sometimes feel like I can be normal and live like a normal guy or person. I would like to out for walks with my dog. I think we both need the exercise. At home I try to talking with everyone there. I take medicine four times a day and I think they are helping me recover from whatever I'm feeling. I've been learning a lot and I can say I'm getting better. Seeing other persons in groups makes me feel like I'm not the only one with a mental illness. I think persons might see me as a crazy person but I'm not; I just have thoughts, feelings and ideas.

Now I get a lot of help from my family. I think they kind of understand what I've been going through, like not wanting to live anymore or feeling hopeless. I try to talk to them the best way I can but sometimes it's difficult making them understand me. I sometimes worry a lot when my family is out somewhere and I'm in my house by myself. I wonder about stuff like who they are with or what they are doing. When I think about myself I think of all the paranoia and it's scary to feel scared and paranoid.

Right now in this moment I'm feeling good about writing about my mental health. Some persons might think that persons with mental problems can't do anything right. I disagree. I think I can accomplish things, like waking up early every day and going to CRP. I'm seeing a therapist on a weekly basis and I think it's helpful to talk to the therapist, letting her know how I'm feeling and how I'm improving at home and, most of all, getting better mentally. I just need to get some exercise.

I'm coming out proud and saying I'm getting better in my own mind. The streets, the persons, the places, everywhere you go there's someone thinking, having ideas, living their life. What I'm trying to say is that if someone knows about me, they should step up and say they know about me and this is what's going on. Sometimes I tell myself, "I know this, I know that, but I don't know this, and don't know that." So it can be complicated, struggling with a mental illness and everything that comes with it. I take medicine. I see a psychiatrist. And I can say that I'm improving and that I can relate to a lot of persons like me.

My name is William Vasquez. I'm from Chicago, IL, from a street with lots of good persons. This is my story of overcoming the stigma of mental illnesses.

What's There to Be Proud Of?
Jenny Otto

I have to be honest about my mental health. I can no longer deny or avoid my feelings and emotions. I like to use the word "surrender." I surrendered a massive burden that at times had total control over me. I relinquished the shame from traumatic experiences that were destructive and paralyzing, both mentally and physically. I am free.

I have experienced sexual abuse, anxiety, major depressive disorder, suicidal ideation, a suicide attempt, and several inpatient hospitalizations. I have also had to deal with my mother's major depression and suicide attempts, my father's alcoholism and schizophrenia, car accident that caused the deaths of a brother and sister-in-law, suicides of two other brothers only 10 months apart, suicide attempt of a sister, and suicide of a friend at age 18.

I now believe that I have experienced mental health challenges since I was very young. I don't remember a lot about my childhood. My spotty memory all began to make sense when in my early 20's my sister commented to me about a relationship that I was in. She said that it reminded her of our brother. This triggered intense anxiety and confusion. The brother was the one who had died in the car accident. I began to have flashbacks of him sexually abusing me at the vulnerable age of five.

I began to see a therapist and started to understand certain parts of my childhood, for instance why my brother was sent away and not allowed in our house. My parents were always guarded when he was around. I have a memory of sitting in a big leather chair in an office talking to a man. I now know that he was a therapist. Not knowing what these flashbacks meant, why I was in this strange office, or why this was happening to me was frightening. No one had ever talked about this and over time it was just forgotten.

I obviously did not completely forget, though. I remember having strong feelings of sadness at times and crying very easily for no apparent reason. I was afraid of male teachers. I was always uncomfortable when boys showed interest in me because I didn't know what a healthy relationship was like. I felt confused and thought there was something wrong with me. This period caused a lot of self stigma.

The flashbacks, my father's sudden death from a heart attack, a new relationship, and work stressors contributed to my first major depressive episode. I was 26 years old. This was when I began to take medication, attempted suicide, and spent time in an inpatient unit of a hospital. Self stigma set in fast and furious. I was determined not to be like my mom. I feared that everything that had happened to her would happen to me. My mother lived a life of despair, isolation, apathy, inactivity, and physical illness from being over medicated. This was my only knowledge of what mental illness was like. When I was hospitalized and saw and heard the other patients, I again thought, "I am not like them." I began offering support and guidance. In fact, I practically started running the group. Another patient once said to me, "Why don't you take some of your own advice?" I was avoiding my own situation, living in denial.

For over 12 years I was on and off medications and in and out of therapy. At times I thought my mental illness was gone for good. I was "fixed." When I was open with others about what I had been through, they were scared and did not know what to say. This made me feel terrible, as if I were damaged and different. Talking was a release of self stigma, but reactions of others and lack of support increased my feelings of isolation. I was stigmatized. To others I was a far-off blur that they could not quite bring into focus. No one really understood. The self stigma kept coming back, and I was caught in a vicious cycle.

Later on, in my thirties and after the suicides of my two brothers, I really began to embrace the idea of recovery. For so long I had looked to others to see what I was supposed to say, how I was supposed to respond, and how I was supposed to feel about mental illness because I was so confused. My family was large, and everyone dealt with mental illness differently. Some wanted to deny its existence and just say that the second brother had died of a heart attack. I realized that they were reacting to their own fears and worries about what others might think or say about our family, especially after what happened to my brothers and me. Mental illness was once again something to be forgotten and not discussed. Were my family members ashamed, scared, or perhaps genuinely unable to talk about it? I concluded that mental illness is hard to talk about because most people just don't know how. This was pivotal for me on my journey of recovery. I wanted to stop the cycle of persistent illness and shame. I made a commitment to educate myself and others.

The more I learned about mental illness, the more I heard myself saying, "I am not defined by my illness; it is something I have had to experience in my life." At times my disease was scary and dangerous. Not anymore. My defense lies in being proactive. After all, knowledge is power. Learning has helped me manage my mental health. I have learned far more from my struggles, challenges, and illness than I would have if I had not gone through them. I began to be more honest, open, and even proud of my experiences. I have so much to offer, so many stories of recovery and resiliency to share. I am no scholar, but I have an honorary degree in mental health. I am proud to be an advocate and a teacher. Sharing stories of illness, strength, and recovery are vital to our public perception of mental illness and the way society deals with it, now and in the future.

I am now working at a behavioral health hospital on inpatient units, and have learned the importance of setting therapeutic boundaries regarding personal disclosures to patients. Yet I feel that it is also important to challenge these boundaries. I remember on several occasions saying to patients that I understood what they were feeling--that I, too, had been in the hospital and live with mental illness. Afterwards I always asked how it made them feel to hear this. I received many positive responses, such as "I feel a whole lot better," "This makes me feel hopeful," "I feel better knowing that I am not alone," and "If you got better, I think I can too." I almost see the resolve forming right before my eyes. I believe that when you feel pain, sadness, fear, and grief so deeply, you also have the ability to feel joy, happiness, peace, and creativity just as deeply. Our potential is endless.

This journey of recovery has given me a new sense of purpose. I have served on an advisory board to create a new key corporation that focuses on mental health education, storytelling, and stigma reduction. I also work on a committee for a statewide initiative for stigma elimination. My passion is working with today's youth to help stop the cycle of shame for the next generation. Hopefully, using my "gift of imperfection" will pave the way to empower others.

Today my journey continues. I learn daily and challenge myself. I am looking forward to exploring more opportunities to share my story and teach others about this experience I call "the mindful journey." We all need to learn how to let go of stigma and not be afraid of our own mental health issues or those of anyone else. Let's continue to learn from each other. We are all human. We all have a brain. We all have mental health. Let's use our collective experiences and abilities to work for better mental health for all.

Identity Narrative
Amy C. Watson

Stepping back to reflect, I notice that the status of "person with mental illness" has varied in the extent to which it has defined who I am during different periods of my life. By age 10, I was depressed, at times suicidal and generally felt that I was not fit for this world. I saw other kids making friends and having fun while I watched from the sidelines. I did well in school, baby sat for a neighbor and had a couple of friends. But I remember always feeling tired, alone and depressed. By age 11, I developed anorexia nervosa and was well on the way to starving myself to death before I was hospitalized in a pediatric psychiatric unit for six months. Once discharged, I started 7th grade midyear. While some classmates (mostly girls) envied how skinny I was, everyone else just knew there was something wrong with me. I did too. While I was physically healthy, I felt I was just not as good at living as everyone else. I felt like my master status was "broken and not good enough girl."

I managed for a while and kept my weight up enough to stay out of the hospital. I ran seven miles a day-it was the only thing that came close to helping me feel okay. But fall of my freshman year of high school, I developed a hip stress fracture and was told I could not run for six months to a year-and had to avoid most other types of exercise. I came unglued. I was anxious and agitated while at the same time I was too tired to drag myself to school. I ended up in an adolescent psych unit, this time, for over a year. While there, I was put on lithium and imipramine, learned how to make myself throw up, started smoking cigarettes and tried drugs and alcohol for the first time. I also made some good friends and developed a new master status-"angry screwed up girl" that I liked better than "broken and not good enough girl." It was not as lonely and on occasion, it was fun. I was finally discharged to return to the last quarter of my sophomore year at school.

"Angry screwed-up girl" caused my parents a lot of distress and worry, but I managed to go to school and pull decent enough grades. I had some friends that I hung out with, and to my parents' dismay, drank and partied with regularly. I guess I was lucky I did not get myself in too much trouble. During this period, I really struggled to keep going, but deep down felt I was too damaged, weak, messed up or whatever you want to call it to make it. I decided that I would kill myself by my 18th birthday-that was my light at the end of the tunnel.

A few weeks into my senior year of high school, I got so depressed I quit going to school. I decided this was it, I could not go on living, I just was not capable of carrying on. I chased a full bottle of imipramine down with half a bottle of whisky I stole from my parents' liquor cabinet. At some point, in my drunkenness, I must have felt some regret, as I called a friend who came and drove me to the hospital.

A few days later, I woke up in intensive care hooked up to a bunch of tubes and monitors. I was embarrassed that I was still alive. I couldn't even do that right. I was transferred to the adolescent psych unit, but this time only stayed a week. They told my parents that there was not much more they could do for me, and recommended they send me to the Menninger Clinic for residential care. My parents chose not to, and brought me home. I tried to go back to school, but there, I was now "suicide girl." I did not have the energy to try to act like I was okay-so I just stopped going. My parents were angry with me and rightfully worried about what would happen to me if I didn't finish high school. As it turned out, I had enough credits to graduate. When I spent over a year in the psych unit, I went to "school" year round-and earned credit year round, although I am not sure how legit the credits were. After arguing with the school, they finally agreed to give me a diploma, and I was done. Apparently, the rumor going around school was that I did not come back because I was pregnant. I was not pregnant, but preferred the rumor to the truth.

For the next few years, I lived at home, got into college but didn't go, worked a few restaurant and retail jobs, had a couple of boyfriends (one at a time), partied and fought a lot with my parents. My new status was "mentally ill f*#k up girl." Whenever I argued with my father, he would threaten "maybe we need to up your meds." That is what you say if you want to see my head spin.

After a while, I started taking classes at the local community college and began to re-engage in school, the only thing I had ever been good at. I had been talking a MAO inhibitor, but once Prozac was approved by the FDA, I switched. It worked well for me. I met the man who would eventually become my husband and father of my children, and transferred to a university to complete my degree. I did very well in school and set my sights on a job as a probation officer. Many of my professors encouraged me to go to graduate school, but I wanted to prove to myself that I could support myself. I had become "over achieving girl with a secret." At this point, few people in my life knew about my past. Outside of my family, only my soon to be husband knew any of it, and he loved me anyway.

In the next few years, I got the probation officer job I wanted, got married and bought a house with my husband. Things were looking up. Still, in many ways, I felt like a fraud and worried that people knew my secret. I supervised a probation caseload of clients with serious mental illnesses. Strangely, while I felt I was damaged, messed up and not good enough, I did not necessarily identify as "mentally ill." I had started to separate my current and professional self from my past self. I was running from the "mentally ill f*#k up girl"-trying to convince myself she did not exist. Then something terrifying happened. I developed a severe allergy to Prozac and had to stop taking it. I feared that everything would fall apart and I would revert back to "mentally ill f*#k up girl." I was convinced that Prozac was the only thing that had let me put her behind me. Fortunately I was wrong. Not only had I developed much better coping skills and a good support system, I also responded well to the more recently approved SSRIs.

With that crisis averted, I started the evening MSW program at University of Chicago. I still worked full time during the day as a probation officer and took classes and did field placement hours in evening and on weekends. As I was completing my degree, several people encouraged me to apply to the PhD program. I was hesitant—how could I go from basically dropping out of high school to a doctoral program at the University of Chicago. I applied anyway and was admitted. At the same time, my husband and I decided to have our first child. I gave birth to a healthy baby girl, Shannon, one month into my doctoral studies. My son, Sean, was born a little more than two years later. They are the best things that have ever happened to me.

As I completed my dissertation, I was offered a position working as the project coordinator for a NIMH funded Research Infrastructure Support Program grant that funded the Chicago Consortium for Stigma Research. Pat Corrigan was the Principal Investigator on the grant and my boss. I remember the first day of the job, Pat asked me if I was a primary or secondary consumer. I lied; I said secondary, that I had family members with mental illnesses. Actually, that is not really a lie, I do have family members with mental illnesses. But for some reason, I felt bad about not being fully honest, so the next day I told him that I also have lived experience with mental illness. He did not bat an eye, and told me a little about his own story. That was the first time I started to feel that maybe my secret was not so horrible after all.   While in most areas of my life, I continued to be "over achieving girl with a secret," I started to recognize that previous versions of myself were part of me-and perhaps had some value.

In the decade plus since then, much has happened in my life. My marriage ended. My children survived that and have grown into really beautiful teenagers who are still willing to talk to me on occasion. I have moved into a social work faculty position and now have tenure. My work focuses on police response to persons with serious mental illnesses. I also continue to do some stigma work. I have been fortunate to have wonderful mentors and to work with really smart and passionate people. I now have opportunities to mentor others-which just seems like such a fabulous privilege.

I am also beginning to integrate "mentally ill f*#k up girl" and all those who came before her as a valued part of who I am. As I have become more comfortable with who I am, I have shared some of my experience professionally. My first 'outing' was in a person first essay I wrote for Psychiatric Services. After that was published, a number of people emailed me supportive comments thanking me for sharing.   The second time I shared publically was in the context of being publically considered for a contract. There was concern that the candidates for the contract did not include persons with lived experience of mental illnesses on their teams. Given that concern, I felt it was appropriate to acknowledge my own experience, although I did not share details. Another candidate did the same. A mental health advocate who attended the interviews later wrote testimony stating that the candidates trivialized the experience of mental illness by acknowledging their own. I guess she made some assumptions about how serious our mental illness experiences were. Perhaps we did not currently look down and out enough to support her stereotypes. At this point, I found myself wanting to prove to her just how ill I have been and how much a valued part of my identity "mentally ill f*#k up girl" remains. Go figure.

At this stage of my life, I don't think my identity can be summed up with a few words. I am a proud single mother, daughter, sister, aunt, social worker, teacher, researcher, colleague, friend, mentor, mentee, and person with lived experience of mental illness. Oh, and my team got the contract.

Malia's Extra-Ordinary Adventures
Malia L. Fontecchio

I.

My name is Malia. As a toddler, my favorite movie was "Ahhhh ah ah." You may know it better as "The Little Mermaid." Instead of a mermaid who wanted to be a girl, I was The Little Girl who longed to be a mermaid. I was in the wrong world. I wasn't the same as the people around me. I felt it in my bones. There had been a mistake, a mix-up. I longed for another life, one under the sea, one where I would feel right.

Malia Fontecchio

The Disney channel aired a movie "The Thirteenth Year." In the movie, the boy turned into a mermaid on his thirteenth birthday. That must be what was going to happen to me. I just had to wait another year or so.

At thirteen, I lay in the bathtub, looking at my legs. This was it. I would grow my tail and go to the ocean. Near the shore my mermaid family would be waiting for me to, at long last, come home. I would feel that fuzzy togetherness, that similarity, and connection of belonging, of finding where you fit. No longer would I feel separate and different. I waited and waited. Nothing. No fins, not even a scale appeared on my tan skin.

I went to the ocean's purple sunset and sat on a large rock. I felt a pull from the ocean and a longing. I wanted to walk into the ocean and just keep walking. Salt water trickled from my eyes, down my cheek. I wasn't going to become a mermaid. I wasn't going to find a place I belonged.

~

I found solace in my books where a lonely boy with shaggy black hair finds out he's a wizard, and a group of kids walk through their wardrobe to find a large magical lion who watches over them and is always there when they need him. I could feel the lion's solid furry body as I imagine leaning into him, resting my head against his muscular shoulder. A feeling of protection encapsulates me. That felt real. Those places made sense to me. When I peeked up above the cover of my book, I found dullness. No wizards. No lion. My cat wouldn't even talk to me, no matter how long I sat looking into her green eyes and coaxing her to talk.

II.

As a child I remember darkness and a glowing light that I perceived as an angel or spirit. It was beautiful and magical. As a teenager I remember sitting in a chair at my desk, my hair standing up as I felt a finger trail along my forearm. I was alone. Sitting in the car I felt a hand pat my head. On the stairs of my high school library I felt a hand pat my behind. Again, I was alone. Always, I was alone. Sometimes these feelings scared me, but they also made me feel protected. Like maybe there were spirits around me, watching out for me. It made me feel less alone, and special.

III.

The summer after my freshman year in high school, I started taking a class at the local community college. You had to be 16 to take a class, and I had been waiting until I was old enough. I loved school; I loved learning new things. Throughout my high school years, I took psychology, biology, philosophy and counseling classes at the local community college at night and during the summer.

Around junior year, the peers in my AP classes started wearing a new face accessory: an SAT book. During lunch and between classes, they walked through the halls, across the quad, went to the bathroom, all while studying SAT vocabulary and math. I was an editor of the school newspaper, the president of the Best Buddies club, a ballroom dancer in a troupe, taking college classes, and enrolled in AP classes. I didn't have the time or the desire to study those huge SAT books on top of my already full schedule. I had a 3.7GPA, but that would never get me into Berkeley.

During senior year my father's girlfriend bought a brand new sprawling white million-dollar mansion on the top of a hill. My siblings and I moved in with my dad and his girlfriend and her two sons in this new house. She decorated the house with gold sculptures, columns, large Asian vases, rich burgundy and gold blankets. The floor was made of large limestone slabs. She cooked delicious dishes: salmon topped with a rich sweet white sauce and French onions, quail egg soup that when you bit into the egg it burst and filled your mouth with warm gooeyness.

It was nice to have a mom and a dad again and two new brothers. We were a family. But then some sexual abuse occurred. That morning and the days that followed were just like every other day. I wondered if I had imagined it. I watched behavior for clues that hinted that it had occurred. Nothing ... until it happened again.

I would find out later that this individual had done this to two other girls and that he experienced sexual abuse himself when he was younger. I hate to talk about this and I rarely do. It's ugly and uncomfortable, and I'd rather just forget it. But I've realized that it is part of my story. In order to understand my extra-ordinary experiences, you have to know what preceded them.

One night, I lay on my bed and closed my eyes.

Through my eyelids I could see the eggshell white walls of my room, the large windows, my thick maroon and gold comforter, and a black horned demon standing beside my bed.

"Lightweight," he whispered. I jumped up and ran to my brother's room, terrified. My father came in and I explained to him what happened.

"That's enough," he said with finality. "We have to take you to the doctor." The way he said it alluded to a pattern of events or symptoms that he had been noticing, but I was unaware of. This was the final straw for him.

IV.

In front of the concrete building was a box with two rows of buttons with names next to them. I found the doctor's and pressed the button. Shortly afterward, a man approached me claiming to be the doctor.

"How do I know you're the doctor?" I asked.

"Are you paranoid often?" he asked me back. This was already not going well. I followed him up the stairs. One wall in his office was made of bricks. I told him a few of the things that had occurred, including the demon next to my bed. He asked me if I had been awake, if my eyes were open. I know what I saw. I wasn't sleeping. I had just lain down. I wanted him to believe me, and I didn't want to argue and have to convince him of what I saw, so I said that my eyes were open. The doctor diagnosed me with schizophrenia and gave me antipsychotics.

V.

My new "mom" had similar experiences as me. She was born and raised in the Philippines. She had symbolic visions and God would possess her and speak through her. In the Filipino community she was revered as an elder of the church. My father called her a saint.

She liked her house to look like a polished museum. In order to pay for the house she worked two jobs, which meant my dad, my siblings, and I were supposed to pull the weeds, clean the bathroom, clean the rooms, etc. This new "mom" and my dad were very strict. This was a big change from being unsupervised and taking care of myself. I was none too pleased. I refused to do the chores, I yelled at my dad, I ran into the woods behind our house and stayed there for hours. I waited and waited for the day I turned 18.

On my 18th birthday I celebrated by going to Disneyland with my boyfriend. My dad called to ask where I was, when I told him Disneyland, he yelled at me, and I hung up. I knew then that my age wasn't going to change anything, so I decided to leave. I lived in my boyfriend's SUV for the next few months while still going to school. One of my teachers let me use the computer in the hall to do my homework and I'd lock up when I was done. My boyfriend's work had showers so he'd sneak me in there to shower or I'd hop the fence of an apartment complex's pool and use the outside shower. My boyfriend and I lived on fast food. We'd drive to different neighborhoods every night so that no one ever got too suspicious. I pulled the sunroof open and looked up at the blue sky. I was happy and I was free.

I got a job as a hostess and quickly moved up to being

a waitress. Since I went to high school during the week, I only worked on the weekends. By the time it was the weekend, I had already forgotten everything on the menu and the different sides and I couldn't remember which soup we had on which day. I was a lousy waitress. As a naturally lethargic person with a terrible memory, waiting was hard and overwhelming. Sometimes I would cry in the back. But somehow I was able to scrounge up enough tips so that I could pay for half of the rent on a room in a condo with my boyfriend.

VI.

Again, my dream school was UC Berkeley. With my 3.7 GPA there was little to no chance I would get in. I could probably get into another UC school, but I had my heart set on UC Berkeley or UCLA, which were both out of my reach. After graduating from high school, with mostly A's (except for in some classes like AP Calculus, which I barely slid by with a C), I continued to go to community college. I became the editor of the school newspaper, which I revamped from a newsletter to a newspaper. I was also very involved in the Honors group. Because I had taken AP classes and summer and night community college classes, I completed my A.A. in one year.

I had a 4.0 college GPA and by making some inquiries around school, I learned that I was the only one with a 4.0, thus making me the valedictorian of my class. Yet, I was called to have a "speak-off" with another Honors classmate who was a friend of mine. Since we were friends, and we had talked about our grades, I knew that his GPA was slightly below mine because he had one B. While I didn't feel that a speak-off was required under the circumstances, I complied with the school authority member. We prepared our valedictory speeches and presented them. Later I received a phone call saying that I was not chosen as the valedictorian because my male classmate had a louder voice. I was devastated. I felt like crawling into a hole and never emerging again. It wasn't fair. Yes, he was a better speaker. I am a small shy (half) Asian girl. But the valedictorian is the student with the highest GPA, not the loudest voice.

I worked in the school library at the time and was good friends with the librarian. He insisted that I was the rightful valedictorian and that I should fight for it. He wrote to the vice president who was new at the school, and explained to her what a valedictorian is. When the story got out around school, others supported me as well. A friend of mine from the Honors group contacted his friend who was a reporter. The reporter said that if the school doesn't recognize me he will set up a broadcast of me reciting my valedictory speech at the same time as the graduation. I also had the head professor of the English department back me, and write to the Vice President that microphones were invented to project voices, and that men's voices are often louder than women's, and that has nothing to do with who is the valedictorian. The vice president called me into her office and apologized, saying that at her last school they did things differently. I had nothing against my guy friend and since he had already told his family members the news, I agreed that we could both be the valedictorian, and on the program mine said "4.0 Valedictorian."

I tell you this story because it was a defining moment in my life when I realized that by advocating for yourself and gaining support from others, you can accomplish things that otherwise would have felt impossible. As a student, I didn't think I would be able to stand up against the college vice president and win my case, but I did. Others, oftentimes mental health workers, ask me how is it that I was able to be successful despite my mental health challenges. I believe they would want me to say medication or therapy or some other mental health treatment was most important. And those things did and do help, and for some I'm sure they are the primary factor, but for me, it's my character. Resilience, perseverance, and downright stubbornness. Ever since I was a toddler I was very patient and very determined. If I wanted to open something, I would sit there and try this way, and try that, and try the other way, long after most toddlers would give up, until I figured it out. I joke that I always get my way, but it's pretty true. I set my mind on something and I don't give up until I get it. I plan, have patience, field obstacles, and find a way.

VII.

After graduating from community college, I was accepted into every school that I applied to: UC Los Angeles, University of Southern California, UC Riverside, UC Santa Cruz, and UC Berkeley. I packed up my belongings and drove up to Berkeley in my silver Camaro named Slinkstercat. This was the first time I was away from friends and family. I am not very good at making friends and I spent a lot of time brainstorming about how to make friends. Do I just look for someone who looks like she has similar interests as me, walk up to her, and say, "Hey, do you want to be my friend?" That didn't seem natural. It seems kind of bizarre. Again, I'm shy. In the past, girls just gravitated to me. In elementary, middle, and high school, there were cliques and the girls who seemed to think I was a right fit, just came up to me and I followed their lead. College was not as easy. For the entire two years I was at Berkeley I didn't really make a single real friend from campus. I think it was harder as a transfer student, and a financially poor one at that. Most students seemed to have made their friends at the dorm or the cafeteria. I couldn't afford the student meal plan and mostly lived on the $1 Naan from Naan & Curry. I definitely couldn't afford the dorms, and I wouldn't want to deal with an RA anyway. I finally made a friend only because my boyfriend knew her and asked her to be my friend. She was a local and not a student though. There were a few other friends I finally made as well, which drastically improved my mental health.

I really enjoyed some of my classes like the creative writing ones, and the Berkeley Fiction Review magazine, which I would become the managing co-editor of. I also enjoyed dancing and competing with the ballroom dance team. However, I was really struggling in my other English classes. I am a very slow reader and the assigned reading was physically impossible for me to complete in the assigned time. Also, much of the reading was old Victorian novels or written in old English. It felt like I was trudging through mud. I loved reading, which is why I was an English major, but I love reading magic realism and fantasy, not the stuff the professors assigned. And then my papers were coming back to me with Bs and Cs on them. I had never seen a C on an English paper of mine before. I felt like the professors were looking for something specific and I had no idea what that was. I started to hate reading, hate the books they gave me, I stopped reading, I stopped touching my books. They all lay in a pile in the corner of my room. They piled up, a physical representation of my inadequacy. They loomed over me forebodingly. They were surrounded by darkness. I felt that if I touched them, my limbs would fall off. Their presence taunted me. I wasn't supposed to be at UC Berkeley. I had gotten in through the backdoor as a transfer, and I wasn't smart enough to be here.

I went to the counseling office on campus. I thought I would get in there, admit my problem, get fixed, and leave. Talking to the counselor, I started to realize that this would not be a quick fix. With this realization I felt helpless, and hopeless. My arms felt heavier, my fingertips tingled, I didn't have the strength to move my arms; they were like lead. This feeling spread down my body so that I could only move from my shoulders up. The counselor was visibly terrified when I told him what was happening. He called an ambulance. After about an hour, some men came in with a gurney and strapped me in. By then I was starting to regain some movement in my body. They brought me to the emergency room. When the doctor came in to see me I already had regained full movement of my body. She said I was the most functional schizophrenic she had ever seen. She discharged me pretty quickly and wrote on my form "psychogenic paralysis."

When I got home I looked up psychogenic paralysis. I didn't really find anything on Google, and the counselor's terror made me feel like maybe the professionals didn't know what was happening. Maybe the doctor just made something up that sounded medical.

Still suffering with my issues, I stayed in bed. There was a loaf of bread in arm's distance and a box of Hot Tamales, which would be my sustenance. At UC Berkeley many of the classes are held in auditoriums. You are a small face in a huge crowd. The professors didn't know my name, nonetheless notice that I was absent from class. I didn't have any friends to notice either. I started to dream of death. I had a gorgeous gold ballgown I had purchased from a vintage store on Telegraph. I would wear that dress, do my makeup and hair, find gold shoes, and a gold rope, and hang myself up in front of the full-length windows. When I was found, I would resemble a beautiful angel. I imagined laying in my coffin and having all of my loved ones gathered together around me saying nice things. The room would be full of love pouring into me. These thoughts are the only things that gave me relief and respite from the darkness. On Halloween I managed to haul myself out of bed and back to the student counseling center once more. The counselor was a young woman about late twenties to mid-thirties. She had curly brown hair, and wore a tan knitted blankety cardigan. Her office had warm tan walls, and comfy chairs. It felt like a sitting room. I felt comfortable speaking with her and had already let my plan slip out of my mouth before I had realized the consequences. Shortly thereafter I was on my way to the Herrick psych ward.

~

In the psych ward I immediately made a friend. He was a Berkeley student as well and was in for taking too many drugs. The professionals thought it was an overdose, although he said he just had accidentally taken too much. In the TV room a horror movie was playing about an insane asylum where the patients became homicidal and started gruesomely torturing and killing the doctors and nurses. This was Halloween night and the staff in the psych ward must have not noticed what we were watching.

During my stay, I remember having three roommates. My first roommate was a lovely girl about my age. She had long stringy golden brown hair. My first night she whispered to me about cameras in the bathrooms. I was nervous when I had to go pee, wondering if the camera was inside the toilet. But I told myself that that was nonsense. She also warned me to stay away from the windows because of the snipers. She spoke about a white bunny and secret messages on car license plates.

In the hospital I didn't feel like myself. I couldn't feel my body like I usually did. My body felt disconnected from me. I rolled off my bed onto the wooden floor. Thud. That felt reassuring. I got up onto my bed and rolled off again and again. The feeling of the wooden floor thud against my body made me feel real again.

The staff took my bed away leaving me with just a mattress on the floor. When I entered my room to meet my next roommate, I said "Hi." "You can see me?" she asked. "Uh, yeah," I said. She was African American with long black braids. She was also my age and a UC Berkeley student.

After a few days in the psych ward, I was released. Everywhere I looked there were dangerous things that I wouldn't be allowed to have access to in the psych ward. I could jump off the balcony, I could drown myself in the bathtub, I could get a knife from the kitchen and slit my wrists. I had to go outside. I felt compelled to go outside. On my way out, I glanced at my shoes near the door. Ahh who needs shoes? I walked around Berkeley, ending up at my old apartment. I ran into a friend who still lived there. I was trying to jump off the staircase and also thinking about throwing myself down the stairs. He called my boyfriend who came and got me. He drove me back to the psych ward. The doctor who came out to speak with me was a midget or a small person. Going through some kind of psychosis, this made my head spin even more. He gave me a pen to sign some documents, which I ended up scrawling on the wall with. The doctor wasn't pleased with my boyfriend bringing me there. It wasn't protocol that someone be dropped straight at the psych ward. Usually a clinician called in after doing an assessment. But the doctor decided that I was clearly unwell and mentioned something about regression, and so I was once again admitted to the psych ward.

Through the patient gossip I learned that the side I was on was for dual diagnosis patients and the other side was for mental health. It also sounded like on the other side of the wall was more young people. I spoke to the doctor about getting transferred over, which she arranged. At some point I remember a black woman leaning into my doorway and saying, "Hi, I'm the patient's rights advocate," or something and then leaving. Somewhere in there I was given papers saying that my 5150 had became a 5250 and that I was now not allowed to ever own a gun.

There was a menu for meals and you could put in your requests, but it took a few days. A staff member told me not to bother because I probably wouldn't be there long enough anyway. Well, after a week or so, I wasn't sure that I was going to get out anytime soon so I went ahead and put in my orders. I ordered pies and green teas, and all sorts of good food. I hid my bread buns and gave it to my anorexic friend later at night. People complained about the food there, but I thought it was great. Then again, I was used to living on Naan and sliced bread.

A few of the friends I had made there were in there because of anorexia. They had a different program that they went to during the day. You could tell who was anorexic because when they came they had their bags packed with pajamas and slippers and robes and different sets of clothes. They were able to prepare and pack. Those of us who were in there because of psychotic breaks didn't get a heads up to pack. I had the outfit I wore when I came in, which didn't even include shoes.

The patients with anorexia also went for a daily walk with staff. When I asked staff if I could go on the walk, they said only voluntary patients could go. I asked if I was voluntary and the staff said yes. I said in that case I would like to leave. She said, well, you are now no longer voluntary. There went my walking privileges.

I remember looking out the window of my room at a woman rolling down the street in her wheelchair. I envied her. She could feel the fresh air on her face, and go wherever she wanted. She was free.

The floor below us was the children's unit. If I was a couple years younger, I'd be on that floor. I felt like I had more in common with those kids than the patients up here, many of which were in their 40s or something. The children's unit had an enclosed porch and I would look down at them through the window running around and playing basketball. I wished I could go outside too.

One of the patients was a man in his 40s. White with glasses. Some mornings he would be rolled away in his hospital gown to receive his electroshock treatments. Over lunch a woman spoke to me about her electroshock treatment. She told me that the antidepressants didn't work on her, but she felt so happy after the electroshock treatment. I wanted electroshock treatment. I wanted to feel happiness.

In the hospital I felt very creative. I wrote in my journal a lot, I wrote poetry, and I made artwork with pastels and paint. I created a nightly poetry group. Many of the other patients were poets and they had some wonderful poems. We had a computer on this side of the floor, and I submitted a few of my poems while I was in the ward and a couple of them got published. One of them was a poem I wrote together with another patient. I got "Come Visit Me in the Psych Ward" and "Our Psych Ward" published.

Of all my time at UC Berkeley, I felt most at home in the psych ward with the other patients. You'll remember that I was always looking for a place to belong, always feeling different, and at long last, I found others like me. In the psych ward, people were free to be themselves. They didn't have to pretend or wear masks. If you wanted to be naked or smear your feces on the wall, you could. Well, probably technically you weren't supposed to, but the other patients wouldn't think less of you for it. We were all crazy, that's why we were there, and there was something beautiful about that. We all accepted each other for who we were, our true selves.

I enjoyed dance group and doing art. One of my paintings depicted my open hands bleeding at the wrists surrounded by words like "loneliness." The staff confiscated this painting, but not before I took this picture of it.

I would often ask my psychologist when I would be released. She was an Asian woman with long black hair, probably in her late 30s or early 40s.

"Tomorrow," she would tell me every day. But tomorrow never came...

Until one day when some staff members called a meeting with me and my boyfriend. Let me preface this by saying he had previously talked to me over the phone and tried to break up with me. I pleaded

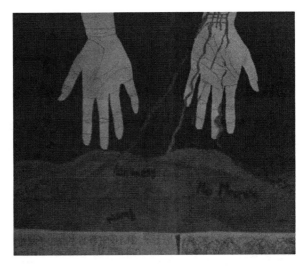

with him and cried and told him how much I needed him. He said I was like his favorite MR2 car that broke down and had to stay in the shop for a while. Being compared to a broken down car didn't make me feel any better. He decided not to break up with me after my pleading. I really did need him. I had no family, not nearby anyway.

Back to the meeting. So the staff told him that they wanted to release me and wanted assurances that I would be released into his care and be staying with him. He told them he thought I needed more time. Bear in mind, he has no training in psychology, he had no legal authority over me, and he wanted to break up. I don't think it was fair that his opinion had any weight when it came to my freedom. I told the staff that if I couldn't stay with him, I'd stay in People's Park. Just let me go. The staff took that as proof that I was still insane. But only someone who had never been locked in a psych ward would question someone who says she or he would rather stay on the streets than be locked up. And so I remained.

VIII.

I was sitting in the TV room one day when I heard my name called. I turned around and no one was there. I went straight to the nearest staff member and told him. He was a pudgy man in his late 40s who resembled a bull dog.

"So what?" he told me.

I went to my room and cried. I was so alone and even the staff member who was supposed to help me was a jerk. His words swam around in my head, "So what? So what? So what?" It was like a mantra. Their meaning morphed into something else, "So what?" So what if I have these extraordinary experiences? I have had these all my life, and I need to keep pushing forward, just as I always have.

~

I saw the psychologist every weekday. In addition to speaking with me, she would look at my journal to see how I was doing, look for themes. In the beginning were words in capital letters repeatedly scrawled over and over again. Words like "HOPELESSENDDEATHNOCURELONELINESSEND." It was barely legible. But this repetition soothed me. It gave me a feeling of moving forward. I was doing something. It was a brief respite from the sinking monotonous black emptiness that so often encompassed me. As time went on my writing was no longer all in caps, and actual sentences emerged, albeit macabre ones. After a few sessions where she looked through my journal, I started writing only good things in my journal, and I wrote any bad things in the back of the journal where she wouldn't see it.

After a while of this, I was released on the promise I would attend a full day program. I would have agreed to anything if I thought it would get me out. I never went. I would have liked to continue with groups and seeing my friends, but I wanted to go back to school, and I couldn't do that if I was attending a day program. All in all I had been hospitalized for 30 days and my dad was sent a very big bill. I don't think it's fair to force someone into treatment that they don't want and then send them the bill for it.

After being released from the hospital, I took the bus home. When I got on the bus I felt like everyone could tell I was a psych patient. The next day, I returned to school. In the hospital I had managed to send a couple of emails to students in some of my classes explaining to them the situation and asking them to tell the professor. The student from my Anthropology class did as I asked. She was silently supportive and didn't press me for details or overly worry about me. My co-editor of the Berkeley Fiction Review acted similarly. She covered for me while I was gone and allowed me to seamlessly start back up when I returned. Their responses were exactly what I would have wished for. No one made any sort of fuss, and I was able to jump right back into my schoolwork.

One might think it would be awkward returning to school after a psychotic break, and staying in the psych ward. I thought the students might act strangely around me or keep their distance, but they all surprisingly behaved just as they did before. I think many of them were too concentrated on their papers and finals to even notice or care that I was gone. Upon my return, especially in the Berkeley Fiction Review class that I co-lead, I was very confident in myself and not ashamed of my experiences. My co-editor was a girl in a mohawk so I think the class was used to its facilitators' eccentricities. In my creative writing class I submitted pieces from my journal from my stay in the psych ward to the professor and for the other students to read and critique. As a writer, if anything, I think my extra-ordinary experiences gave me some credibility.

The professors were all very understanding and despite having a semester of incompletes, I was able to make up all of my work the following semester. I also switched majors to

Social Work. This helped immensely. Now I was studying articles and papers that I was actually interested in and getting good grades, mostly A's again.

One day in my social work class the professor played a video on schizophrenia. The people in the video were homeless, yelling at the air, or were family members saying they didn't know where their loved one was. The one man who was the epitome of a successful schizophrenic volunteered at a flower shop. I left the class and went to the bathroom and wept. That was my fate. My mind would gradually deteriorate until I was homeless and yelling at invisible hallucinations or, if I was very lucky, I might hope to volunteer at a flower shop. I would never accomplish my dreams, my goals.

But I decided I could give up and give the illness a head start at ruining my life. I could just wait for the illness to eat away at my mind, or I could keep moving forward and accomplish everything that I could before my mind deteriorated. And so, I wiped away my tears, and went back to class.

I was able to graduate from UC Berkeley on time with my Bachelor's in Social Work. Actually, if you'll remember, I completed my A.A. in one year, so I graduated with my Bachelor's a year before my peers.

After graduating I worked for a year as a residential counselor in a group home for severely emotionally disturbed adolescent girls and then as a behavioral therapist working with children on the Autism spectrum. I loved both jobs and the children. I knew I had chosen the right career path. It was very fulfilling work. And yet, in order to progress anymore in my career, I needed my Master's degree. I met with admissions counselors for UC Berkeley and the Wright Institute, which was my fallback school. Both counselors said that with my GRE scores and GPA I was a "shoe-in". In my essay I wrote about my mental health experiences and how I believe it makes me a better social worker because I am able to relate to my clients. I applied to three schools and was rejected by all three of them. Well, I knew it wasn't my scores and numbers, so it must be my essay. I changed my essay and took out any reference to my having personally experienced mental illness and applied to the University of Southern California (USC), where I was accepted.

At USC I interned at The Painted Brain. The first day of my internship Painted Brain members spoke on a panel about their mental health experiences to USC Occupational Therapist students. After seeing the panel I wanted to share my story as well, and I jumped on the panel that afternoon and shared my story.

~

I mentioned before that I usually get what I want. Well, my dream guy has always been a tall skinny guy with pale skin, black emo hair, and electric blue eyes. One who writes me songs would also be great. He'd be a combination of Edward Scissorhands and Victor from the Corpse Bride, both of which, it is to be noted, are  not real people. It turns out that this combination is pretty hard to find. But, one night, after last call at a Hollywood hotel party, there he was: leaning against the wall smoking a cigarette. Now, I never approach guys. I'm shy and old-fashioned as well. But tonight something was in the air, I had a supercharged dose of confidence, maybe it was the alcohol, maybe it was the desperation that comes at 2 A.M. when LA closes and you're not tired, and you haven't found what you were looking for. But I called out to him. We started chatting about the bay area, about LA, about the night. I said there's nothing to do after 2 A.M., and he agreed with me, except, he said, to go to the beach. And so, I said, let's go. He hopped in my red convertible and we drove to the beach to watch the sunrise. Two years later, he brought me into a cave on Jalama beach where he played for me a song he wrote for me and proposed. Shortly thereafter we were wed.

IX.

After graduating from USC I was hired full-time as the Stigma Discrimination Reduction Coordinator for Project Return Peer Support Network. I just had my one-year anniversary at my work and was honored with the Woman of Courage award from the Women Who Hide agency. I am proud to be mentioned in the preface of the COPp manual for my work on the program, and am included in the upcoming research article because of my coordination of the Southern California Coming Out Proud program research study.

To this date, I have shared my story three dozen times to audiences of up to 500 people, nationwide. I facilitate the Coming Out Proud program (COPp) and facilitate speaker's trainings. Being a naturally shy person, having a career that largely involves public speaking is somewhat ironic, and at times, uncomfortable. But it does get easier with practice and is even exciting. I often receive comments like, "You don't look schizophrenic!" or other mental health consumers saying that I inspired them to return to school or mental health professionals say they can now more honestly encourage their clients to pursue work, school, and success in general. And that's why I do this.

When I was first diagnosed with schizophrenia, there

weren't any role models that I could look up to who were successful with this illness. I've decided I want to be that for others, to provide hope. I find this to be very rewarding work.

I still struggle with depression and suicidal ideations, among other mental health challenges, but I have a fulfilling full-time job, a wonderful husband, a car, a little backhouse, and two cats. I consider myself very blessed. I hope that my story gives you a better understanding of psychotic disorders and serves as proof that recovery is possible.

Beyond Stigma
Mary Esther Rohman

I've been around for about 66 years, and I've been the identified problem for at least 50 of them. When you are seen as the identified problem, everything becomes your fault: your family's substance abuse; your own substance abuse; your family's homelessness; getting into trouble at school; your family's mental health problems; having mental health problems of your own; the fact that you've never had children; the fact that there was never enough money. You take the blame for anything and everything, even as a child.

I came from a working class family nestled up against the New Jersey Turnpike, right next door to what used to be called the Standard Oil refinery. My childhood was shaped by mental illness, drug abuse, alcoholism, violence and homelessness. Needless to say, I came out into the world angry, depressed, and ill prepared to do anything but react self-destructively with drugs, alcohol, sex, and food. My mother's friend once told me, "You were always a weird little thing, weren't you?" School counselors sent me home for dressing indecently in short skirts. The only clothes I had were hand-offs from my landlady's daughter who was 4 inches shorter. My mother, on the advice of teachers, sent me to counselors who told me to join the Girl Scouts. My high school guidance counselor barred me from math classes and told me not to bother going to college. I learned algebra with my head on my desk to avoid getting hit with flying objects. Nevertheless I got straight A's in geometry until the final when the questions were asked out of the order in which they were taught. My ability to memorize exceeded my understanding of the subject matter. But instead of tutoring or anything as radical as real teaching, the administration black listed me from college track math. (My algebra teacher eventually was arrested for receiving stolen goods from students.) I was very, very angry.

After about 20 years of treating my rage and depression with unremitting use of alcohol and other drugs, I tried to deal with the unmanageability of my life by getting sober. It wasn't easy. I couldn't do it alone. The worst part was not being able to avail myself of the community afforded by self-help groups. I didn't speak to anyone; I couldn't speak; I couldn't reach out for the support offered. I thought I was invisible. I literally ignored other people, thinking they didn't see me. In turn, they thought I was ignoring them. I was making myself invisible.

In 1984, newly sober, I proved my high school wrong by getting a Ph.D. in social policy and research methods at Brandeis. I got a great job and a motorcycle; I thought I was invincible. Only I wasn't. I still couldn't fit in socially and my emotional problems got much worse without the drugs and alcohol to "take the edge off". Self-hate raged and I started again to hurt myself, this time with a vengeance.

There was my eating disorder; I either binged and purged or was totally anorexic. I inflicted physical pain on myself with razor blades and pieces of broken glass to counteract my intense emotional pain I was experiencing. I wanted the world to know that I hated myself as much as everyone else hated me. Perhaps then they wouldn't hate me quite so much. That was the logic, such as it was.

That logic escalated into attempts to end my life by suicide, many times. I was in and out of psychiatric hospitals for about a year, and in and out of the ER. I had to be supervised continuously. They gave me several courses of ECT, which did nothing but wipe out my memory of people, places and things that were happening about that time. Once my mother was driving me home from the hospital after an ECT treatment, and we were about a half-mile from my home in a town where I lived for 20 years. I could not have found my way home by myself if my life depended on it. That's how ECT works. But I didn't forget my depression, or the reasons for it.

I barely escaped being committed to a state hospital as incurable during that time. A young, new doctor who had optimism and compassion intervened. Eventually he found the right medication, which encouraged me to speak, so that talk therapy became possible. Medication was the key that unlocked the door to give the pain another way out. At the same time, I got lucky by meeting a counselor who took the time to re-parent me, doing all the things a mother should have done, such as teaching me to love myself and take care of myself. I saw her several times a week for about 15 years. At the same time, I earnestly took whatever suggestions were given to hasten my recovery. I sat on the front porch of my home, reading in the rocking chair, wondering if I would ever have a life again. I had to write down everything I was supposed to do in a day and the times I would do them, or I'd just sit there and rock.

Then one day I promised myself I would say yes to any new opportunity that came my way, regardless how much it scared me. That decision resulted in getting me involved with a peer group of mental health survivors, where I really found my life again. There were several of us learning to speak together. The group taught me two critical pieces of information: I was okay just the way I was; I was not the identified problem I thought I was. I learned I had the right to be treated with dignity and respect. I was not invisible. For the first time in my life I felt seen and heard.

It is hard to put my feelings about this group into words. I felt part of the group, a new experience. Everyone had similar problems adjusting to each other, yet we treated each other with respect. It wasn't always possible to understand, but the respect was unwavering. We listened to one another. I always needed a few extra seconds of silence to speak into and once the group figured that out, I always got what I needed. I remember clearly the realization that I must really have something to say because of the way the group listened and took my point of view into consideration. Soon they were asking me what I thought. No one ever did that before. And this happened to each of us. We became a group, a family.

The proudest moment came when we crashed a sensitivity training session in Washington D.C. for all types of service providers. It was held sometime in 1999. There were a variety of cultural/racial/age groups represented. But our small group of mental health survivors stole the show. We got up in front of several hundred professionals and told our stories about the adverse effects of stigma and discrimination on our lives. There wasn't a dry eye in the room. I got up and explained what it felt like when, on a recent trip to my hometown, a lady I used to know as a child told me to my face "but then you always were a weird little thing, weren't you?"
We mesmerized the audience. People with mental health issues were not on the agenda when the audience came to this diversity training. But they were rapt. When I listened to my peers tell about their moments of grief and rage, I was so proud of them. I knew what it took to revisit that pain in front of a large audience of strangers. The experience solidified us. We knew each other inside and out. When I spoke, I felt the release of years of pent up pain and rage. In my mind I was making sure that none of these people would make anyone feel as diminished as I was made to feel. Afterwards the group met to decompress. We were all feeling an adrenalin rush and more freedom than we had ever known. And we were a solid unit, beyond intimacy.

I worked hard at recovery: peer group support; leadership training; CBT therapy; self-help groups; counseling; psychopharmacology; nutrition counseling;

exercise; and meditation. After about 8 years on SSDI and a 100% lifetime disability, I was ready for the world again. In 2000, I was well enough to return to work as a research professional for an agency that helped people with disabilities. Of course my history was "leaked" to senior management shortly after my arrival. I was "out" whether I liked it or not. Everyone knew I was a "consumer", but most people didn't talk about it (at least to my face). In all fairness, most people were kind and understanding in those early days, when it was difficult for me to adjust. At the beginning, I didn't feel totally "normal" or accepted as a "normal". Having an incident like a fellow worker running from my office, yelling at me "you're crazy, you're totally insane" at the top of her lungs, didn't build my self-confidence. But over time, I felt more and more at home. With increasing positive feedback from coworkers, I developed personal and professional self-confidence and took pride in my work. It was clear that my history had no impact on my performance. I began to let people in, to talk about myself. I made disclosures to the people who were close to me or who were survivors themselves. As time went on, my past mattered less and less. I felt comfortable, accepted and even liked. I began to feel, for the first time in my life, like the kind of person a stranger would identify as being similar to themselves rather than "a weird little thing". What mattered was how I felt about myself. I was one whole entire person, a feeling that put me beyond the emotional reach of stigma.

It no longer matter what people knew or how they felt about it. I was proud of what I had accomplished. My work was excellent and I had a good reputation. It is true that when I announced my retirement after 15 years, I was beyond their reach in terms of coming out, but I was also free emotionally. I had come to believe in myself. I now know in my heart that I am okay just the way I am. Not that there isn't room for improvement, but there isn't any basic flaw or characteristic that makes me less than anyone else. I have nothing to be ashamed about. My peers have shown me that I can be proud, for I walked through the gates of hell and came out the other side.

A few months after I retired I came out once again, this time as an attempted suicide survivor. My story was published on a website featuring a different attempted suicide survivor every week, and the article was published in a biweekly newspaper run by and for the homeless or formerly homeless. Many of my friends and former co-workers saw the article. Most were surprised, and happily, uplifted. I never saw my experience with suicidality, homelessness and self-injury as having any potential benefit for other people. But it changed not only my thinking, but also the course of my life. I've become very involved in the attempted suicide survivor movement, and although there is a lot I have to learn, I've come to see it as a field of my expertise. Again, the personal feeling was one of freedom from blame, of putting rage to rights through constructive action helping other people.

There are many reasons why I am able to write about my past and sign my name to it. I'm retired after a successful 15 year professional career. I'm still involved in the field of addiction recovery, and now, suicide prevention. Twelve years ago I married my soul mate and we live happily in a home that we own. I have friends and colleagues, and inherited a new family through my new husband. I'm a grandmother now. But I also feel that I am beyond the emotional reach of stigma in regard to my mental health problems, substance abuse, former homelessness or suicidality. Although being retired puts me at an advantage as far as stigma is concerned, I am comfortable with myself, and my journey. I am fortunate. I am at peace. And it is time for me to give something back for all the help I received along the way. That is what I'm hoping to do.

Life with a Common Mental Health Problem
Nicolas Rüsch

Born and raised in Germany, I went to Oxford University to study classics as a young man. One evening

Nicolas Rüsch

while I was having dinner in the beautiful hall of Corpus Christi College, my hand began to tremble. I felt intense anxiety, had no idea what was going on and was pretty distressed. I had never experienced anything like this before. It happened again, so I wondered whether I was going mad. This thought looks strange, almost nonsensical, in retrospect, since today I would say my anxiety and how I felt at the time was part of the ups and downs of life. I was pretty new at the university, lived abroad for the first time and was struggling with my decision to switch to medicine after a Masters in classics the following year. But back then I had no concept of mental health or of anxiety disorders and was unaware of such symptoms being pretty common in stressful life circumstances.

While I did not understand what was going on, few others around me did either. Most people thought that I was doing great academically, having won a prestigious scholarship to study at Oxford. But that was not the whole story. Fortunately, an older relative and a friend of our family with whom I was close both were wiser. They normalized my experience, putting it in the context of my biographical situation, which was enormously helpful. When I disclosed to others, they reacted mostly sympathetically, though often they did not know what to say. However, I rarely disclosed since I felt quite embarrassed by my own anxiety. Today I would say that this non-disclosure made life harder for me on the long term.

Later on, I sought help to get rid of this anxiety. Despite the promises of modern psychotherapy, this proved not entirely successful. In the end I took a different approach, assuming that this anxiety is just part of me and will occasionally show up again. I found this new perspective more helpful. So nowadays when I am tired, which happens easily when you have small children, or am stressed out by something else, I feel this anxiety now and then. But it is transient and rarely distressing. This confirmed, many years later, the wisdom of my relative's initial advice to „net amol ignoriern" (not even ignore, in Viennese parlance) the anxiety.

My Personal Identity

Do I consider myself a person with mental illness? Not quite. While my anxiety has troubled me, it never seriously interfered with my ability to study, work or have a fulfilling relationship and friendships. What I experienced does not even get close to what people with schizophrenia and bipolar disorder live through. However, there is a continuum between the extremes of perfect mental health and severe mental illness and diagnostic yes-or-no boundaries are artificial and unhelpful for our purposes here. It shall suffice to say that I see myself as a person with a history of mental health problems. Like everybody else, I have lived in different roles at different times of my life. Currently, I am husband, father, son and brother, and friend of my friends; I work as a psychiatrist and psychotherapist; I am a researcher and professor with an interest in the stigma and discrimination associated with mental illness; and there are other roles. All this shapes my identity. My history of mental health problems is not central to, but is part of it.

Pride?

Am I proud about my history of anxiety or proud of disclosing it here or otherwise? Not really. Taking a step back, I can see, however, that I have succeeded to integrate the anxiety as a pretty normal experience into my life, unimaginable initially, and to have built my life as it is today, blessed with my family and friends. Occasionally I still experience the embarrassment that comes with anxiety. I know very well that my anxiety is nothing to be ashamed of. Still, shame reactions are automatically activated in the situation, no matter what I rationally think. Therefore I see myself in the middle ground between shame and pride.

My Professional Identity

Has my experience influenced my work? Definitely. Even my limited experience with mental health problems has greatly increased my respect for people with severe mental illness and how they manage to go on with their lives and to cope with symptoms and disabilities. It has also certainly stimulated my interest in what it means to have a mental illness and the social consequences of (self-)labeling and discrimination. Even the hard sciences have realized that there is no neutral observer and that researchers, inevitably and often fruitfully, bring their individual perspectives to their work. This is even more relevant for medicine, psychology and the social sciences. Therefore I believe my experience with mental health problems has helped my work in many ways, increased my empathy and sharpened my mind. Given the prevalence of mental illness, substance use disorders and suicides, most psychiatrists and psychologists out there will have experienced mental health problems, either directly or indirectly in their families. It is just something that most colleagues still decide not to disclose.

Why I Tell This Story

First of all, this is due to my friendship with Pat, editor of this book, to whom I am grateful in too many ways to mention here for everything he has done for me ever since our paths crossed in Chicago many years ago. Second, this story is part of who I am. Third, younger people who struggle with some kind of common mental health problem might possibly find stories like mine useful. No matter how much you suffer during transitional crises or from making decisions as a young person, things will probably get better later on. Life itself will let you mature. And getting help helps. Just look for someone with experience, a sense of humor, empathy and common sense; stay away from ideologues, no matter whether of psychoanalytic or other backgrounds, who think they know it all. Look for someone who, despite her or his training and professional (de)formation, has kept an open mind and will understand that you have many questions to which you do not and cannot have the answers yet. Some of those questions are who you are, what to tell others and whether to disclose.

About the Author

Nicolas Rüsch is a German psychiatrist and researcher. After studying and working in different European countries and in the US, he is now based in Ulm and Günzburg, Germany, where he lives with his family.

Coming Out Proud
John Dick

My Journey began over 26 years ago in Coming out Proud. At the time, I was readying myself to be discharged after almost a two-year stay as an in-patient in the Whitby Psychiatric Hospital in southeast Ontario now known as Ontario shores center for Mental Health Sciences. A flyer was being circulated around the hospital-seeking volunteers to help in developing what would be known as a Patient Council. This caught my interest and I decided to put my name forward.

I recall my interview with palms sweating, knees knocking, thinking to myself "What am I doing here". I knew little to nothing about developing a group and only about participating in therapy sessions. I was sitting in a boardroom with a panel of three people who all looked like they were professionals; including one man I believed to be a psychiatrist. His look and dress just screamed psychiatrist. They asked many questions about the hospital, treatment of patients, about choices, feelings. They were what I later recognized as recovery questions, but it seemed like that information could and would be used against me. The hours of question felt like deep inquisition. I remember the relief in leaving that boardroom and going back to my unit thinking, "Soon I'll hear that my discharge date was going to change".

About a week later I received a phone call informing me I was successfully selected to be a steering committee member, effectively the first Patient Council at Ontario Shores. The words 'successful' was a foreign feeling. I had not been successful very much my life was filled a trail of disappointments for which I deemed myself responsible. At the first committee meeting, three panelists from my interview were sitting at the long boardroom table as the rest of us cautiously took our seats. Each of us wanted the seat nearest the closet exit. The introductions began with us (the consumers). For the first time I felt that I could honestly open up about who I was and how I had arrived here. The fear of what people might of thought about me was lifted as I listened to others speak about themselves. We stated our names, respective units and a bit of personal information. The professionals were then introduced and a seed of hope was planted and I felt proud to come out. We met Margaret, the assistant administrator of the hospital, Cathy a bank teller who was also a consumer of the mental health system and the man I thought was a psychiatrist Doug. I mislabeled Doug; he was and became my first mentor and a close friend until he died four years later. Doug had a way of listening that I admired. He spoke passionately about his journey. In Doug, you could always count on his sense of humor to lighten those stressful moments. His knowledge of the mental health system from a patient's perspective always amazed me. Doug not only talked the talk but he would always walked the walk. I would sit for hours with him as he explained policies and procedures to me. He taught me the language the professionals used and what to look for in that language. One of the biggest lessons I learned from Doug was that it was much more powerful to give than it was to receive. Doug's process resonates with me "Let's just sit back, grab some jelly beans and a solutions will come to us". I was honored to be a pallbearer at Doug's funeral. Doug will always instill hope in my life. His encouragement helped me speak openly about my journey.

During the first meeting we discussed the mental health system of Ontario's was goal of involving consumers within decision making process. This came out of a document produced by the Ontario Government called, *Putting People First*. This document stated that the mental healthcare system needed consumers involvement to make relevant changes. This included hiring two people with lived experience to be coordinators for the patient council. To my surprise I was selected to chair this meeting and assist in the hiring process. I was a leader during the next few months before I was discharged from the hospital. Engaging in the patient council was empowering and aided in my continued recovery.

During council meetings, I shared my lived experience with depression, post traumatic syndrome and addictions. For the past two years in therapy, I talked about challenges in my childhood and adulthood. What had happened to me as a child and adult. What I shared is what I felt defined who I was. I was the accumulation of many losses beginning a 9 years of age with mother's death. I grew up in a large family and never felt that I fit in. Being placed in a special class at school and being picked on and bullied relentlessly the moment I stepped into that portable behind the school. Years later when I reflected on the name of that class I feel that if you are going to call a place "special" it must feel special and not be a misnomer. All the friends I had at school were suddenly gone because they did not want to be associated with the retard from the portables.

School was the most difficult place to be and I stopped caring about everything. I was introduced to pot at the age of 13 and found this stopped the pain. I had no friends and spent most of my time alone, isolated in my own world, which only increased my depression and drug use. In high school I remember hearing, "Let's watch the retards dance," as stones were thrown at us outside the portable of misfits and rejects. At age 14, I was sexually abused for the first time. This happened many more times and I felt like a cast aside person. I had felt like a cast aside person that no one ever noticed. I was there only when those who wanted to feel powerful could target me as a scapegoat.

I often refer to my recovery as planting a garden. We plant seeds even if we do not know which ones will take root and flourish or which will not. Nevertheless we still plant the seeds hopeful that all our seeds will sprout. Within my recovery sometimes planted seeds of hope, did not take root. That does not minimize my efforts as less important, but just as a seed may have needed caring people to help seeds grow and flourish. Finally, hope itself became a seed.

One seed that grew was being involved on the patient council. A couple of weeks before I was discharged from the hospital, the administrator of the hospital Ron join a council meeting. I sat on pins and needles as he spoke about recovery and his vision. The vision Ron spoke about was one that a patient would discuss a length in private moments when no staff were around. He spoke of a system that included the voice of patients and how patients were important to the system. He spoke about the need to get away from the paternal system and move toward patients being partners in the system. At the end of the meeting he walked over to me, and shook my hand thanked me for helping with this very important venture. For the first time, I felt proud of myself. Finally, Ron handed me a key TO THE ENTIRE HOSPITAL! It opened every door on every unit. Ron said I want you to have access without any barriers. The patient council seeds blossomed with colours like a rainbow.

Seeds of hope may not grow the very moment we plant them. They may not flourish today, tomorrow, this week, this month or this year. Sometimes seeds are waiting for the right moment. All these seeds will always matter in someone's life and are important. We should never stop planting. The harvest will show itself to us in its own time, and rewards will be plentiful.

My own coming out proud began 26 years ago, a glorious adventure. There were frustrating times as we grew the patient council, but these provided amazing learning opportunities. We wanted an effective, active council that was making real decisions and changes within the mental health system. We sought to be proactive, not reactive. We decided not to moan and groan at our meetings, instead leaving our personal "system" complaints outside the meeting rooms. We didn't want our personal issues to bog down our opportunity for improvement. We had open discussions about the issues and tried to find solutions.

We attended weekly patient meetings on each unit to facilitate conversations about opportunities on the patient lead and run council. Many patients were pessimistic, believing the mental health system would never listen to our input. A year later the council became a reality. We had no idea what the turnout would be, but food is an amazing carrot! I am always reminded of the movie Scrooge when the businessman is discussing attending Ebenezer's funeral. "I will attend his funeral only if they feed me. If they do not I will not go, so we had food."—Charles Dickens 1843.

Over 100 patients were in attendance at our first council meeting. I firmly believe that the main reason we were and continue to be successful is that we spoke openly with patients in a language they understood. We spoke to them from our lived experience and from a patient perspective of the hospital. Many of us do not understand clinical language with the acronyms that professional's tend to use; we spoke to everyone in a manner that they understood. We elected our first patient council and I was chosen to one of the members. I proudly accepted the role and was elected the council chair as well. At first, the professionals felt a little awkward sharing the decision making table with us. After reflection, change is never an easy valley to navigate and the mental health system is no different than any other system. We were given opportunities to educate ourselves about the system many professionals helped us to understand the importance of having us involved and played key roles in seeking us out for advice this in turn gave us a sense of being a partner, in building an inclusive mental health system. One of the first things that is lost when you suffer from a mental illness is trust, we first lose trust of others and then we stop trusting ourselves. What happened here is that trust started to come back first the trust of being capable to make a decision on our own and second the trust that if we spoke openly that we were not going lose anything because of it.

I remain in awe about those first years of the council when a group held one common goal, to be a voice for those we served. We were busy with all kinds of decision making committees, planning groups and obtaining patient input. When the hospital employees held a strike, services were effectively stopped. I gathered patient input about the strike's impact. Overwhelmingly patients commented about the lack of things to do. Patients inquired about opening the canteen to get off the unit to at least buy a coffee. In collaboration with the hospital administration, I became responsible for the canteens operation. For the next 21 days and nights I stayed at the hospital 24 hours a day slept in make shift rooms and ate with all the managers and administrators of the hospital. This was huge for me, we all slept in the same building as it was increasingly harder for people to get in and out as the picket lines were set up. The canteen was not deemed an essential service so I stayed at the hospital just like every other staff member who was not a part of the union. To help keep the services, we offered to keep them running.

After 25 years of lobbying efforts the hospital was approved to be rebuilt to accommodate a changing population and different services. The patient council consulted patients about the design of the new hospital. The old hospital had a cottage like setting, built close to Lake Ontario. On the grounds there was a farm enabling patients to get out and help with the farming and other areas of the grounds. We helped gather feedback from the patients and offered our own expertise as the design progressed. I was part of the ground breaking ceremony and delivered a press release to the media.

The opening ceremony of the hospital was held in the main lobby. I welcomed those in attendance. The facility itself was praised as state of the art. In my opening remarks I said it's not about the bricks and mortar. It's about those we serve that's really were our focus should be.

I have been on a journey of a lifetime for quite some time now. I have no regrets and am not alone on this path of recovery. I talk freely to audiences large and small on a regular basis. Each and every time I open up I feel a sense of enlightenment. I often refer to this as unloading the baggage that I carried by myself for so many years when I was in a dark place with no hope or sense of belonging. I was given an affirmation in a treatment center that I carry in my heart each day. "My name is John. I am a giving person who cares for himself and others and I "BELONG".

A Life Worth Living
Robert Koptik

I have struggled with mental illness for the last forty years. It has been a tragic and debilitating thing. Hospitalized more than forty times in the thirty years I have been in treatment, I was seen by a host of different doctors, therapists, and social workers, who gave me differing diagnoses, ranging from *Borderline Personality Disorder* to *Psychomotor Epilepsy.* I have also been put on a veritable cornucopia of medications and have been in myriad aftercare programs.

Robert Koptik

To tell you the truth, the treatments themselves—especially the medicinal treatments—proved largely ineffective and, instead of stabilizing me, left me feeling incompetent and sluggish, and still susceptible to symptoms of depression and even rage. It has only been over the last decade that I have felt any significant improvement, which is mainly due (I think) to the fact that I was given the opportunity to recover. For the majority of the time I was in treatment, I had never heard the word "recovery" mentioned outside of the context of addiction or dependency. Surely, people with mental illness could not recover. Told in the beginning that mine was a permanent impediment, it was simply something I would have to learn to live with and find ways to work around. It was a disability, wasn't it?

The people who really lacked the most understanding were my so-called peers. Stricken with this disorder ever since I was a little boy, I was made the proverbial "whipping boy" at school. Beaten, ridiculed, called "a retard" or "mental," I made no attempts at defending myself against the mistreatment of the other kids. This was mainly due to the fact that Mother would not allow her little son to fight. She had given me the strictest instructions not to resist the abuse, but to report it to the teacher . . . or run. I would not tell the teacher, for fear of further punishment. Yet, when I did not resist the torment of the other kids, they called me a sissy and would later come to question my sexual identity. To make matters worse, I came out of a very dysfunctional home where I was neglected and abused as a general principle.

Now, normally, Mother was the ideal doting parent. But Mother had a secret. She drank excessively, to the point of becoming insensible. When she walked me to school in the morning, she took the alleys so she could imbibe without being seen by the other neighbors. I watched the transformation occur as we made this trek every morning. When she came to pick me up after school let out, she was in worse condition and the other students saw this, which gave them further cause for ridiculing me.

My parents divorced when I was seven and Father was granted custody of me. Father was a strict disciplinarian who took no guff from little boys. In other words, he expected perfection. He would say things like, "Thinking people do not make mistakes," and call me "careless, irresponsible, and negligent" at every turn. At one point, I brought him in to the guidance counselor at my school, telling her that he had physically mistreated me. I will never forget his words: "I believe in the Old World standard—spare the rod and spoil the child."

And Father did prove neglectful of my needs, both physically and emotionally. I never had clothes that fit and he made me unpalatable food to take to school with me for lunch. The other kids would see me wearing pants that hung above my ankles, so tight at the waist I had to fasten them with a diaper pin. The children would chant, "The floods are gone, the land is dry. Why do you wear your pants so high?" The uniform shirts we were expected to wear were skin tight on me and, as we were required to wear them buttoned to the collar, I was constantly being written up for being out of uniform. The shirts were simply too tight to button.

Eventually, though, the anger and hatred I felt toward my dad came spilling out of me like gushing lava. It was doubtless just a matter of time. I remember being a freshman in high school, with Father being an invalid with emphysema and a bad heart. I had to help carry him up the stairs to our apartment. I had to help him clean up and dress. One morning, I was tying his shoe and the lace broke. It was frayed. Dad, however, told me I'd pulled it too tight. Then he cuffed me. He never hit me after that. Indeed, he confided in Mother that he was afraid of me.

At the age of fifteen, I held my father hostage in the apartment. I was determined to make him pay, by showing him what it was like to feel all the fear he had heaped upon me over the years. I unjacked all the phones so he couldn't call the authorities and told him to sit in his accustomed living room chair. I told him if he didn't behave himself, I'd have his head.

The following morning was a Monday. He asked me if I was going to let him go to work. I agreed to let him go. He didn't call the police on me or try to have me institutionalized, as I'd expected. When he came home, however, he told me I was sick and needed help. I told him I was no sicker than he was and meant it. In the opinion of the family, the man was called everything from a sociopath to "the devil incarnate." Mother, certainly, had endured his abuse for years before she finally left him. Sometimes, there was bloodshed, though my sister said, "At least Mom got in a few good licks." Both my parents were alcoholics, so it was common for the apartment to turn into a battlefield.

"You drunken sot!" Father bellowed. "You can't fight your way out of a paper bag."

I would lie in my bed, with my eyes held tightly shut and my hands clasped over my ears, thinking that if I could drown out the chaos going on in the other room everything would suddenly turn normal and we would live happily ever after. It never happened. But I started thinking there was more going on here than met the eye. I believed the house itself was evil. I believed it was haunted by a diabolical presence and that this "big dark thing," as my sister had once called it, was trying to take possession of my mind. In any case, I had even seen the thing on one occasion. It had actually crawled into bed with me, a huge ebony figure—a shadow-man—without feature. I watched it eventually get out of the bed and leave the room. I never did see it again, but I knew it was there, waiting.

My mother was separated from me for the most part, though the judge afforded her weekend visitations. I would generally spend time at her suburban apartment, though, in truth (because her drinking had frightened me so terribly) I did not want to be there. Father said, "It's been ordered by the court. I have no other choice." He would drop me off at the dental office where she worked. My brother, who was still living with her at the time, would pick us up and drive us back to the apartment. It was while there that I saw another apparition. This one was likewise huge, but misshapen. It looked as if pieces of it were flaking off as it walked through the living room where I was sleeping on a cot. I was actually awakened by the chiming of the grandfather clock. I saw the creature go in the kitchen, making garbled noises as it went. I followed in its wake, but by the time I got to the kitchen, the room was empty. The monster had disappeared.

Until I was put on a high dosage of Prednisone, I had never had such vivid hallucinations. Nothing of this sort would recur until much later in the future, when I experienced a bout of full-blown psychosis that lasted for over a year. However, my time for treatment was coming soon enough. My father was leery of me. It was just a matter of time before I would go off again. This time, I stormed out of the apartment into the snow with the intent of never coming back. Father got my best friend on the phone (the only one I had) and told him to go after me. Wild Bill came running from his home a few blocks away. He was only in his sock feet and it was winter.

"What are you doing?" I asked the boy.

"I'm following you," he replied. "Wherever you're going, I'm going too."

"In your sock feet?"

"I don't care," he said. "I'm not leaving you."

"Well," I said. "I'm not gonna go back there. No way."

"Let me tell ya something," Bill said. "Your dad loves you very much and he's not gonna do anything to hurt you."

"Right now," I replied, "he's bombed out of his mind."

"I'm telling you, he's gonna be alright."

"Well, I'm not goin' back."

"I'm not leaving your side."

"Why?" I asked Wild Bill.

He said, "Because I love you."

I asked him about his gender identity and he punched me in the eye.

"What you go and do that for?"

"I love you like a brother," he said to me. "Now, why don't we go back to the apartment? I won't leave your side."

I did go back to the apartment and there was a police wagon parked in front of the building.

"I'm not going in there," I said.

"It's alright," Bill tried to reassure me. "I'm not gonna leave you."

I hesitantly climbed the back steps to our second floor apartment. When I opened the kitchen door, a cop was standing right there. He told Bill to go home.

"What seems to be the problem?" the young officer asked me.

"That man abuses me."

"You don't look abused," the policeman said.

"He's drunk," I insisted.

"He doesn't appear to be drunk," the officer said.

I turned on the police officer in a fury and shoved him into the kitchen table with all my might, sending him and the collapsing table to the floor. Then I ran into the living room. Almost. Another cop, an older, bigger police officer, tackled me in the dining room and handcuffed me on the spot. He asked his assistant if he was OK. The younger cop said he was.

The officers loaded me in the back of the wagon and took me to a city hospital. Both my parents showed up before I was admitted. The man at the desk told both of them, "If you've got any other place to take him, don't leave him here." They didn't. Instead, my dad arranged for me to see a psychiatrist at a private facility, who did recommend inpatient evaluation. So marked the beginning of my treatment history. I was fifteen years' of age. I had secreted my illness at home for all this time until I could contain the depression-turned-anger no longer. It burst from me like water from a dam (or like "heat in a pressure cooker," as the psychiatrist explained it).

Two years later, my father passed away. He had already attempted suicide once before and frequently threatened it—and once even feigned his own death, just to get a reaction from me. I had awoken one morning with no apprehension of what I was to find. My father often worked out of the house and had a large desk set against the mantle in the living room. I found him there, slumped over his typewriter, with drool hanging from his lip. He was still semi-conscious. There was an empty vial of his heart medication beside him.

I called 911 and an ambulance came to the apartment. By the time the paramedics got my father to the hospital, he had actually come around some more. I went to tell one of the nurses about what I had found, with regard to the empty bottle of his medication, but Father flagged me to the bedside and said, "Don't tell them that." I abided by his decision.

That evening, alone in the apartment, I sat in the hallway at the telephone table, hoping he would call. He did. "Son," he said, "Before you say anything to me, I want to ask you a question."

"Go ahead," I affirmed.

He paused and it seemed as if the air around me congealed. The silence was thick. Finally he spoke. "Son," he said, "Will you forgive me?"

My breath caught in my throat. I fought back the sobs. This was coming from a man who could torture my pet hamster and laugh about it. This was the man who had made me carry one of Mother's valises to school as a book bag just to humiliate me. He was asking for forgiveness?

"Dad," I said, "Before I answer your question, I want to ask one of my own."

"Go ahead, Son."

"Do you forgive me?"

My Dad didn't pause. "Of course, Son," he said. "Of course I forgive you.

"Then I forgive you too." Those were the last five words I said to the man.

The following morning at school, something told me to get to the pay phone outside the gymnasium and call the hospital. I ran like a flash, inserted a quarter, dialed the number, and waited for someone at the Nurses' Station to answer. I was told he was "in procedure." They said they couldn't tell me anything more.

When I got back to class, a voice came over the intercom, asking that I report to the office. The Principal ushered me into her office and I sat down in front of her desk. "I'm sorry to tell you this," she said, "But your Dad died." I was given the rest of the day off. My mother was with me when I went to the hospital and they wheeled his body out on a gurney. Although my every instinct should have told me this was coming, I couldn't believe it. It wasn't him. It was just a body, a hollow shell.

Arrangements were made for the wake and funeral. The Principal of my school was there. The entire Student Council showed up as well, as pallbearers. Very few people came to visit Father and pay their last regards. Only the people who worked for him showed up. Now, at seventeen, I was fatherless. I would have to live with my Mother. I told her I wanted to be emancipated, but she would not agree. I had positively winced at the idea of seeing her come home from work and drink herself into a stupor on a nightly basis. My brother was no longer living with her now—he'd married and moved to another suburb—so I had nobody to turn to if things became heated between us. And they would. The rage I had experienced toward Dad only escalated now. I became so infuriated with Mother's drinking I could not contain the explosion. And every time I went off on her, I ended up at the local hospital. It was like a revolving door for me—literally. I must have had these "rage attacks" dozens of times. Then, I would go into a funk and occasionally threaten suicide.

By this time, I was seeing a psychiatrist regularly on an outpatient basis. I had never told him about the rage attacks and he never once mentioned them to me. It was an unusual relationship. He had changed my diagnosis from *Borderline Personality Disorder* to *Bipolar Disorder*, and I was being treated with lithium. The numerous hospitalizations must have come to his attention, though I don't recall saying much about them either. The doctor did not talk down to me or treat me like a child, as some clinicians do with the mentally ill. He evidently regarded me as an equal. He treated me like a friend. Years later, when I heard of his passing, it choked me up, even though he had ceased being my doctor long before.

I never followed up with the doctors I saw in the hospitals. I would be admitted for a week or two and then be discharged back into Mother's care. After several years, it finally got so bad that while hospitalized at a different facility, my family got a petition against me stating I could no longer see Mother unless accompanied by another adult. Even the doctor at that hospital seemed to be afraid of me. He had taken a CAT-scan of my brain and found atrophy in the left temporal lobe region. He recommended some kind of surgical procedure. I said no. He then recommended electroconvulsive therapy. I refused this too. Finally, he committed me to a state facility. Just before I was transferred there, one of the workers at the private hospital confided, "If you want to get along in that place, just make the patients think you're crazier than they are."

At nineteen, this was the worst hospitalization I ever experienced. I saw drugs and booze being smuggled into the place. I saw prostitution, an attempted suicide, gang rape, and a stabbing in the cafeteria. I saw people reduced to shells of what they must once have been. I saw patients abusing other patients. It seemed the people working there did not really care enough to stop it. I used drugs and had sex while in the hospital myself.

The girl with whom I had relations was the first for me. She was older—twenty-four—and had a child from a previous involvement who lived with his paternal grandparents. She needed a place to stay and they would not release her from the hospital until she found one. I told her that when I was released, I'd get an apartment and bring her to me. Up until that time, I was living in a townhouse with a number of other mentally ill men. Initially, I sneaked her in there, but within a few days had made other arrangements to move to another complex. I knew this woman was an alcoholic, much like my mom. She also did drugs, but she said she would stop. That never happened. My relationship with her was unlike any I'd had with anyone, save the other kids at school who ridiculed and abused me. She made fun of me sexually and told me I was insufficient. She pilfered money from my wallet to buy drugs. She even pulled a knife on me once, because I went in her purse to retract my keys. I tried in vain to get her into a rehabilitation program. When finally I did succeed, she walked out the following day. It was while with her that I made my only serious suicide attempt. At the time, she was visiting her son in another town, so I had the apartment to myself. I took an overdose of pills. Just as I was ebbing out of consciousness, she called and I told her what I'd done. Ironically, she called the paramedics and saved my life.

Still, the relationship was destined for failure. In the future, there would be several others involving addicts, all of which would go sour. An acquaintance of mine at a work rehab program told me the reason I got involved with these women was because my mother had been an alcoholic. He said I was going for the familiar. In retrospect, I think it was actually a little bit more involved than that. I used to think I had to get Mother to stop drinking. I thought if I could play the rescuer and fix these women, I would be vindicated. I was living with another alcoholic when my Mother passed away. She had been diagnosed with cancer and expired rather quickly, though it was a painful, horrible death. I ended up being hospitalized for a short span just before she died. Mother was in hospice at my sister's when the monitor finally went blank. My brother was the last to see her go. The previous afternoon, I had stood at her bedside and held her hand. I could have sworn she tightened her grip around my fingers.

On the day of Mother's wake, my girlfriend was too intoxicated to show up. The whole arrangement was exquisitely done, compared to my dad's, where they had him made up like a clown and gave him an open casket when I requested a closed one. I ended up putting him in an unmarked grave. I never returned to it. Mother had a piano player, flowers, a pink casket, and a pink granite headstone.   I did revisit the grave site with my sister, but I never went back after that. I never really believed in visiting cemeteries.

When Mother died, I was twenty-five. I had broken up with my girlfriend after this and my brother's wife put me up for a short time at the apartment complex she managed, under the agreement that I go back to work. I'd already had many jobs, in sales, janitorial, landscaping, and advertising. I got hooked up with a temp agency right away, but I was too grief-stricken and mentally sick to endure it. I didn't have the emotional stamina to handle a job. All the stuff I owned had gone into storage. I left my sister-in-law's complex and went to live out of church shelters, using my old Buick as a means of transporting myself from place to place. I hooked up with a couple of homeless men there and we three hatched the notion of going to Colorado, where one of my road partners supposedly had family. We got as far as Davenport, Iowa, where I was robbed by the very man who had suggested the trip.

When I returned to the Chicago area, I ended up went back in the hospital. While there, I made the acquaintance of another lady who invited me to come live with her. She was suffering with inoperable cancer. I couldn't take it. She owned a large house, which she had actually opened to people who suffered with terminal illnesses. I got back in my Buick and drove to southern Illinois, where I had lived for a while before at my mother's behest, but this time it proved disastrous.

First my car broke down in a February blizzard and the mechanics bled me dry. With no money with which to rent a room or a studio, I ended up at the Salvation Army. I stayed the winter there with the other homeless people. In the spring, I moved to a nearby rescue mission. I had made the acquaintance of another young woman, who helped me to get assistance from the city so we could rent the upper floor of a bungalow. I ended up impregnating her, though she did not carry full-term. This relationship, likewise, ended in disaster. I left and fled to another town, not wishing any further encounters with this street woman. I stayed in yet another mission until a back-check from Social Security gave me the means of going back to Chicago. I got an apartment with another young man in a Chicago suburb, but that didn't work out either. This time, we got into an altercation over a stupid leather jacket. He almost put me in the hospital. He left and never returned.

While in residence here, I had found myself in yet another private hospital in a nearby town. I probably broke down five or six times to end up back at this hospital, which was like a country club compared to some of the facilities I'd seen. After the place closed, I moved out of the county, got engaged, found employment as the yard manager of a local nursery, and even re-enrolled in college. Then things went from bad to worse. I had always felt uneasy around people and had lived like a shut-in when I wasn't cohabitating with someone. Now I was being integrated into somebody else's family and I freaked out. I ended up quitting my job and going back into the hospital. I lost almost everything again. I was already on the verge of psychosis, although my fiancée never knew it.

So, I returned to Chicago and ended up staying at a rather disreputable hotel. Aside from contracting scabies and getting infested with bedbugs, I had to deal with people scribbling obscene graffiti on the walls, starting fights in the hallway, and igniting the garbage cans. And the psychosis only worsened. I began to suspect that this hotel was a front for some secret underworld society. I believed they saw me as an infiltrator and that I was marked for death. The delusion had become so intense I was starting to hallucinate. I took off running and fled back into the suburbs on foot. I was sure these people were after me. I was certain that every car on the street was being driven by one of them. Finally, weary of going further, I returned to Chicago by train and tried to lose myself there. It was nearing Halloween. The decorations in the store windows were giving me indications of how I was going to be tortured and killed. When I came to a police station, I went in and explained that I was surrendering. I thought the station was just another front for this dark society. I must have passed out, because the next thing I remember was coming to in a hospital holding pen. I knew they'd gotten me now. It was just a matter of biding my time until they decided to murder me slowly.

I must have been hospitalized four times while I lingered in this psychotic nightmare. I believed these people had even gotten into the hospitals. I hallucinated that they were there. I had conversations with people who looked just as real, just as palpable as actual human beings—only they were never really present, outside of my mind. One gave me instructions to kill a man and even drew diagrams on a dry-erase board. Another told me in my room that I was being watched from the street. Programs on the TV or the radio were somehow about me. Even outside of the hospital, I believed I was getting messages on billboards and business signs. One told me I was a fugitive. Another told me my ex- fiancée had been killed. I was missing in action for a significant stretch. When finally I arrived at my ex's townhome, she seemed thunderstruck. But there would never be any reconnecting here. We remained distant friends for a number of years, but this too eventually faded away.

Now, I was diagnosed *Schizoaffective.* A more recent MRI revealed even more lesions in the left frontal and temporal lobe areas of my brain. I'd been tried on a host of different medications and would learn later that some of them have been "demonstrated" to have this effect. But that was still years and years in the future. For the time being, I still believed this brain damage was residual to an automobile accident I'd suffered as a boy of ten. How it had increased, however, was anybody's guess. The psychiatrist at the hospital apparently believed that this brain injury had compromised my ability to function to the extent I should be placed in a nursing home for the mentally disabled. I told her she was barking up the wrong tree. I valued what little independence I had and was intent on keeping things just as they were.

Another hospitalization followed, with subsequent involvement in a related day-program. When it was discovered that I was unable to pay my "percentage" of the bill, however, I was asked to resign. Another patient at this program suggested a public outpatient facility not far away. I was still numb from my psychosis, I had no idea what this new place would be like, but I had nothing better to do with my time. Anyway, I needed a doctor and a therapist. I called intake and scheduled an appointment to go in. My waiting time was not long. It was even recommended that I join their PSR (Psycho-Social Rehabilitation) Program. I'd never heard a day-program referred to as this. I went along with some trepidation.

I was surprised by the differences I saw here. We weren't even called patients in this place. We were "mental health consumers" (or consumers, for short). They also spoke of something I had never heard referred to outside of the context of an AA meeting—RECOVERY. This was the in-word here. This Behavioral Health Center was on the cutting edge of this new Recovery Movement that would soon overtake the field of psychological healing all over the country. For all my life thus far, I had never really conceived the day that I should be able to "recover" from this terrible illness. Here was a welcome opportunity, an open door. I was afforded the chance to get better, to take back control of my life to the fullest extent possible. I was skeptical, of course. I thought this was some kind of hype.

It was all very different to me. For most of my life, I had been made to feel inadequate and inconsequential. It began at home and in the school (it lasted through much of high school), but it also occurred on the job (for instance, in my early twenties when I worked for the newspaper). Much later, when I worked at the nursery, the assistant manager still referred to me as "an enigma." One of my co-workers did even more to ridicule and harass me, though I tried to take it in stride. The job itself was the problem. It wasn't that I wasn't relatively good at it. I drove a lift-truck, I took care of all the plants outside, I serviced the customers—I probably did the work of three men. But I had always felt insecure and inferior. When I first took the job, I felt so anxious about messing up, I came in early with the runs. I was always so afraid that I would do something wrong, I ended up causing damage to the property. One day, I was on the dock and I pulled the heating unit out of the wall where it was mounted. I was grounded from using the forklift until I transferred to another outlet closer to where I lived.

My father had helped to turn me into this eternal perfectionist. He had me feeling that I could never measure up. I was always having accidents or making mistakes. He told me my problem was I didn't think about what I was doing. My problem was he made me think about things too much. At home or out in public with him, I was expected to be a perfect little adult. At school, I was usually in too much of a state of shock to remember much of what I "learned." Not that that mattered to Dear Ol' Dad. I could have gotten straight A's and he would not have recognized it. He was indifferent to my accomplishments, but hypersensitive to my errors. So I stopped caring after a while. He was indifferent in a lot of other ways too. He was never there for me if I had emotional problems. I was not allowed to cry. That was for babies. Anyway, he expected me to solve my own problems— whatever they were. When I was real little, I was not even allowed to be in the same room with him except on special occasions, like birthdays and Christmas.

Father was also accusatory. He would blame me for doing things I never did. Once, for instance, he misplaced one of his cufflinks. "Where's my &*(^%#$ cufflink!" he'd roar. "What did you do with my cufflink?"

"I didn't touch your cufflink," I told him truthfully.

"It's not here," he grumbled. "So what did you do with it?"

"What would I want with one of your cufflinks?" I asked him.

` "Don't get smart with me. Just give me back my cufflink."

Sometimes, I thought the interrogations would never end. Like the time I took my allowance to buy lunch outside of the school cafeteria. On route to the hamburger stand, I was jumped by two older boys.

"How'd you like to join our club?"

Before I could get the words out, the second boy came up behind me and shoved my head face-first into a brick wall. I was a bloody mess.

"How'd you like joining The Wall Club?" they said, laughing.

There was blood on my uniform shirt and my lower lip was lacerated and swollen. I would have to conceal both from my dad; otherwise, I knew there would be hell to pay. I never did get to eat lunch that afternoon, which was no different from any other. Usually, my dad made me lunches—cream cheese and butter sandwiches, with equal parts cream cheese and butter on alternate pieces of the bread. I almost vomited trying to ingest the things. I wasn't even able to give them away. So I ended up trashing my lunch and going hungry until dinner. It was terrible. I'd have the shakes long before school let out. Why should this day be any different? I never told him about throwing away my lunch. He'd kill me. If he knew I'd gotten blood on my uniform shirt . . . Well, I had to hide that too.

He started on me as soon as he walked in the door that evening.

"How come you're not wearing your uniform shirt?" he inquired.

I lied. "I was hot, so I took it off."

"What did you do with it?"

I was squirming. "I put it in the clothes hamper," I said.

"Why did you do that?" he asked. "You've only worn it for a few days." (Around our house, clothes were worn for about a week.)

"I dunno," I said.

"Was it dirty?"

"I don't think so."

"Well," he said, "Don't you know so?"

I just shrugged. My jaw was quivering.

"Why don't you go in the hamper and show me the shirt?"

I opened the hamper, dug around, and withdrew my hand. "I can't find it," I said.

"What do I have to do?" he demanded. "Find the fool thing myself?"

He thumped to the hamper and dumped its contents on the floor. "Now, show me the shirt."

I did.

"What's this?" he said, inspecting the garment for any traces of foreign matter. "What are these little brown flecks?"

"I dunno," I said.

"This looks like blood. Why don't you explain why there's blood on your uniform shirt?"

I told him everything. He glowered at me. "I should punish you," he said, "But I won't. I think you've learned your lesson."

I merely stood there, shaking my head.

"You had it coming, you know," he said to me. "You disobeyed me by not eating your lunch in the school cafeteria."

"I can't eat those sandwiches," I said.

"Why not?" he said with a scowl.

"I don't like them," I said meekly.

"What have you been doing with your lunches?" This was the killer question. I lied again.

"I've been giving them away."

"You mean to tell me I've been throwing away perfectly good money to feed some kid that's not even my own?"

It was like this all the time. Bad, bad, bad. Shame, shame, shame. Stupid, stupid, stupid. Don't forget, "Careless, irresponsible, and negligent." But Father was not a well man. He demeaned everybody—behind their backs. He was prejudiced, chauvinistic, bigoted, egotistic. The man made Archie Bunker look like a Saint. He corrupted me in more ways than one. He used vulgarity in my presence. He indulged in obscene things. He let me drink. For my fifteenth birthday, he was going to set me up with a prostitute. He taught me dirty songs. The man was a terrible influence, especially given the fact that he was a wife-beater. The people he affiliated with— well, he was an ex-con, among other things. He'd been disbarred as an attorney and had served time in the federal pen.

The man often spoke of his life and his past, but I know much of this was fantasy. Indeed, the man had been a mystery to me up until the time he died, when Mother set me straight about who he really was and what she'd really felt about him at first. The man was an inveterate liar. He had everybody convinced that he was still a dyed-in-the-wool lawyer. Mother was the only one who knew better, I guess. The only things he told me that I accept with any legitimacy is that he probably was shot in the war (his hip was shattered by machine-gun fire) and that he did graduate from DePaul law school, in 1941 (I'd seen his yearbook).

Yes, Father was not exemplary. He was not a good role model. He taught me to doubt myself, my integrity, my ability, and my value as a person. I would carry this forward well into my adult life and I have to admit, I still feel the sting of his influence in the present from time to time. Whatever he inculcated in me, it smelled of hate, contempt, intolerance, and emotional instability. I have every reason to believe that the rage I experienced around Mother had derived principally from my previous experience of Father's spousal abuse. For much of my early life, it was "the norm." My home was a warzone.

I also watched my father drink and smoke himself practically to death. It was only natural that I followed suit. In my youth, I had one of the highest alcohol tolerances of anybody I knew. I could drink almost anybody under the table. I'd hit the bar almost every night. Or I'd go to my girlfriend's apartment and drink with her until I finished off most of a case. I also smoked to an excess until, finally, I too developed acute emphysema—and I'm currently only forty-seven years old. I'm already on oxygen.

So, given all this, one might think I've had quite a miserable and unredeemable life. Roughly thirteen years ago, I blundered my way into that public city clinic and my life changed irrevocably—for the better. To begin, I was put on a stable regimen of medication for the first time ever. Then, I gained a therapist who was instrumental in opening up so many doors, allowing me to literally bloom in so many ways, I cannot begin to imagine where I would have ended up without her. Yet, like I said, in the beginning I was a skeptic. I thought all this recovery talk was just that—talk, with no substance. But the more I came into my faculties, the more I came to realize what I'd needed to know all along.

Knowledge, of course, is an acquired thing. Or so I had thought. What was coming to me seemed almost like revelation from above. It was as if it just occurred to me, like something out of the ether. Eventually, it was spilling out of me—mainly, onto the blank page—like water from a tap. Had I been keeping this stuff repressed inside me for all this time? Was it stuff I had picked up piecemeal, without even realizing it? Or was it intuitive? However the seeds had been planted, they were certainly germinating now. I was, evidently, seeing the results of a lifetime, arranging themselves spontaneously on the printed page. It seemed like magic to me. My mind just seemed to be conjuring it up as I went along.

And I was flooded with memories. I'd had flashbacks in the past, but this was different. Perhaps, it was even more vivid. Things that had happened decades ago—over forty years ago, in fact—seemed as fresh as if they had happened months ago. Like the memory of my Mother coming to school under the influence. Or my having to negotiate my way back home from kindergarten without her. Mainly though, my focus seemed to be directed around the little retarded girl. I had met her, indirectly, through my best friend, Wild Bill. He had come pounding up the back stairs to my apartment one afternoon and rapped insistently on the back door.

"Wudduh ya want?" I said.

"I got this guy I want you to meet," he replied. "He's new in the neighborhood and he's real cool."

I was reticent from the beginning. When Bill explained a little more about him, I knew there was trouble ahead and I wasn't biting.

"He's seventeen?"

"Yeah," Bill said, "But he's real cool."

Wild Bill and I were only thirteen. There was a four-year discrepancy here. This just didn't sound right. How did Bill find out about this kid?

"I don't think so," I said. "I've got homework to do."

"That can wait until later," Bill insisted. "You just gotta meet this guy."

"I'm busy," I told him flatly.

"I'm not taking 'no' for an answer," he replied. "Come on. You gotta come."

I knew I was going to regret this decision. I had no idea what was going to unfold, but I had a foreboding about it, like this was going to prove horrendous. I was right.

The kid's family had moved into a third-floor apartment about a half-mile from where I lived. We accessed it from an open stairwell in the back. The older boy came out the screen door and stood on the back porch. He proffered us both a Marlboro cigarette and, of course, being idiots, we partook. We stood there, looking ridiculous, when a young girl came to the door.

"Are these your friends?" she asked her older brother.

The boy growled at her, "What'd I tell you about not coming out of the bedroom?" He rapped his fist against the screen door for further emphasis. At first, the girl recoiled, but she shot back, "I can go where I want." Then, she stuck out her tongue.

"Get back in the bedroom!" he yelled at her

The older boy turned back toward Bill and me. "Don't mind her," he said. He used a word to describe her that I had never heard before.

The girl was smiling in my direction. "Who are you?" she asked.

I introduced myself and she invited me into the apartment. I commenced to follow her lead, but Bill grabbed my arm and attempted to restrain me. "Don't go in there," he said. "I'm warning you." I didn't pay him any mind.

Yet, when I set foot inside the kitchen, I could appreciate what he meant. Dishes were piled everywhere in disarray. Newspapers littered the table. I could see where food had congealed to one of the plates. No one had cleaned this place up. And the air smelled rank. I couldn't tell where exactly the odor was coming from, or what it was. The girl, however, would show me.

"Come see my room," she said happily.

Before we'd left the kitchen, we were standing face to face. She looked dirty and disheveled. Her hair was braided at the sides, but it looked as if it hadn't been washed in a while. Her freckled face was smeared with traces of whatever she had last eaten. I also noticed she was cross-eyed and that she spoke with a lisp.

I got in the bedroom. She and her brother slept in bunk beds, hers, evidently, being on top. I knew what the stench was now—ammonia. I put my hand on the upper bunk and realized the sheets were damp. The girl directed me to a box beside the radiator. "Wanna see my toys?" she inquired. I glanced inside the cardboard box and saw little figurines befitting a six year old. I asked the girl her age. She told me she was twelve. There was no questioning the fact that this girl was mentally challenged. She directed me into the living room. I sat beside her on an old sofa.

"Where do you live?" she asked me.

I told her. She then said, "Where do you go to school?"

I answered again, and then posed the same question to her. She said, "I don't go to school." I excused myself. I told her I had to get back with Wild Bill.

"Isn't she a dog?" Bill said.

"How can you say that?" I told him. "She hasn't done anything to hurt you." I left. I wasn't going to listen to their prattle. On the way home, though, I thought to myself, "I'm not going back there." I wouldn't have to. Without realizing it, Wild Bill had opened up Pandora's Box. All the evils inside that Box would soon be spilling out into my life and I was totally helpless to do anything about them. But I had no sense of the future. I felt relieved that I would never see that girl again.

Nothing out of the ordinary happened at school the next day. Other kids still said I had "cooties" or complemented me on being a total dweeb. But after school let out, the girl was standing on the sidewalk in front of the public elementary, waiting for me. Her brother must have brought her to me as some kind of cruel joke. I knew she couldn't have gotten here by herself.

"What are you doing here?" I asked in astonishment.

"Waiting for you," she said with this big, crooked grin.

I just stood there, dumbfounded. I didn't see the other boys assembling behind me, gathering stones from the asphalt. Before I knew it, though, they were pelting us with the rocks and chanting nonsense about the retarded girl and me having a baby. I was incensed. The girl shouted, "Don't hurt my boyfriend!" One of the boys raced towards us and pushed the girl onto the pavement. She was crying. "Go!" I told her. "Go over there and wait for me." I pointed in the direction of a red wooden fence on the far end of the block. I turned on the boys with fury in my eyes. "Get out of here, now!"

One of the kids shot back, "What're you goin' to do about it?"

I guess the expression on my face said it all, because the lot of them took off running across the schoolyard. I gave chase for a while, but I didn't think it worthwhile to pursue any of them further. Anyway, I had to ditch the little girl. I didn't even think that she wouldn't be able to find her own way home. I just wanted to get away from her as quickly as possible. I ran across California Avenue and didn't stop until I was halfway across the yard of the neighboring parochial school. That was because I head footfalls behind me. The girl had caught up to me. "Where you going?" she said, huffing.

"I'm going home," I said.

"Can I come too?" she asked.

I said no. "My father won't let me have anyone over when he's not around. Sorry." I was lying through my teeth.

The girl was smarter than I thought. "He won't know if he's not there."

"He might come. Then what?"

"Please," she begged me, "Can't I come."

It was another decision I would live to regret. "OK," I said. "But you can only stay for five minutes. Then you have to leave."

Although she agreed, she did not hold true to her word. Never in my wildest imagination could I have foreseen what would happen that afternoon. I am still, to this day, shaken at the thought of what transpired. This would be a real turning point for me, a series of days that will live in my mind indefinitely.

When we got to the apartment, I showed the girl around. "You have to leave now," I said.

The little retarded girl had other ideas. She sat on the living room couch and motioned for me to sit beside her. "You have to go," I said again.

"First," she said, "You've got to tell me if you're my boyfriend."

"I guess I'm your friend," I said.

"But are you my boyfriend?"

I didn't know how to respond. I said, "I'm a boy and I'm your friend."

"Then you are my boyfriend!" she cried gleefully. She got up from the couch and grabbed my hand.

"I told you, you have to leave." She wasn't listening.

"Come here," she said. She was pointing toward the hall closet. I had no idea what she wanted now.

"What do you want in the coat closet?"

"You're my boyfriend. I want to show you how the French kiss."

I had absolutely no comprehension of what she was talking about. "You want to show me in the closet?"

"That's the way it's done," she said. I was not about to comply.

"We're not going to fit in there," I said.

It was a horrid experience. She tried to show me other things. This was so wrong.

"Who showed you how to do these things?" I asked her.

"I can't tell you that," she said.

"Why not?" I asked.

"Cause my boyfriend, he said he'd hurt me if I told anyone."

"Nobody's going to hurt you," I said, trying to reassure her. "You can tell me. Who's your boyfriend?"

She was hesitant. She looked scared, almost like she was going to cry. "You promise you won't tell?" she said.

I did, but I had plenty to tell.

"He's my daddy."

I could not believe what I was hearing. "Your daddy is your *boyfriend?*"

"He loves me," she said. I felt as cold as ice. I knew right then what I wanted to do to this . . . monster. I would do it with relish.

I took the girl home. When I got back to the apartment, I considered my weapon of choice. I was prepared to take justice into my own two hands, if it would save the girl from that creature who masqueraded at being her father. He wasn't even fit to be called a human being, as far as I was concerned.

First, I would try to talk this over with my dad. Maybe he could help to resolve this in some other, less desperate way. When I told him about what happened earlier that afternoon, however, he misconstrued everything.

"What did you do to that girl?" he said.

I told him I didn't do anything. He wouldn't believe me.

"That's statutory rape," he said. I could be sued."

"You know who showed her these things?" I asked him.

"Of course, I know," he said. He called the girl's family an "inbred clan of Arkansas hillbillies." He said, "I want you to stay away from that little retarded girl. I don't want you bringing her back in this apartment." Then he said, "Boy, you really are stupid. I should disown you for this." I left the room and reconsidered my plans for the following morning.

When I got to school the next day, I had the weapon tucked into my trousers and hidden under my shirt. I figured I'd go to the girl's apartment when school let out that afternoon and wait for her dad to get home from work. I assumed Wild Bill would understand my intentions. I just knew I could confide in him.

"You are sincerely crazy," he said. "Don't you know they'll send you to juvy. Then they'll send you to prison. You can't do a thing like this."

"But that man has been having sex with his own daughter."

"How do you know *that?*"

"She told me herself."

"Do you think anybody would believe her?"

"Why would she lie?" I asked him.

"You can't do this," he reiterated.

"I'm going to," I told him. I also told him there was nothing he could do to stop me.

"If you don't promise me right now that you're not going to follow through with this crazy scheme, I'm going straight to the Principal's office and telling him you brought that *thing* to school."

"You wouldn't do that."

"Yes," he said. "I most certainly would."

"Then, what about your dad?" I asked him. "He's a cop. Can't he do something about this?"

"You can't prove nothing," he said.

I just shook my head.

"Promise me you're going straight home after school and put that thing away."

I told him I would.

Unbeknownst to my father, I did continue seeing the girl. I could, at least, befriend her. Nobody else would. My dad, surely, could have done something to stop what was happening, but he too turned a blind eye to the whole thing. Before this was finished, a number of people in the neighborhood had been informed, but no one was willing to help this unfortunate incest victim.   I still adhered to a crazy dream of my own. I conceived in my mind that one day I would take the girl away from all this. We would go to some other place, where things of this nature did not happen and people would accept her. I had to believe there was such a utopia. I had to believe I would find it. Otherwise, life made no sense at all and there could be no justice in this world.

What followed, however, was a travesty. One day, a bunch of the kids in the neighborhood had grouped up not far from where the little girl lived. I was with them. Wild Bill had been elected as their spokesperson. "If you don't ditch the little retarded girl," he said, "none of us are gonna have anything further to do with you."   Now, they were threatening to ostracize me. I wasn't even allowed to be her friend.

"Are you serious?" I asked Wild Bill.

"Yeah," he said. "We're all serious."

I was more than crestfallen. I felt totally dejected and alone, like the whole world was turning against me. Even these so-called friends of mine were threatening to abandon me if I favored the retarded girl.   And then I saw her, coming up the alley.

She came to me and I said, "I can't be with you anymore. I'm sorry."

The girl was totally uncomprehending. To her, I was her "boyfriend," her rescuer. Now I was going to abandon her. She dropped to her knees and started crying. "I love you," she said. I don't know if this girl had any real understanding of what love was, but in this moment, I guess I assumed she did. In her own warped way, I believed she really did love me. I tried to make her feel significant. And wanted. Now, I was tearing that all away.

"I have to leave," I told her. "We can't be together anymore."

"But I love you," she sobbed, grabbing hold of my leg. "I love you."

I racked my mind for words to say. I told her the truth. "I love you too," I said. And I meant it. But I wasn't being given any other choice. If I stayed with her, I'd have nobody. We'd both be completely rejected and alone. Life wasn't fair. And I did love this girl. Not in a romantic sense. Not in an intimate way. I was only a child of thirteen and all that was quite beyond my understanding. I loved her as a human being, as a person worthy of having life and respect. I said, "I love you, but I have to leave. We just can't be together."

What I was watching really grieved me. I turned to Wild Bill and the bunch on the opposite side of the street. There was no way around this. "Go," I said.

"No!" she cried. "I love you. I love you." She wouldn't let go of me. I struggled to break away. What could I do? Maybe, I thought, I could scare her away. I looked across the alley to an empty lot behind an auto repair shop. There was a tire iron lying in the gravel. I managed to get free and ran for the crowbar. I picked it up and brandished it over my head. "Go," I demanded. "Get the hell out of here!" She was off and running now. I heaved the crowbar after her and sent it somersaulting down the alley. Before it left my hand though, I heard a shout from behind. It was Mike. "NOOOOO!" he called after me. He evidently believed I would hurt her. He ran out into the street to stop me, but he never made it across. A car pulling off the main thoroughfare hit him.

For the longest time after this, I lived as a relative recluse. I preferred my seclusion. My introversion. Aside from the relationships I had with troubled women, I didn't think people were worth it. They would never accept me anyway. The kids didn't accept me in school. My father didn't accept me at home. I was always screwing up. I was mentally ill. I considered myself an inferior and principally worthless specimen of a man. Nothing I did was good enough. Nothing I did was acceptable. Many years after the incident with the retarded girl, I holed myself up in my apartment, kept the blinds closed, and lived like a shut-in. I did seek counseling from a number of sources, including the church. I joined a group to reconnect with the faith, but was summarily dismissed when it was found that I was mentally ill. If even the church rejected me, I saw little hope for the future.

I never did find out what happened to the little retarded girl. I think she will haunt me until the day I leave this mortal flesh. Maybe, I saw her face in my other relationships too. She was not the only victim. Even I, on one occasion, had been sexually accosted. I know a woman today who feels shamed as a consequence. She is certain others will regard her as a freak. But people can be violated in so many ways. It is liberating to know now, it doesn't have to be this way. I know my value as a person does not depend on the normalcy of my past—or the lack thereof.

Now that I had found the new Behavioral Health Center, new opportunities opened up. My counselor was pivotal, getting me back into school and seeing to it that I was certified to facilitate Recovery Groups at the PSR program. I was also allowed to create an informative journal for other consumers, describing after a fashion, my own personal journey "along that sometimes rocky road of recovery." My therapist was the one who titled this bi-monthly publication. We called it *The Recovery Principle*. It is still used in a group today.

But the main reason for my recovery, I believe, was my affiliation with other consumers. Through my relationships with them, going out to coffee shops, lending a discerning ear, helped me rediscover the true meaning of what love is. And that, in my opinion, is the essence of my recovery. It didn't come out of a pill bottle, or a self-help book, or a therapy session. It came out of the ability to honestly love others and myself. I even came up with a new definition of what love is. I called it "the freedom to be." It is something underwritten in the fabric of reality. It gives definition to everything in the Universe. And it is inescapable, because it is ground into our very being. All we can do is ignore it. Otherwise, we have had it in us and with us all the time.

I do not feel ashamed of my mental illness anymore. I am not exactly proud to be Bipolar (my current diagnosis), but I regard my experience with this illness as something more than just a tragic quirk. It has given me good, serviceable experience, which I can use for the benefit of other consumers—or anybody else. So, in this sense, the illness has helped shape me into a better person, a stronger person. A more capable person. It has afforded me the ability to grow and to improve and to regain my mind and even to be happy. That was something I yearned for—that one day, I would just wake up in the morning *feeling good*. Eventually, I got that wish. And though I still have to deal with refractory symptoms, I can tell you this. The weather still looks good to me.

We have to stop the nonsense that says people with mental illnesses are rejects or defectives. They are, by and large, not so very different from everybody else. The illnesses are not reasons for being disqualified. A person with mental illness has enough difficulty just accepting herself. Fighting depression, coping with psychotic symptoms, struggling with manic episodes—I've dealt with all this. And that's the fact of it. I have DEALT with it. I have resolved to get on with my life, doing whatever it takes now to build a future that I can respect and truly be proud of. I personally believe in something I call "infinite potential" or "open possibility." No one can ascribe limits to the human mind. We are capable of so much more and we must wake people up to the reality that mental illness need no longer be the second leading cause of premature mortality and disability in the industrialized world. People with mental illness are no less human, no more violent or destructive, no less capable of functioning. They are just ordinary people whose lives operate at different frequencies. Their experiences are not so grossly different from the norm. Given all this, we should accept them and respect them for the wonderful contributions they can make. I know we are vital to the welfare of this society. A person with a mental illness has "a life worth living."

Happily Mental After
Diane Mintz

Diane Mintz

The day is still vivid in my mind, though it was nearly thirty years ago and my mind endured a turbulent ride with many obstacles. It was a warm, sunny day just before Christmas and I was feeling *very merry*. It occurred to me that I would feel even more fabulous if I put on my bikini with my fur coat to sunbathe on my balcony. As I was basking in all my grandiose glory, I had an epiphany that Jesus wanted to meet me at the airport.

I changed into my red silk dress, high heels and headed out to the San Francisco International Airport. As I approached every corner, I whole-heartedly anticipated meeting Jesus face-to-face. To show my great faith, I tossed my entire set of keys into one of the trash cans. After several hours, I started walking towards the freeway where a nice couple picked me up. I rambled on so quickly, but I don't recall if I told them that I was stood up by Jesus.

I had several manic episodes during my ten years on the bipolar roller coaster when I was clearly out of touch with reality. I had some crazy ideations during those times of psychosis, which led me to do some wacky things, but it was not a permanent state of mind. Psychosis is a treatable mental illness syndrome, but when people see odd behavior in us, they think we will never be the same.

Once my grandma was given an insulin shot by mistake just before she was released from the hospital. It was frightening to see her suddenly become unresponsive and unable to formulate words. My natural reaction and immediate fear was that she was going to remain in that state forever and we'd never be able to communicate normally again. But thankfully with proper treatment, in this case sugar, she was back to normal just hours later.

My psychosis eventually stopped once I was properly medicated, but it took a very long time because I loved the feeling. Who wants treatment for feeling fabulous? Everything was full of meaning and purpose. There were signs and meaningful symbols everywhere. The TV and radio were talking directly to me or about me. There were deep levels of connections which suddenly all made sense. I could connect every dot, understand everything about everything and it was all *very* significant. I thought I had the secret decoder ring to life itself and it was overwhelmingly fantastic!

I can laugh at my manic episodes now, but when those of us with mental illness are feared or ridiculed because we suffer from conditions that affect our behavior, it can keep us hiding in shame. If people had a greater understanding of our afflictions then we might be treated with greater compassion and respect.

It is messy to be involved with a sick, mentally ill person, but my family never gave up on me. If not for my mom, I would be on the street, in jail, or dead. She had experience working in a psych ward in nurses training, so she had some understanding of bipolar disorder. The understanding of mental illness along with compassion saves lives – it did mine.

The onset of my mental illness was a debilitating depression which lasted almost a year. Suicidal ideations weighed heavily on my tortured mind. When I finally agreed to go into the hospital after six months of mind-numbing nonexistence, I very reluctantly conceded. I couldn't understand how I could possibly get better when I would forever be labeled a mental patient. On a good day, I didn't know how to deal with that. A lifetime of stigma heaped on my pile of insurmountable problems was too much to bear.

The only solution I could think of was the permanent solution. For the entire three months I spent in the hospital, I spent the majority of my free time planning my suicide. Then I finally gave in to my obsession. When I saw what my suicide attempt did to my family, I promised that I would never try again.

The most despair I've ever felt was the downward spiral of that first clinical depression. I could not see a flicker of light at the end of the tunnel. The path was unfamiliar. The flashbacks of my life as a cheerful social butterfly were disjointed from the dark, isolated life of despair that I was trapped in. I truly believed I would never function again.

The missing element during my first clinical depression—was hope. Because I could not believe the misery would end, my recovery was hampered. My unstable mood ride had only just begun, but I was the only rider I knew. I wish I could have observed others and gotten advice like I do when I see people get off an amusement park ride. At the end of the roller coaster, I can observe if riders are laughing or look queasy and ghost white. When I have witnessed other people make it through the chills and spills, I feel more assured and less fearful. I don't obsess about falling off the ride to my death. If only someone had blazed the way before me and showed me how they got through their dreadful experiences because it would have given me hope that I could get through safely too.

Instead, I was the lone rider on my decade-long ride of ups and downs. My illness was called "manic depression" back when I was diagnosed and I was the only person on earth that I knew who had this disorder. Then I heard about Jimi Hendrix. The extremely talented musician suffered from manic depression and wrote a song by that name. Then one day he took an excess of sleeping pills and died choking on his own vomit.

Depressions after manic episodes were devastating and full of humiliation. The fact that the unlimited energy and euphoria was gone was bad enough, but the thoughts of my outlandish, embarrassing, manic behavior made me want to crawl under a rock and hide.

After my first steep fall and rise, I got my life back on track and landed a great job. The life-saving, job-saving benefit was the fact that the vice president's sister suffered from bipolar disorder. Even though my co-workers were baffled by my behavior when I got ill, they were all very supportive; thanks to the guidance of my empathetic VP and his patient assistant. Because of their compassion, I enjoyed a fifteen-year-long progressive career, despite long hospital stays and difficult transitions back to work. That kind of support was key in my recovery.

Most of my manic behavior happened behind the scenes, but sometimes everyone knew—like when I ran out of gas on a bridge in the company car; it didn't faze me in the slightest. I had been drinking at lunch and planned to continue, so I left the car parked on the bridge. My boss didn't know what to do with me when mania took over the controls and alcohol further impaired my judgment.

Several things kept me sick during those ten years of severe mood swings. Certainly non-compliance played a big part. When I was in a manic episode, no one dared to tell me there that something was wrong with me. I was more than fine, I was new and improved. Therefore, why would I need medication if I felt so good? It's a hard pill to swallow.

The sensible thing to do when I needed medicine was to take it when I felt bad and then stop taking it when I felt better. I learned that the effective treatment plan for bipolar is unlike taking aspirin for a headache until it feels better. This treatment plan is more like taking a low dose aspirin every day to prevent another heart attack. For several years, my problem remained because there were long periods when I felt fine and didn't care about prevention. Then when I got sick, I had to use my brain to treat my brain.

Little did I know, what looked like denial to others was actually a symptom of my illness that accounted for my lack of insight called *"anosognosia."* This symptom of my brain disorder prevented me from realizing that I had a brain disorder! This not only impeded my recovery, but was cruel and unusual punishment for my family and friends who were trying to help me!

I put my parents through hell when I was ill. My mother's nurturing gifts were taken to the limit. She didn't know if I was dead or alive, but when she went to work she hid her anguish. At the time no one talked about mental illness at all, so how could anyone understand the pain of having a mentally ill daughter that was running wild in a manic episode? Mental illness takes a terrible toll on our loved ones when they feel they must carry the heavy burden secretively.

I continued to try to mix my own medication plan of street drugs and alcohol with the doctor's plan of mood stabilizing drugs. My substance use masked and mimicked my psychiatric symptoms, which made my bipolar disorder difficult to treat. I enjoyed alcohol and the drugs I chose because I thought they made me more social and interesting. It was counterintuitive to take prescriptions that made me feel flat and boring compared to being high; especially compared to the fireworks of my manic neuron activity.

If only I could have accepted sooner that *I can't drink,* I would have had an extra decade of life progress instead of roller coaster chaos. I couldn't get off the pity pot and appreciate how people deal with temptations and live to tell about it all the time. Certainly my friends with peanut allergies are enticed by the smell of delicious peanut butter cookies and would love a peanut butter cup sometimes, but bad things happen when they eat it so they abstain.

I didn't know about the strong genetic component of substance abuse in families, nor did I realize that alcoholism was rampant in my extended family. It is crystal clear to me now that I had a predisposition to addictive disorders. Eventually I realized that it really didn't even matter if I was technically an alcoholic or not because I had extenuating circumstances. Eventually, I realized that I was indeed an alcoholic.

The problem was that I had to use ping pong treatment of my dual disorders. I had to bounce back and forth from twelve-step programs to psych wards. Recovery seemed impossible when it was left up to me, the impaired one, to integrate treatment. I was either too depressed to follow the directions of the twelve step program or I had partied too much to care about therapy or meds— either way, my mind got in the way of treatment.

Therapy helped me to dig up issues, but at the core I found a spiritual malady. I tried to fill the hole in my soul with something that couldn't fully satisfy me. I discovered that my Creator designed me with a God-shaped hole, so that He and He alone could fill it. But unfortunately, I made other things my god. I stuffed that empty space with drugs, alcohol, sex, food, and every other self-centered pleasure-seeking thing I could try.

On the other hand, I often come across well-meaning people who firmly believe spiritual help alone is enough to treat mental illnesses and addictions. Prayer works, but when I had chest pains, I was expected to go to a doctor and seek treatment too. It sounds odd, but we actually need to teach people that the brain is an organ of the body. Their ignorance can make someone with mental illness feel worse about themselves when they don't get better from prayer alone.

Sometimes we are even told that we do not get well because of our lack of faith or our sin.

I have also heard people claim that their bipolar is cured. I totally believe in supernatural healing because I have witnessed some inexplicable miraculous healings and heard about many more. However, it is too dangerous for me to make an assumption that I have been miraculously cured because my condition impacts cognitive reasoning. I could be mistaken though. The error of my judgment may not show up for months or years. If I got ill again I may never get back on track. It just isn't worth it.

After many attempts, I finally got sober in Alcoholic Anonymous in 1991. When I was newly sober and on the stabilizing medication alone, I thought my creativity disappeared. I failed to recognize how the incredible creative spree only lasted until the illness became unmanageable. I bloomed with creative energy, then it wilted and withered. During a manic episode, the amazing abilities of Super Diane never lasted long enough to really take root and be fruitful before the ride twisted, turned and plummeted. I didn't realize I had the same basic qualities before I got ill, but during my long season of extremes, these characteristics either exploded or faded to oblivion. The truth of the matter was that my gifts and talents didn't just vanish. My brain just had to recalibrate.

I have taken my medication faithfully and have stayed within a manageable mood zone ever since I got sober. But, my adventures with mental illness were not over.

After I was two years sober and sane, I met Greg in a twelve-step program. We had a lot in common, but a history of mental problems, addictions and food issues were not on my ideal-mate checklist. However, the things Greg had overcome and the recovery he spoke of was impressive and inspiring.

Greg's illness was a mystery to us both. He was not correctly diagnosed with schizoaffective disorder until a few years after we were married. Greg has symptoms of bipolar, schizophrenia and attention deficient disorder all in one. Greg had learned how to hold it together in front of the world and hide his struggles, but after we were married I saw him fall apart. Then he realized that he could tell me all that was going on in his head… and it didn't freak me out. Once he was convinced that I loved him no matter what and wanted to learn how to support him, we were able to get real help for him.

I began to be grateful for my illness. I had experienced mental illness from the inside out, so it helped me to deal with mental illness from the outside in. It is a heartbreaking battle with an invisible foe. I still felt helpless when Greg was really sick and I didn't know what to do to help him. It was a lot of trial and error.

I learned that sometimes Greg's mind is quiet and peaceful and sometimes the voices he battles aren't bothersome because they seem to be a room or two away. Oddly, we never gave credence or even considered the word, "voices" until very recently. Greg always referred to his realistic, phantom, unwanted mental input as "intrusive thoughts." For almost three decades, he never used the word "voices" to describe the negative input when discussing his experience with anyone, not even his doctors. Perhaps, he unconsciously dismissed the word due to stigma. How could anyone embrace a word that people clearly associated with crazy people? We still find the word "*thoughts*" to be more applicable because they are so intertwined with rational thinking and because Greg has learned how to distinguish between true and false input.

So it turns out, truth is a really big deal, - not just for getting sober, but for dealing with Greg's delusions and the delusions which confounded my thinking when I was manic. A delusion is a distorted or irrational belief. They can be mild delusions, like the thousands of tone deaf people who believe they can be the next *American Idol*; or it can be a dangerous delusion if you believe you can fly.

On our spiritual journey, Greg came to believe the truth that only God knows our thoughts and no mortal is privy to another person's thoughts. So, when he believes he can hear other people's thoughts he recognizes this irrational belief as a symptom of his illness and not reality.

I believe one of the many problems we face in getting proper treatment for these complicated conditions is the fact that the world of psychiatry deals only in the emotional, mental, and physical state of a person. They miss the very important spiritual component. We are complex beings in how our mind, body, and spirit interact. In order to recover, we need steps toward spiritual healing. This is a challenge in a secular society which tells us that relying on a Higher Power is just a crutch. Yet relying on a few cocktails to cope with a problem or dealing with emotional issues by overeating seems to be no big deal.

Today I believe I am responding to my real message from God - to share our story in order to change people's minds about mental illness and provide genuine hope for recovery. Greg and I have gained insight into what very few people understand and despite of what society hears about people with severe mental illness, we live full and successful lives.

To tell our story, I wrote a book called *"In Sickness and in Mental Health: Living with and Loving Someone with Mental Illness."* My amazing mother was my inspiration because she took care of my father, a heart patient, diabetic, double amputee on kidney dialysis (while dealing with me), but she never complained about all she did for her husband. She truly loved him in sickness and in health.

I am active with various mental health organizations and on three speaker's bureaus. It is my mission to tell everyone I can that there is no shame in having mental illness and it is not a hopeless life sentence. Greg and I have a ridiculously good life despite our diagnoses. I hope that everyone I speak to and people who read my book will find a safe way to talk about mental illness, so that stigma doesn't stop people from getting help.

My husband and I are blessed with two awesome kids, a beautiful home in a gated community, many close friends and a loving family. We own and operate an IT company, which we started in 2005. We are active in our community and in our church. Connection with others is very important. We must sometimes make an extra effort so that we don't isolate.

Our wellness is all about balance. Greg and I both require medicine and therapy along with spiritual development and growth to remain sober and sane. Recovery from these very complex illnesses requires full commitment to every aspect of treatment. I am very grateful that my husband and I have overcome so many challenges. Even though we are not cured, I am now proud to share what was once shameful.

Before my book came out, Greg and I knew we had to commit to full disclosure. We had many people in our close circle that knew of our illnesses and supported us, but others were very shocked to learn that average folks like us live with these severe illnesses. As I have been speaking out I am finding that people are just ignorant – they just don't know any better. One colleague from the Ukraine said that he thought of a person with a chainsaw when he hears about someone with schizophrenia. Clearly, people haven't heard very much about the silent successful people like us.

I was uneasy at first to find out how our business community would react to the fact that they have been doing business with two people with serious mental illnesses. I attend a business networking group each week and they knew I was writing a book. It was just a matter of time before they knew what it was about. When I shared the title, the members with mental illness or with loved ones with mental illness were anxious to read it. Their response was very encouraging so I decided to shock the rest of them. I gave a presentation about mental illness and shared our story. The response was overwhelmingly positive.

The fact is, when I look back, I can see that as we began to receive acceptance and compassion from people who we disclosed to, it did wonders for our mental health. It actually accelerated our recovery! We started with someone safe and eventually felt better after we shared and continued to talk about it. It was scarier in our own heads. Isolation with shame is dangerous. Our brain is not our friend when we are ill – that's where suicidal thoughts fester.

Not everyone who shares about their experience with these issues and be accepted, but it sure is wonderful when it happens. It opens the door from the darkness of disgrace to the light of liberty. It also allows others to feel safe to come out of the dark shadows themselves. Many years ago, when Greg and I disclosed to our connection group from church, a small group of twenty people, we were shocked to learn that one friend had bipolar disorder and another schizoaffective.

I envision the day when mental illness is no longer a taboo, shameful subject. Breast cancer finally got the proper attention, so I believe with all my heart that we are moving toward the day that society will support people dealing with mental illness in a similar way.

It may take many years to change the way the Hollywood and the media have demonized us, but once we focus more on those of us living successful lives and managing our illness, the more people will feel comfortable coming out of their shame and getting support. Someday people won't think of shooters at schools when they think of mental illness. They will think of people who have survived and thrive, people like me and my husband.

We need the media and Hollywood to change their focus. The news reports of tragic murders and other violent crimes are rare, but sensational due to the senseless nature of the crimes. We are more comfortable with daily reports of violence when there is a motive of greed, jealousy or envy to pin it on. If a violent act is caused by an ill person who has not been able to get complete, on-going treatment for their condition, then it makes no sense at all.

Imagine a world without stigma where treatment for the mind is as common as treatment for the body. Since so many deaths are attributed to physical ailments, which actually stem from untreated mental illness, why not give attention to the root cause?

How many tragedies could be avoided if early detection was commonplace because those suffering didn't feel the need to isolate and hide their problem from a "judgemental" world? What if we screened and treated warning signs of mental illness like cancer; and offered complete treatment - *without shaming the person*?

What if we viewed the killer disease of addiction more compassionately to make it safe for alcoholism and addictions in families to come out in the open? Maybe medical professionals won't need to wait to recommend treatment for substance abuse until the late stages of the disease when physical health is severely affected. Maybe people won't resist treatment until it is court-ordered due to trouble with the law. In both scenarios, there is already so much damage to repair that the chances of recovery are slim. People feel utterly hopeless.

If there was a paradigm shift of society's view of the disease of addiction where early treatment was expected and applauded, I believe it would manifest into widespread improvement in all kinds of mental and physical illnesses.

Loved ones need to understand that relapse is a part of recovery. It is hard not to shame or give up on a person when they stumble because it is so disappointing. It is also heartbreaking when cancer comes back, but people respond differently. How often is the cancer patient blamed? I doubt the blamers could take on the two no-fault illnesses of addiction and mental illness (which mask and mimic each other) and overcome them with their upstanding moral character.

In the twelve-step program we learn to be responsible for our actions, but it can be challenging when the mental illness causes behaviors we can't control. Sometimes we just have to keep cleaning up our messes in order to be responsible and gain trust. It would be wise for the person in early recovery not to shout from the mountaintops that they are sober, lest they fall. After I was on solid ground, I found it helpful to disclose to people that I also have the disease of addiction and alcoholism because it keeps me accountable. I would want people to call me out on anything that might get me into trouble.

Even in a perfect world without stigma, people will continue to cover up their addictions due to pride and determination. They don't realize that others can see through the façade. Frustrated loved ones can't convince them to acknowledge a problem. Denial, lying and secretiveness are the pitiful pillars of addiction. It is the nature of the beast.

My husband and I always get a "good for you" when telling someone of our two-plus-decades of being clean and sober. In meetings we applaud people with days or even hours of sobriety. Would it help the prideful to know that on the other side of the perceived deflating, demoralizing admission of defeat, folks will cheer for them?

I wrote my book and speak publically about our experience in order to bring about a change of perception, so we can eradicate the negative judgment associated with mental illness and addiction. When stigma keeps sick people from seeking help it impacts everyone in their life.

Relationships are destroyed and families implode. The power of stigma not only impedes recovery, but sometimes the impact is permanent when the ultimate consequence of stigma is suicide.

With so many people touched by mental illness and addiction, it is vital that people are willing to understand these diseases and adopt a new attitude. It is truly a matter of life or death.

I don't look for Jesus at the airport anymore. Greg and I can find Him at the center of our lives. Our spiritual journey and healing journey have been intertwined. Our lives have been completely transformed and our marriage has reaped the benefits. We are very grateful that we have overcome so many challenges and are able to live happily mental after.

Three Poems
Gina Misner

Black Eyed Suzie
He loves me, he loves me not,
That's what Black Eyed Suzie says
Whenever she talks about her fat lip
and her blackened eye.
Nowadays she doesn't know what to think
she's been knocked around so many times.
If you were to ask her if he loves her
Black Eyed Suzie has been known to reply,
"He loves me, He loves me not",
but she doesn't really know the reason why,
because he's picked her self-esteem away
slowly;
One petal at a time;
Leaving her devastated,
and ruining her pride.
Next she began to exhibit untreated symptoms
caused by insomnia;
Her remedy?
A bottle of wine.
Then there were the Holidays
spent abused and bruised;
Unable to hide her fat lip and her blackened eye;
It wasn't until Christmas Eve,
when he'd nearly broken her neck
that she began to realize;
That he'd done nothing,
but beat and cheat on her
until all she could do was cry.
Finally she came to the conclusion,
that her life was one big mistake,
she had been living a lie.

She began to ask herself questions, like,
"Why does he insult my intelligence?
along with my mind?"
Then there were other times
When she was seen leaving her job
On campus,
sobbing,
with her fat lip and her blackened eye.
There was nothing that her friends could say or do
except sit idly by;
As he destroyed her life
With a blink of her blackened eye.
It was when she finally decided to leave
that he revealed his rabid side;
By following her all over the city;
Wherever he thought she might reside.
It was then that Black Eyed Suzie
asked the police for help,
in them she knew she could confide.
She explained to them and the judge,
"He's been stalking me and that's a crime!"
"This time sorry doesn't cut it,"
she told the authorities as
she signed the restraining orders on the dotted line.
"I'm sick and tired of his countless apologies
because I've learned that they're just another one of his
pathological lies."
"I know he says he loves me,"
she told the Police Officer,
"But his rap sheet proves that he's the abusive kind."
 Unable to escape the fact that he was following her
She decided to return to New York
with an angel by her side.
She left the bright lights of Denver behind her
but as for her hopes and her dreams

she brought them along for the ride.
Thirteen-hundred miles she drove
in a moving truck
until she reached her mother's house
where she parked by the roadside.
Safe and sound she thought,
but the damage had already been done to her mind.
Many years later...
After she'd finally received treatment,
She decided the moment had arrived,
For her to share her courage,
about how she had survived.
She wrote her story down,
In detail;
each sentence using reason
along with rhyme.
It was if God was sending her a message,
an omen;
Yes He was giving her a sign.
A sign that things will get better,
but until then,
She'll kiss it up to God,
and leave it all behind.

My Advice
I was just sitting here
Thinking about my past,
and wishing I'd never left home.
Back than your were only a baby
and I was just a kid myself;
about seventeen or so.

No words can express how sorry I am
For missing out on so much
So I'm taking the time to let you know

That I wish I could turn back the hands of time
But I can't,
And that's just the way things sometimes go.

I'd like to share with you a thing or two about life however,
And that is,
If you let it,
It can lead you down a rocky road,
And because there are no guarantees of your success,
It's important that you cling to your dreams,
even when you're growing old.

I'd also like to give you some advice,
which is to think before you re-act,
'cause it's the consequences that will keep you from reaching
your goals,
and try not to predict the future
for tomorrow is a mystery
so take things nice and slow.

What I'm trying to say is,
Don't hurry when making decisions
'cause trust me your mistakes are all your own,
And if by chance you become confused
Just remember to ask for help,
'cause you're never really alone,

And even though I can't be there with you,
I hope you get some comfort and relief
via the words of this poem,
when I tell you how proud I am
of your accomplishments and how beautifully
you have grown.

The Changing of the Seasons
As the leaves begin to change I listen to the rain drops tap on my window pain for what might be the last time before winter's snowflakes glitter like diamonds as they fall to the ground.

Over the years it's become normal for me to sit and ponder about the things that I've missed out on;

Like the special moments I wished I could have shared; the barbeques, the holidays, the graduations, the wedding ceremonies, the birthdays, and even the deaths.

I thank God that the hands on the clock keep ticking as I seek out an inner peace that allows me to adjust in an atmosphere that is filled with so much chaos;
an environment that scrambles my brain like an egg.

At other times I snap like a tree that's weathered a storm; my limbs broken like that of an ancient Sycamore.

Let me relish the moments as they go by; adding up to the days that are like that of the Maple tree in the fall; the beauty of it's existence found in the depths of it's foliage, as its colorful leaves bleed into one making the season festive.

I have come to realize that I too change as the seasons change.

This is why I find the need to mention the New Year which I always hope will bring happiness to those who I hold dear.

Let me never forget the coming of Spring;

It's Forget Me Knots and famous Jack in the Pulpits; their greatest royalty being the first signs of spring.

Spring; bringing with it it's freshly made batches of nature's sweet syrup, and the buzzing of beehives.

Then there are the tulips that burst into bloom signifying that of a painters palette during summertime, the warmth of human bodies covered with tanning lotion; reflecting the rays of the sun.

As I think back I begin to ponder about all that the Seasons have given me; then I bow my head and pray to be given another chance to appreciate the glorious parts of mother nature; The greatest gift that God ever gave.

To Disclose or Not to Disclose:
The Story of Linda Ma

Linda Ma, Aisia J.B. Lu, and Hector W.H. Tsang

I am Linda Ma, a Chinese young woman born and raised in Wuxi, a picturesque city of the Yangtze River delta. Like most people born in the 1980s, I was an only child. During my childhood, my parents surrounded me with love and care. I was cheerful, obedient, outgoing, and loquacious. I liked playing with my peers, singing, and doing handicrafts.

Linda Ma

Unfortunately, this happy time came to a sudden end with the divorce of my parents when I was 6 years old. I went to live with my mother. She raised me all by herself. Our life was full of hardship and excruciating moments. I no longer understood the word "pleasure." Even worse was that my mother did not allow me to get close, either physically or emotionally, to my father. Because of my lack of paternal love, I always felt that other children were happier and luckier than me. A question always haunted me: why did other children have a father, but not me?

When my mother remarried I was forced to accept a stranger as my "stepfather" and to live with him for nearly 20 years, which was a dreadful experience. It felt like I had fallen into an abyss. I had terrifying encounters with him.

My stepfather was a grim, unfriendly, and violent person. Whenever he was at home, I was breathless and almost petrified, fearing that something dreadful would happen. Every word I said and every movement I made was scrutinized. He was easily ruffled and whipped up by any minute mistake. He magnified it and then belittled me. He often pointed at my head and cursed me, "You are nothing but a parasite." I loathed him.

I had no way out when he tried to beat me. I would desperately rush to my room and lock myself in, to escape from his anger. He did not usually give up easily. He once pried open my bedroom window using an iron bar to get in. I screamed and cried hysterically. I pleaded for him to leave me alone. Fortunately, my mother protected me. After this chilling incident, I was always jittery and was frequently woken up in the middle of the night by nightmares in which a monster was chasing me.

Onset of Mental Illness

When I was fifteen studying junior high school, something strange happened. "Linda! Linda!" I heard someone calling me in a daze. "Hey!" Someone kicked me twice and the pain brought me back to reality. "What are you doing?" the teacher asked me with a raised voice. All my classmates gazed curiously at me. I was so embarrassed that my heart seemed to be pounding out of my chest. Obviously, the teacher noticed that I had been daydreaming. "Answer the question!" I stood up slowly. My face turned red. I could not get out a single word. My classmates were whispering to each other, trying to guess what had happened. The teacher scolded me angrily, "Linda, you used to study hard and be attentive. What has happened to you recently? You often daydream in front of me. Your grades have dropped. You'd better try to figure out how to improve!"

My teacher was still talking, but I no longer heard the words. A strident buzzing filled my head. I felt like my brain was going to explode. What was happening to me? Why did my memory not work? Why did I not pay attention in lessons? It must be my poor sleep the night before. There shouldn't be any other reason! I needed to sleep well tonight to avoid this happening again.

The situation did not improve. The same nightmare woke me every night. When I awoke, I knew that my situation was still miserable, that I was still at the mercy of my stepfather. What could I do to save myself? Where should I go? I had no answers to these questions. The only thing I could do was to tolerate and submit to my suffering without complaint.

Living in a family devoid of love, my academic performance plummeted. My memory was deteriorating. I could not focus on classes at school. The questions raised by my teacher in class made me choke, as I was not able to give the right response. It became a vicious cycle. The more nervous I was, the harder it was to answer the question. The stress over my studies was exhausting.

With the release of the high school entrance exam, I managed to gain admission to the accounting course of a technical school. My condition improved. From the first year, I often had a giddy feeling like a tumor was growing inside my brain. This sensation of having a "foreign body" in my brain was intolerable. Eventually, my memory became so poor that I failed to attend classes or take exams. Finally, I was required to defer my study for two years.

"Who am I?" was a question I often asked myself. Sometimes I felt that I was just a clown who made people laugh. I fell behind in my studies. Nobody liked me. No one talked to me. My stepfather was right: I was just a parasite in my family and society. I had no way of escaping to live away from the family home.

One day I felt as though my soul had become detached from my body. "Does this mean I am free?" I asked myself, "I don't know!" I told myself, "It's great; it is a wonderful moment. I finally have power! I can do what I want!" There was a loud voice talking to me: "Think about how insignificant and pitiful you are. You have been a parasite so long. What will people think of you?" I continued to tell myself, "No! I am not afraid of anybody, I am not the person I used to be." "I will show you that people around will be scared of me. See!" My hand was no longer under my control and began to hit my mother. "Get away, I hate you people! You are all bad! Ha ha ..." I was emboldened. "If someone bullies me, I will hit back ... I will kill you! Kill you all ..."

When I opened my eyes and wondered where I was, I saw my mother sitting at the bedside with red eyes. I began to realize that I was in a mental hospital! I had gone mad! The diagnosis my mother told me was unbelievable! Ha ha! I was a mental patient. Finally, I understood that I did not need to do anything with myself. My life had come to a dead end!

Discharge from Hospital

After my discharge from the hospital, I could no longer tolerate my stepfather. We had frequent squabbles. The worst period was yet to come. It seemed that my personality had changed and I had become another person. I was not sure if this was due to my mental illness. I became cranky and the tension ran higher and higher. My stepfather often reeled off terms like "crazy," "insane," and "nut" to insult me. My mental condition fluctuated and I had several relapses. Because my mother did not want my condition to deteriorate further, she ended her 20-year relationship with my stepfather.

After the separation, we began again in a new house and lived an impoverished life. My mother dedicated all her time to taking care of me. She tried to protect me and put me in the role of a sick person. She often said, "You're a patient. You need to take more rest. You don't need to do anything. Let me do everything for you." She never allowed me to do any housework. She served me every meal in bed, thinking that I had a serious medical illness. I was treated like an infant, fed and dressed. From the onset of my mental illness, my mother never left me alone for a second. She seldom allowed me to go out. When I did go out, she would ask where I went, who I met, and what I did. She urged me to go home whenever I had been out for a while. She was preoccupied with me, becoming more and more exhausted. I rapidly put on weight. I did nothing but sleep all day. I was reluctant to wake up and groom myself. I often saw my mother weeping in secret. I asked why she cried, but she did not respond.

Discrimination

When my condition was more stable, I went back to school to continue my studies. I looked forward to learning and socializing with my classmates as we had in the past. I sensed that their attitude towards me had changed. My deskmate was so frightened that she asked our teacher to change her seat so she could keep a distance from me. Nobody was willing to work with me for group activities. I wanted to express my feelings to classmates with whom I had been close in the past, but they found excuses to stay away. It was obvious that they didn't want to be near me. It was likely that they had heard about my mental illness. But they should have felt sympathy. Why did they opt to estrange themselves from me? I had already recovered from my mental illness. I no longer spoke nonsense. I could control my behavior. Why didn't they understand me? Why didn't they show concern for me? When I saw my overweight body in the mirror, I hated it. It made sense that my classmates and friends didn't like me, that they mocked me. Who would want to socialize with a gawky, stupid person who slept all day? In order not to be avoided, I decided to keep to myself. This situation persisted until I graduated from technical school.

Sometimes I accompanied my mother to the market to shop for groceries. There was a hawker selling vegetables who knew my mother well. She once saw me and asked, "Is this your daughter? Oh, I have not seen her for a long time! She looks chubby." I was nervous and wondered why she had said this. Did she know about my mental illness? Did she want to mock me? I'd better stay at home and not go out.

Gradually, the neighbors in my community found out about my mental illness. When we met in the lift, I felt that they looked at me with curiosity but I dared not look back. What are they looking at? Am I a monster? Are they worried that I'm a degenerate and violent? They probably used words like "mad" and "insane" to describe me! I was distraught! I no longer wanted to go out! I thought this would shield me from the stigma and discrimination of my mental illness. The door isolated me from the outside world. Staying behind the door gave me a sense of peace and security.

Every day I took the prescribed medication because my mother said it was good for my health. I had to listen to her because I lost control and beat her during the first onset of my illness. I must be mad to have hurt my mother! I had to take my medication to prevent my aberrant behaviors. I fully understood that my mother was suffering. She often cried secretly and fretted about my future. Because of me, she had left her husband of 20 years! I knew that my mother still loved my stepfather. She had to shoulder the burden of taking care of me. We had been living hand to mouth. She had to bear enormous psychological stress because I knew she cared about other people's opinion of me. I understood that she prevented me from going out so that I would not hear their negative comments and get hurt! But I could do nothing! I just lay on my bed and felt drowsy all day. What else could I do? I was unable to share my mother's burden, even the chores, not to mention work. I felt totally worthless and hopeless! I was disinterested in most normal daily activities. I was a burden to my mother, contributing to her hardship.

Concealing my Mental Illness

My mother rarely smiled after I was diagnosed with mental illness. I knew that she suffered more than I did! She always sighed, sobbed, and told me, "Don't tell other people anything about your illness. The family shame should not be revealed!" I definitely wouldn't tell anyone about my illness. It was shameful for my family! When classmates, friends, and neighbors looked at me, their gaze was like arrows piercing my heart. It was so painful that it went beyond description. I was so sad that such ordinary life experiences as work, dating, marriage, and giving birth were luxuries beyond my reach. Who would want to live with a mad person? To protect myself from others teasing and hurting me I couldn't disclose my mental illness to other people.

The Recovery Journey

Time flew. In 2010 I made a successful application to a charity service, and now had financial support allowing my admission to the Wuxi Mental Health Centre to receive psychiatric rehabilitation. This was the beginning of my long journey of rehabilitation and recovery.

It seems like everything was determined by fate. When God closes a door, He opens a window! The center was a paradise to me. There were many people who had similar problems to mine. Thanks to this common experience, I felt that I was not alone. We didn't look down at each other. The professionals in the center -- psychiatrists, nurses, occupational therapists -- did not see me through filtered glass as the public did. They were warm, always smiled, and often encouraged me, "Linda, you can do it!" "You have made great improvement!"

Living with mental illness, I felt no pleasure in life. But there were plenty of interesting social activities at the hospital. I remember clearly the singing contest that transformed me. As the contest needed to recruit participants, they asked me if I wanted to join. As I had never sung since my mental illness began, I hesitated to take part because I was afraid of failure. The occupational therapist encouraged me and helped me choose songs and practice over and over. Finally I had the courage to stand on the stage and sing with commitment. I almost forgot that I was mentally ill. I saw many pairs of supportive eyes before the stage, and heard the sound of acclaim, which was so encouraging. It came as a big surprise to win the singing contest! I received the gold prize! This was the most wonderful experience I had had since my mental illness.

I gradually built up my confidence and life pattern in the rehabilitation program. I made friends with some co-patients. I became more cheerful and willing to go outdoors. My mother and I felt that the best thing was that my mental state became increasingly stable.

I was fond of handicraft activities. The occupational therapist allocated me to work in the handicraft workshop. At the beginning, I was inattentive and impatient, but eventually I made my first product. The experience further boosted my sense of worth and confidence. I became increasingly skillful and able to produce different types of products. People praised me for my skill. My handicraft products were so popular that they easily sold out in the hospital tuckshop and brought me some income. I was excited because it was the very first time I had been able to earn money by my own efforts. Although the amount was minimal, it was a tremendous achievement for me. I realized that I was capable of earning money and I could make a contribution to the rehabilitation department. Because of my talent, I even thought about running my own business, opening up a handicraft stall. Then a very important question emerged in my mind. Was I able to get a competitive job? Was I able to earn money to survive on my own?

Supported Employment

In June 2013, knowing that I wanted to try for competitive employment, the occupational therapist referred me to the Integrated Supported Employment (ISE) program, which was an experimental joint project between the Wuxi Mental Health Centre and The Hong Kong Polytechnic University aiming to help those with severe mental illness to get open employment. I was assigned a case manager for this purpose.

At first, I was not sure I would succeed in finding work as I had never had a job and I was troubled by past unpleasant experiences. I saw job advertisements clearly stating that people with mental problems or physical disabilities need not apply. I wondered whether employers were aware of my mental problems and rejected me because of it.

My case manager gave me much emotional and practical support. I told her my worries on finding a job, she listened with patience and asked if I wanted to learn interview and communication skills in preparation for my job hunt. In addition, she took initiative to help me with ways of handling psychological stress. After a period of training, I had gained a lot of confidence. Despite this, I didn't have the courage to disclose my mental illness during job applications because I believed that employers would reject me because of my psychiatric history.

One day in May 2014, I was walking in the street and was attracted by the delicate products of a handicraft shop. I was gazing at the display window when suddenly a middle-aged woman asked me if I would like to purchase anything. To my astonishment, she showed appreciation of the bracelet and necklace that I was wearing and asked where I had bought them. I was delighted and told her I had made them myself. She was so surprised by my talent. Then we started to chat. I learned later that she was the owner of the shop. After our conversation, she asked me if I was interested in working there. She gave me her contact number, asking me to call her if I wanted a job.

I was overwhelmed and immediately phoned my case manager to tell her about my special experience. She was excited too and immediately helped me to prepare for the job interview. I succeeded. I got a job in the handicraft shop. I loved the job so much. I looked forward to it.

Disclose or Not to Disclose

I had a very good impression of the shopkeeper because she appreciated my handicraft skills. She was friendly and sincere. I felt very comfortable when I talked to her.

On the first day of work, I was unfamiliar with the routine. I felt tired, nervous, and appeared slightly restless. My employer noticed. She cared about me and asked whether I was sick. I felt scared and worried that she already knew about my psychiatric history. During our conversation, she happened to mention that one of her friends suffered from depression and had a tendency to try to commit suicide. This made me more tense, and scared. Was she aware of my illness? What should I do? It had been so difficult for me to get a job and I loved this one so much. I couldn't afford to lose it. I replied in panic, saying that I felt ill, and reassured her that I would be better after a few days. She allowed me to go home to rest and resume my duties once I had recovered. She even comforted me and told me that I could tell her if I had any problems, and encouraged me with the words "where there is a road, there is hope."

To disclose or not to disclose? What a dilemma! I was distraught. I wanted very much to tell her about my illness. When I recalled how my classmates had isolated me, how my stepfather belittled me, and how my neighbors teased me, I put a halt to my urge for disclosure. In the past, I had learned to hide my illness so as not to be discriminated against. If I disclosed the truth now, I would be taking off my shield and exposing myself to the ridicule of people around me. I remember that when I was in the hospital, the occupational therapist asked me in a group therapy session to draw a picture to depict my mental illness. In the drawing, the world was colorless. None of the people around me were smiling. There was a large dark cloud shadowing my head, oppressing my spirit. Someone shouted at me, like my stepfather, speaking words that were very unpleasant; someone was resentful of me, asking why I concealed my mental illness; some people were criticizing me, watching me make a fool of myself. Their actions and words were

Figure 1. Before disclosing my mental illness

as devastating as a thunderstorm. Where could I find shelter? The only thing I could do was hide my mental illness, like a huge umbrella blocking the torrential rain and strong wind. This is the only way I could protect myself from other people … (See Figure 1).

If my employer knew that I was hiding my mental illness from her, our relationship would be sabotaged and I might be dismissed. If other colleagues knew about my mental illness, they would mock and tease me.

My employer always said, "One should be sincere and honest!" She was so sincere and nice to me, and really appreciated my talents in handicraft. She had never been mean. I shouldn't cheat her. If she knew I was lying to her, she would be very angry. She hired me, which implies that she trusted me. Why didn't I tell her the truth? Although many people would undermine me, I still believed that she would be kind to me. I wasn't much different than a "normal" person in terms of job competencies. This was shown by the fact that my boss appreciated my handcraft skills. I believed that she wanted me to be honest, not deceitful.

After reflecting on this issue for a few days, I decided to confess the truth about my psychiatric history. This wasn't a rash decision. I had prepared for the worst – that I would be fired.

Confession of My Mental Illness

"Boss, I want to tell you something!" She listened carefully, with great concern. I picked up my courage and said, "I was more seriously ill than you can imagine!" "What happened to you?" My employer was puzzled and asked, "Haven't you recovered?" I said, "Boss, what do you think about my handcraft skills?" "Very good," she replied. "It is because of your competencies in handicraft that I recruited you. You should know that from the beginning."

"I want to tell you that I learned my handwork somewhere you won't expect, I learned these skills in the occupational therapy department of a mental hospital!" I didn't have the courage to look at her after speaking this sentence. I took a deep breath and continued, "Yes. I have spent time in a mental hospital." My employer was astonished and asked, "Are you depressed? Do you want to commit suicide?" "No, it is more serious than depression. I would not kill myself. I feel tired easily, and was sometimes inattentive," I tried to be as honest as I could, hoping that I would win her trust and forgiveness. "But I have already recovered. I don't have any crazy behaviors. You know my competence in handcraft and you are satisfied with it."

I did not wait for my employer's reply. I continued to say, "I love this job, I hope you might give me the opportunity to carry on working in your shop. I will work hard to your satisfaction." I said this eloquently in a way that I didn't expect. Where did my courage come from? I had no idea. Probably my fear of losing the job. This was the only thing I could do to try to keep it. My heart was about to explode and my palms were wet with sweat. I looked at her eagerly. She replied calmly, "Linda, if you hadn't told me, I really wouldn't have known you were sick. I just thought that you did not feel well." She paused and continued, "Your handicraft is very good'. I need staff like you. You can stay here. Don't worry. Despite your illness, I believe you can handle it."

I couldn't believe what I heard. Did this mean that she accepted me and my mental illness? Was she saying that I could continue to work there? My heart was beating fast and my voice was quivering, "Thank you, boss. I will try my best!" I was so ecstatic that I couldn't hide my excitement and gave her a bow to show my gratitude for her open-mindedness and acceptance. She stroked my hair like a mother and said, "Go back to work!" As soon as she turned away, tears streamed from my eyes. Yet my heart was joyful. I was so fortunate to have met such a kind employer. All of the above showed that I had made the right decision to disclose my mental condition.

Positive Consequences to my Life

Sweeping away the doubt, I unwaveringly devoted myself to my work. This was the first time that someone had accepted my psychiatric illness and offered me a chance to prove myself. I had to be careful. I went to work every day punctually, and took the initiative to communicate with her whenever necessary. I carefully completed all the tasks she assigned me. When there were new products, I learned attentively and effectively.

My employer was more generous than I could imagine. She sincerely cared about me and always supported me. When I felt tired on duty, she gave me a chair and allowed me to sit. During lunch time, she always encouraged me to eat more. She showed concern if my condition deteriorated. She allowed me to take a nap before resuming my duties after lunch. Sometimes, she noticed my lethargy and asked me to go home early to rest. She was never concerned about my sick leave. If I needed a day off, she would readily approve it. More importantly, she didn't tell others about my mental illness. She often encouraged me to discuss anything with her. She often gave me gentle reminders that I shouldn't work too much, and to take breaks if necessary. She gave full recognition to my work performance and ability. Every day I felt very warm and satisfied when I left the shop after work.

Work had gradually become a necessity for me. When I got up in the morning, I looked forward to going to the handicraft shop. Working was now as essential as sunshine and air!

Work had also produced other subtle changes in my life. My mother smiled more. Every day she watched me leave our home happy. She would ask about my job when I got home in the evening. She cooked delicious food for me as a reward for my diligence. After dinner, we would go out for leisurely walks. Our relationship was close and mutually satisfying.

My neighbors learned that I had a job and were surprised. They had never thought that I might be talented in handcraft. They liked my products very much when I gave them as small gifts. With the help of a neighborhood organization, I began to teach people simple handicraft work in the community hall. Although the honorarium was minimal, I enjoyed this kind of community service because it further recognized my competencies. Neighbors realized that my mental condition was more and more stable. Their fear of me gradually tapered off and they started to greet me in the morning.

I told my case manager about all these positive changes. She listened to my words carefully liked my friend. She asked me if I wanted to draw another picture showing how I felt after telling my employer about my mental illness so that I may compare and contrast it with the previous one I drew in the hospital. Instead of a patient, the case manager treated me as her peer and did not give me any instructions this time. Vivid images appeared in my mind when I thought about this wonderful experience and I drew this second picture spontaneously. After I had completed it, I compared it to the first, which was entirely different. In the second drawing, I used many colors. It showed a blue sky and a huge ocean, with a gentle breeze, white cloud, sunshine, and nice weather. In such a peaceful world, I put away my burden and protective shield. I walked away from the shadow and basked in the sunshine to refresh my mind. I had never been so relaxed, like a seagull flying freely in the sky.

I started to realize that life was amazing and colorful! In the picture, I hugged my employer, smiling, which was the feeling I wanted to express to her. I was extremely grateful for her courage and willingness to reach out to me. She was not fearful of my mental illness, she offered me a job, and provided responsive assistance so that I could settle well in the post. My previous worries had vanished. All of this went beyond my expectations. I had absolutely no regrets about telling my employer about my mental illness. Her acceptance made me feel that my decision to disclose in the workplace was the correct one. After telling the truth, my psychological burden was much reduced. I performed better at work. My confidence grew. People no longer showed contempt for me as they had before. Instead, they became friendly and kind to me. At the same time, I could see a ray of hope in my future (See Figure 2).

Message to Readers

That is the end of my story. It is the story of how a cocoon opened to release a beautiful butterfly. The reason why I have shared my personal experience is to let more people have a closer look at life with mental illness.

Figure 2. After confessing my mental illness

It is unfortunate that mental illness is much misunderstood by the public, and that those who suffer it are seen as outlandish and strange. People with mental illness are waging a constant war against stigma. When our mental condition becomes stable, we are in fact no different from the general public. We think rationally and our mood is stable. We long to be treated with care and fairness. Our desire for employment is strong because we need to survive, show others our value, and make a contribution to society. Instead of being sequestered, we look forward to being accepted by the community. Do not think that people with mental illness are monsters based only on our aberrant behaviors during one or two isolated episodes of relapse. We need fair competition for employment in the labor market. This would allow us to live independently and not be a burden on family and society.

Finally, I want to share a few words about disclosure of mental illness with those who are still contemplating this issue. In disclosing their mental illness, I hope and believe that many will have experiences similar to mine, with open and accepting employers and colleagues. Nevertheless, even when others don't accept our condition, we must face the negative consequences in a positive way. We shouldn't give up on ourselves. Instead, we must continue to work hard and live a normal life. One day, you will create your own miracle.

I asked my care manager, Aisia Lu, to comment on my story.

Reflections

This is a beautiful and encouraging story. As Linda Ma's care manager for the past three years, I accompanied her along the path of recovery. I helped her gain employment, and witnessed her dramatic change from an introverted person with a sense of inferiority to a confident person with a stable job and harmonious relationships with her supervisor and mother. It was a process of transformation and self-actualization. Throughout the process, I treated her as my peer. What I did was to facilitate her decision making especially whether she would disclose her mental illness to her employer.

Many people unconsciously treat people with mental illness as targets for ostracism. They will use adjectives like "horrible," "dangerous," "lazy," "filthy," "stupid," and "useless" to describe these people (Corrigan, Roe, & Tsang, 2011). This is the origin of stigma and discrimination towards mental illness.

What can we learn from this story? Linda is a typical case. Her experience allows us a glimpse of the life of a person with mental illness. Throughout my interaction with Linda, I never saw her as dangerous or violent. Quite the opposite. She is a pure-hearted and kind young woman. In the face of her stepfather's oppression, she opted to accept and tolerate it. There were multiple factors that resulted in the onset of her psychiatric illness. She was filled with regret and distress over her history of uncontrollable violence during the episode in which her mental illness emerged. The people around her may have labeled her "violent" based only on a particular incident when her behavior was spinning, temporarily, out of control. However, she never expressed her suppressed feelings in an aggressive way. Instead, she turned all of the negative feelings into self-protection. She neither felt hatred for society nor exhibited any antisocial behaviors. She longed for others' understanding and acceptance. Studies (Rueve & Welton, 2008) demonstrate that only a very small number of people with mental illness display temporary violent behaviors. Unfortunately, many people generalize these isolated incidents to all psychiatric patients, viewing them as a uniform group.

Linda and her mother suffered a lot, mostly as a result of social stigma. The beliefs causing this stigma are contradicted by the evidence we see in the literature of psychiatric rehabilitation. Research (Liberman, 2008) and our Integrated Supported Employment study (Tsang, Chan, Wong, & Liberman, 2009) reported that as many as 70% of those with severe mental illness can recover and find gainful employment. If Linda's mother had given up on her and not sent her for rehabilitation in the psychiatric hospital, Linda would still be struggling. Fortunately, her mother sent her to receive rehabilitation care. As a result, Linda recovered from her mental illness and resumed a normal life. We, and especially families, should not give up on sufferers. Our acceptance and care is critical to their recovery. So how can we describe them as useless?

I wonder if Linda's handicraft skills change your impression of people with mental illness. If you are an employer who knows a candidate in a job interview has a psychiatric history, please recall Linda's story and give that candidate a chance to realize his/her potential.

Similarly, if you learn that one of your colleagues was once a person with mental illness, please avoid treating him/her as an "alien," but give him/her support so that he/she may stay in the job.

Finally, if you know an ex-patient in your neighborhood, please do not be scared or distance yourself from him/her. Instead, greet him/her when you see him/her. This will make a real difference. Let us adopt an encouraging, friendly, and open-minded attitude to this group of people with a view to realizing the aim of social inclusion.

References

Corrigan P. W., Roe, D., & Tsang, H. W. H. (2011). *Challenging the stigma of mental illness: Lessons for therapists and advocates.* Chichester, UK: John Wiley & Sons Ltd.

Liberman, R. P. (2008). *Recovery and disability: Manual of psychiatric rehabilitation.* Washington, DC: APA, Inc.

Rueve, M. E., & Welton, R. S. (2008). Violence and mental illness. *Psychiatry, 5*(5), 34–48.

Tsang, H. W. H., Chan, A., Wong, A., & Liberman, R. P. (2009). Vocational outcomes of an integrative supported employment program for people with severe mental illness. *Journal of Behavioral Therapy and Experimental Psychiatry, 40*, 292–305.

The Cost of Hiding an Eating Disorder, Pretending You Are Okay
June Alexander

Many people who have an eating disorder are terrified of others close to them knowing about it. I refer to people who are able to attend school, attend college, go to work, be a parent. People who have an eating disorder and pretend, to their outside world at least, that they are okay. The cost is high. Both personally and for our community.

For decades I kept my eating disorder a secret too – I worked in a newspaper office, I had friends, who knew nothing about my illness. I felt ashamed of my illness. I felt that I must be weak-minded, not to be able to cope like others – to be like 'normal people'. I envied anyone who could eat lunch and not feel guilty about it! I will never forget the awfulness of wanting to be like others, to belong, to be carefree. Instead of being caught in a vicious cycle with the eating disorder, not knowing which way is out.

To Disclose or Not to Disclose

Welcome discussion is taking place regarding the decision to disclose or not to disclose one's eating disorder history in the work place - including among health professionals who have had, or continue to have, an eating disorder. Reminds me of the gay movement. Which is worse – hiding in the closet in fear and pretending you are someone you are not, or risking being true and open to all? For me, the bottom line is that while we hide in the closet, the eating disorder has the upper hand. This illness thrives on secrecy and darkness. We need to bring it out into the light, and keep it in the light. For me, the benefits far outweigh any negatives.

This discussion reminds me also, of my youngest son, who developed Juvenile Diabetes age 11, same age I developed Anorexia. He is almost 40 now, injects insulin four times daily, and has a successful career. In his professional life, he has always not disclosed his illness because he did not want to be considered 'different' or 'a victim'; he wanted to be considered 'normal' and to be judged on his merits and skills. That is, he did not want to be defined by his illness in any way.

In regard to 'going public' with my eating disorder, I waited many years, until I was 55 and feeling fully recovered and strong within my sense of Self, before sharing my story. Throughout my journalism career of more than three decades I did not disclose my illness to employers, because I, like my son, wanted to be considered 'normal', even if it meant I was functioning on about five per cent of my brain at times. In addition, I feared discrimination and rejection for disclosing a mental illness. One hopes that would not happen but I had good reason for considering that judgement or 'being different' was a strong likelihood. I feared I would lose my job, and would have no hope of advancement in my career.

The Eating Disorder Loves Secrecy

The difference here is that illnesses like diabetes are considered 'acceptable', whereas an 'eating disorder' continues to face suggestive put-downs/ignorance/misunderstandings/weakness/you-cannot-be-relied-upon/cannot be trusted etc. The cost of trying to hide the illness, keep it hidden, is that the illness is not dealt with fully, it has permanent residence in the brain as tormentor supreme.

To remove the stigma that causes many people to suffer silently, I believe we need more people who have recovered from their eating disorder to stand up and show this illness and the community at large that we are perfectly able to recover and live full and rewarding lives. As with other serious illnesses, we may lapse now and then. This is part of life. People with an eating disorder have done nothing wrong! Their experience makes them more reliable, dependable, resilient, empathetic than most. The thing is, to be recognized first and foremost for who you are — as a professional employee, as a student, as a parent, as a partner, as a child, as a sibling, as a friend; that you have had or have the illness, is secondary.

'And By the Way, I Have Had an Eating Disorder'
To confront the stigma/rejection/misconceptions in our communities, including our health care systems, which are a vital part of our society, I believe we do need professionals to stand up, as some already do, and say 'I have all these qualifications and have worked hard on my career, and by the way, I have had an eating disorder'. There are ethical concerns of course, and responsibility and self-care is vital – one needs to be able to say 'I need time out to care for myself right now' when lapse symptoms appear. This occurs with other illnesses; it needs to be okay for people with eating disorders, too. To know that you can have an eating disorder and have a full and rewarding career, be a wonderful parent, be whoever you want to be, is a message we need to get out. Recovery from an eating disorder requires a lot of courage from Self; and for best results, to maintain recovery, it requires openness and acceptance in a village of people who understand and who care.
We hear a lot of stories about people who are suffering the illness, Anorexia in particular (because it is the most graphic for media). To counter this we need a lot more stories from people who have recovered and who, as a result of their personal struggle, are celebrating life deeply, meaningfully, and are able to offer empathy and support in a

way that those without experience of the illness may never know. I am trying to say that we need to 'normalize' eating disorders – they are part of life, and need to be acknowledged openly and in the light. This is the best way of reducing their impact, of reducing the stigma, the fear, the loneliness and the isolation.

- See more at: http://www.junealexander.com/2014/05/the-cost-of-hiding-an-eating-disorder-pretending-you-are-okay/#sthash.ppyMhbVC.dpuf

Sunshine and Obsidian:
Two Worlds, One Life

Lorre Leon Mendelson, Tami Mugler, Harli Kirkpatrick and
Destini Kirkpatrick

Lorre

She walked into my life
and heart in the same moment.
She was so incredibly tiny, with
the smallest buds for ears and
eyes that were not quite ready to
open. I waited quietly, in
anticipation, sitting on the edge
of the whelping box Teri built in
her family room. The room was
home to a beautiful white
cockatoo monitoring the
mewing house kittens from its
cage. Mercedes, beautiful
golden doggie-mom, watched,
then, determining I was safe,

Loree Leon Mendelson

nosed my hand for ear scratches between cleaning and
nursing her pups. There were so many! I opened my heart and
waited to see what would happen.

The puppies practiced using their legs, tripping the
light fantastic around the large wooden box, smelling their
way, falling over each other, touching, licking, listening: it
left me breathless as only new birth can. It was the most
beautiful ballet I had ever seen.

She walked toward me: dark blonde, brownish-red
hair, still getting used to her "land legs", a single curl over the
bridge of her nose. She crossed the box to where I sat and
gently lifted her. We became known to each other. I inhaled

her sweet puppy breath while she leaned against me, learning my heartbeat, my scent, my touch.

Puppy supper may have appeared awkward to others, but was an un-choreographed dance to me, testing the ground, learning her strength as she found Mercedes' nipple to suck hungrily along with her 8 siblings. Each ate enthusiastically until they had their fill or were nudged away by another hungry pup.

Soon they fell asleep in pods reminiscent of Elephant Seals at Año Nuevo State Park, CA where seals gathered and lay in pods on shore.

The only possible name for her was Sunshine, a reflection of her disposition and charm. We grew and learned together. I taught her English, she taught me dog, we traveled together for work, she taught me doggie soccer rules, we went to parks when she was off duty and became completely devoted to each other. She has provided on-going assistance to me when I experience anxiety.

As an incest survivor with PTSD, I trained her to touch my hand if I started to disassociate. If I did not respond, to then jump on me. Later I was delighted to see the same task performed by a working dog on his handler, a soldier also with PTSD. She assists me with panic and has literally sat on my feet, grounding me until I become calmer. Sunshine trained to attend meetings laying for hours by my side, bumping my leg with her head every now and again to remind me she was there. The only time she stood was to go outside for a break.

With a disability others cannot see, I did not know what the community response would be to Sunshine accompanying me. The first few years we were together, when asked, I let people know she was a psychiatric service dog. There were many cautious replies of "um *hum"* *a*nd "I *see"* but as time has gone on, I have found more often when I tell people how she helps me with depression and anxiety, they respond with, "how wonderful" and "how do I get one?" Why did I tell people my disability when I didn't have to? To help end the stigma surrounding those of us who identify as having mental health needs. It is one part of me and does not define me. It is not a crime nor shameful to have a disability. And since many people with psychiatric and other disabilities do not know their rights to own service dogs, I want to let them know it is one tool they can utilize in their wellness box.

I attempt to handle complaints as an educational opportunity. Concerns from businesses, hospitals, fire and police departments have resulted in staff trainings and employee manuals changing to reflect how to work with people with service dogs. In 9 years we have never been asked to leave anywhere because of her behavior.

For every instance where I have been yelled at, escorted out of buildings, challenged to "prove" she is a service animal, and treated with disrespect, I have a dozen more instances of restaurant owners, business managers, store keepers, sales associates, and librarians who greet me asking appropriately. My favorite was going into a barbecue restaurant and before I could tell the owner she was a working dog, he looked at me and said, "get that dog *in* here"!

Many people have asked what she does for me and, in many cases, how can they get a service animal. I have devoted part of my life offering to assist people and businesses how to obtain service dogs, their rights and responsibilities and helping troubleshoot situations such as housing discrimination. I am honored to have psychiatrists, social workers, colleagues and therapists refer clients to me to assist them in getting service dogs. This has culminated in an invitation to sit on a panel for the TN Disability Law and Advocacy Center /Disability Coalition collaboration on service dogs, helping provide information and education to the community.

Teri, Sunshine's breeder, was amazed to learn how much Sunshine does for me and, in a wonderfully generous act, offered to donate a puppy as a prospective service dog to a person with a disability. But, there was more. She wanted me to be the one to select the recipient of the puppy. I was thrilled, and yet what a responsibility! I looked for just the right forever home for this new service-puppy-to-be however, I was reminded that when you are least expecting it, great things happen!

I worked for a non-profit organization that held a conference in middle TN where we live. I was delighted to learn The Mugler family would be coming from Iowa to attend and was thrilled to meet them from all the great stories I had heard about them.

Tami and her two lovely daughters, Harli and her younger sister, Destini came. Harli has Angelman Syndrome. Once I asked what her definition of it was and she described it this way, "brain not broken, just a few curves in the road".

We all really connected at the conference and they loved Sunshine. Tami told me how wonderful a service dog would be for Harli when I mentioned the available puppy. We knew what needed to happen and THAT story belongs to Tami, Destini and Harli!

Tami

There we were walking along the carpeted walk-way heading for our first information session at the annual Microboards Conference in Nashville, TN, when we happened upon her. Sitting there silently but so obviously alert, her head resting on her paw as her eyes darted about keeping a vigilant watch over her charge.

A woman greeting people, handing out programs and giving directions was standing very close by; close enough in fact that every few seconds she would reach down and gently touch the mound of blonde curls at her feet. With her long skirt, loose flowing blouse and long wavy hair she resembled a flower-child
perhaps lost in a time warp. She projected warmth and love with every word, every gesture.

My daughters, Harli and Destini, were immediately distracted by the beautiful golden girl that lay at the woman's feet. Admiring the dog I spoke to my kids as the woman handed me our name badges, "Wow girls, isn't she beautiful?" A bubbly voice responded "Why thank you, but isn't my dog pretty too?" We all laughed at her humor and agreed the dog was indeed pretty, too. I then asked what her companion's name was and her breed. "Oh this is Sunshine. She is a Golden Doodle and she is my service dog". I had never heard of a Golden Doodle, but definitely agreed that Sunshine was the perfect name for this beauty.

We visited a bit about service animals, educating my girls on the various tasks they could perform. My daughter Destini had wanted a dog for many years, but with Harli's disabilities we just couldn't get any lost soul looking for a home. I grew up with many animals and very much wanted my children to experience the unconditional love of a dog, but it just wasn't in the stars, well, not yet anyway.

The woman introduced herself as Lorre and we continued our conversation about her dog, disabilities and life in general over the next few days. Harli continued to get very excited each time she saw Sunshine. Destini, who is painfully shy the majority of the time, finally mustered up the courage to ask if she could pet Lorre's companion during a break from workshops. Destini knew that working dogs shouldn't be pet or played with but she was going crazy to touch that dog's long curls. Lorre thanked Destini for asking first and since we were on break she let Destini reach out to Sunshine who glanced up at her charge for permission. Lorre assured Sunshine it was okay and she and Destini became fast friends.

Being more comfortable now Destini asked what kind of things Sunshine did for her. Lorre was fabulous and explained that she is an individual with an 'invisible' disability and that she has extreme anxiety in crowded places, large groups and sometimes, going to the grocery store can make her heart race. She continued in great detail that Sunshine was very sensitive to her moods and her needs; that when she begins to feel the fear rising, Sunshine moves very close to Lorre, gently nudging her hand to remind Lorre to stay in the present.

Destini asked, "Does it help to pet her when you get stressed?" who had noticed Lorre touching Sunshine's head repeatedly while working. "Yes it does. It helps me a lot in remaining calm. Now I can enjoy many things in life I was missing out
on. I can go out and about much more now. Sunshine has opened the door for me; I no longer stay home due to fear." "I wish I could have a dog. Mom, you should get a dog for sissy and then we could share it."

I responded with a smile "Oh that would be perfect wouldn't it, but service dogs are very expensive." Thus began the conversation that would change all of our lives forever. Lorre talked about Sunshine's breeder, Teri Rowland, who was so impressed with the difference Sunshine was making in Lorre's life, that Teri wanted to donate a pup to someone in need to be used as their service dog. Lorre told us excitedly that Teri had given her the honor of selecting the recipient. Lorre had been watching Harli and Destini all weekend and fell in love with the joyous smile that emitted from Harli every time she saw Sunshine walk by. Her heart tugged knowing how desperately Destini wanted a dog, and mostly she knew the importance of getting the 'right' dog for Harli.

Lorre took me aside and asked if I would be interested in a service puppy as she very much wanted to give this gift to Harli. We emailed the breeder together and explained our unique situation, Harli's disability and her sister's desire to 'help' with the pup. The very next day we were on our way to Teri's and her gorgeous puppies. From our conversation Teri felt that Destini should choose the pup.

Tami, Harli, and Destini in Boston

Upon our arrival it was immediately clear to Teri just how painfully shy Destini is and it became even more important that she be part of the process.

Well it wasn't easy or quick, but Teri never rushed her: she let Destini play with the pups as long as she wanted and talked with us about vet care, potty training, grooming: mostly about how much love would be required. Destini grinned ear to ear at those words, she knew she could do that!

After a thoughtful 2 hours Destini wanted to show 2 of the pups to her sister who was waiting outside with our family friend. Harli was excited to see the puppies and blew kisses at them over and over. Destini knew which was the right pup for Harli and we took him home with us.

On our long drive back to Iowa, the little pup cried relentlessly for his mommy and siblings. Harli surprised us all when she reached out to him offering her 'blankie' as comfort. The pup climbed up on the seat and curled up tightly next to Harli and never made another sound, that is, unless we took him away from Harli!

Their connection was so immediate and amazing! Those two bonded like long lost loves, confirming Destini had indeed made the right choice. A few days later Destini chose a name for our pup, Obsidian. She explained that in folk lore the Obsidian stone is also known as the 'Apache tear' believed to protect us from negativity and harm. Obi, as we now call him, has woven himself into the very fabric of our lives and we cannot imagine a day without him.

He not only warns us of oncoming seizures and changes in Harli's blood sugar, he picks up items that she drops from time to time. But most importantly, Obi has brought us all closer on our journey. After a long day at a crowded holiday festival in a nearby town Destini proclaimed "You know, mom, I think Obi helps me too. People notice me when I am with him and when they ask me questions about him, it makes me talk to more people." Indeed it does! So while Sunshine and Obi live in very different worlds they are living very similar lives and bringing independence to those who need it most.

The Beginning

Epilogue
February 2014, Tami Mugler

Obi has changed all of our lives in so many ways! Destini does have such great issues with her shyness and as she has gotten older now often can suffer from extreme anxiety in large groups or public situations. She really wished she had Obi at college with her! Ha!

She still takes him out roller blading with her or bike riding in the summer months. Some days when we are at a mall she will insist we should have left him home as he will draw so much attention, (which of course she hates) but the day always ends with her snuggled up in the back seat with him telling him how popular and amazing he is.

She spends time in her room and when she lets him in, he knows how lucky he is and snuggles up with her on her bed, or lets her paint his toe nails; he doesn't mind a bit.

While he is amazing at detecting Harli's seizures before they happen, he is just as equally amazing at knowing when Destini needs some extra attention too. When her anxiety is high he is right there at her feet, putting his paw in her lap an offering comfort.

Harli has learned to actually throw a ball, something we spent many years trying to teach her, she learned within a year after getting Obi....she LOVES to throw his ball for him, although it doesn't get far, he will still fetch it and bring it back to her.

She takes great pride in feeding him every single day and has learned to dump out a bowl by doing this. a very hard fine motor skill by the way!

Every day, every year, he teaches us all something. Not a moment goes by that Obsidian doesn't have a great impact on each of us. Every single day we are grateful for having Lorre and Teri in our lives....

Epilogue
July 2014, Lorre Leon Mendelson

Sunshine is now 9, and I am still in awe of her each day. She is a big Doodle package of love, playfulness and immense assistance. Terri, too, has maintained her commitment to helping people with disabilities, frequently donating puppies as service dogs to people in need. She even has a service dog site. I hope you will each come visit us: http://www.goldens-n-doodles.com/ServiceDogs.html.

Journey to New Hope
Angela Willis

My Bible and flashlight are no longer hidden under a dresser. My faith is no longer tucked away in the dark of the midnight hours. My voice is no longer silent and I have made a choice; because I have a purpose and God has a plan.

Angela Willis

I don't recall much of my life as a younger child except my childhood years were filled with abuse. In my conscious mind I can remember instances as far back as when I was 5 years old; however, when I was in my 20's and suffering from chronic flashbacks, I recall some occasions that people told me of where I had acted out prior to the age of 5 years. Most of the years between age 5 and 10 remain empty for me. There seems to be no way of finding even the good times in there. What few things I do recall were abusive with only a handful of good memories. My reasoning tells me to stop looking for those things I cannot remember; however, I keep searching for that part of me that feels so empty regardless of good or bad.

I have had to learn to cope with, accept and above all forgive through the years of my recovery. Too often I just wanted to end my life, not because I wanted to die before God calls me home; but because I wanted and needed the pain to end and the sun to shine in my life so I could see brighter days ahead.

I grew up listening to the jokes at family reunions and many of the family gatherings about not being my dad's daughter and that had weighed heavily on my mind over the years. Was I his daughter? Was another man my dad? I couldn't ask my mother because she had left me when I was 18 months old. So who did I belong to? Who am I?

I wondered time and again if my not being my dad's child is why he was so much different with me than my sister. Is it why he beat me more, molested and raped me, is it why he always did less for me? Was this the reason he never could seem to be proud of me the way he was with her? With every question I came up with my own answer. Right or wrong, I found an answer. I needed to try harder, I needed to talk more like they did, I needed to like more of what they liked, I needed to dress like they dressed and fix my hair the way they did. But no matter how hard I tried I still couldn't win his approval.

Dr. John Charlton III (my Pastor) began showing me I had a voice in 1991. A voice I had been stripped of as a child. It wasn't until 2004, when I was diagnosed with Bipolar Disorder, Post-Traumatic Stress Disorder, and Borderline Personality Disorder that my recovery took a major turn and began setting me free. About 2 years later, in 2006, when I entered into group therapy I began learning how to use my voice, and later I found that I not only have a voice but I also have a choice. God has blessed me with the ability of being able to make choices in my life. Including the choice to recover, forgive, and above all to serve Him with the voice He has given me. Today, I use my voice to show others how God will carry them through their recovery, how He has helped me to forgive the past, and how my Lord uses my illnesses to bring hope into a hopeless world.

The Early Years

My dad and mom were married two months and two days after I was born. In the 1960's, this was a shame factor; young women pregnant out of wedlock were looked down upon and their families were shamed by the young girl's actions. My parents were then divorced by the time I was around 18 months old. My mom had left us behind at a friend's home to run. I don't much know why; however, I believe she was trying to escape her own pain and shame. My dad had to go to court just to get me and my younger sister back from the couple she had left us with. Just before my dad's passing away in 1988, when I was 24 years old, he told me this story.

My dad shared with me that he had gone to work that day. When he came home he found her belongings gone and began calling friends to find out where we were. When he found us the couple she had left us with refused to let him take us home. So he filed the court papers to get us back. When the day arrived my dad said he just walked into the courtroom and told the Judge these are my girls and I am taking them home. He picked me up in one arm and my sister up in another and walked out with us.

I don't know when my step mom and dad were married. I do know it was by the time I was 5 years old. One of the first memories I have as a child, was being beaten with a belt for wetting my pants on my bare bottom. The bathroom was a room in the house I really didn't want to be in. I remember being afraid much of the time. There were times in Kindergarten that I had been sent to school with diapers on to humiliate me for wetting my pants. They were not the disposables like parents use today; they were the cloth diapers that had to be pinned with ducky safety pins. I couldn't do those when I went to the bathroom so I always had to ask a teacher to put them back on me. I have never heard anyone say that through these years I was taken to a doctor for the problem; I was just beaten with a belt buckle for it.

When I was 5 years old, I had spent a weekend with my Grandma and Uncle in the country. They always went to church and took me with them when I stayed. One Sunday morning during Sunday school we sat in a little room not any bigger than an oversized broom closet; it was painted yellow, a small child's table and small chairs for children were around it. There was a flannel board that had a shelf hanging on the wall behind it. Judy Kern was our teacher and she sat at the end of the table. Her knees came just above the table as she sat in one of our chairs. She had a real pretty skirt on that came down to her knees and she put these pictures up on the flannel board as she told us a story about Jesus. She had already put up two or three pictures on this flannel board when she placed one up that had a picture of Jesus with all these children around him. She said that He was telling them a story. At that moment I felt like He was real and Jesus was no longer a story book character to me; but that He would be able to help me even though I never understood how. At this moment I was given hope that would carry me through my life and my recovery.

In my later years when I suffered through flashbacks other forms of abuse came out that took place during that time of my life. Although, much of it I do not remember with my conscious mind; there are some fragments like still pictures that I do remember. Today I deal with these by just looking at the pictures as if they are just a pictures and not memories.

Between the ages of 5 and 10, I have very few memories. I know I went to church when I was allowed to and liked being there even in my fear of those around me in the church. I was living in fear all the time by then and my fear became a way of life. This was not something I would ever get rid of or would be able to ignore. I had to believe in something that I couldn't see to survive. Even though in those days I didn't understand much of the scriptures I read; I look back and think, Hebrews 11:1, "Now faith is being sure of what we hope for and certain of what we do not see."

When I was nine, one night my dad was late at an Amway Meeting. My mom had started cooking earlier in the evening and when she was upset that is what she did. She cooked everything from breads, cookies, cakes, pies, and potato salad. Our kitchen was filled with these things when she was upset. My sister and I were in bed that night when our dad came home from the meeting. She and I snuck out of bed and down the hall when we heard the yelling start. We peeked around the corner, scared of what we would see. Mom was peeling the potatoes by then and had this knife in her hand. Mom turned around and pointed the knife at him because he was very late and had been with this other woman. We didn't know who she was but it hurt mom really bad. As they began to move towards the living room my sister and I ran back into our bedroom out of the way. Mom went into their bedroom and we peeked around the corner again as they continued to yell at each other. Mom was packing a suitcase because she was leaving our dad. After she walked out the door my sister and I stood in the living room crying. Our dad told us when she comes back to get her belongings; if we ran to her, he would send us to our Grandma's to live and give all of our things away. The next night mom came back and we ran to her trying to get her to stay and dad made good on what he said; partially any way. After mom left that night, dad packed us each a bag and took us to our Grandma's to live for a while. He gave most of our toys and that to the kids of the woman whom came between mom and dad. By the time we went to live with our dad again our home was gone and he had gotten us a new place to live. The woman who would then become our "sitter" was around most of the time. It was during this year of change that I became my father's wife and my sister's mother. I don't speak of this horrific change lightly. I was put into these roles and in every sense of the terms. I laid with my dad when he said to, I cooked, cleaned house, did laundry, took care of my sister by making sure she had her bath at night, homework done, cooked her meals while dad was at work, and played with her.

During this time period, my sister also became abusive towards me. One day we were playing with our dolls at the top of the stairs where our bedroom was. She became so angry with me that she had pushed me down the red carpeted stairs into the wall at the bottom of them. Within a couple of weeks my dad was taking me to the hospital as I was having some problems and it was then I was diagnosed with a seizure disorder from being pushed down the stairs. They said when my head hit the wall at the bottom of the stairs; it had caused some brain damage which in turn was causing the seizures. In those days the doctors didn't have surgeries to repair this type of brain damage and today it is not possible for any surgery to correct it due to the time that has passed by.

The "sitter" had also become abusive. She had two tables with plants on them in our basement under black lights. One night while dad was at work she came over to tend to the plants while I was doing laundry. That night she molested me in the basement of our home. I was continuing to be stripped of my voice, my personal power, and I was losing my self-esteem quickly.

I began having my menstrual cycles early on and found how much shame they were too my dad. I was pushed from one person to another to try and learn the things I needed and I found my just being me was a shame to everyone I came in contact with. That even this natural part of life was such a travesty in our family that I was shunned. If it weren't for my teacher at school teaching me and helping me, I am not sure how I would have learned how to take care of that part of me. It was another shame based issue I would need to deal with in my recovery as an adult.

It wasn't long before we had to move to another house. While we were there it seemed things had just gotten worse. I was not allowed to participate in school activities and my role of wife and mom had escalated. The sitter had put a ceramic shop in our home. The dining room was filled with her stuff and the walls of the basement had shelf after shelf of green ware that she was supposed to be selling and her kiln. My seizures were bad during this time. I was kicked out of school because of them. I was assigned a homebound teacher to help educate me and I tried even harder to help make the bills and get food for our house since I was not in school.

On my 12th Birthday, my dad worked late that night again. This was not an unusual thing for him as my sister and I were usually home alone unless the sitter was checking in on us or working on her ceramics, as she had a ceramic shop in our home. She was supposed to be responsible for keeping my dad happy, paying the bills, making sure we had our meds, and the grocery shopping. She had a family of five and her own home to tend to. This night was different and I wasn't feeling well. I had cooked up hot dogs and with macaroni and cheese for supper. However, my stomach was turning in all kinds of circles and I didn't think I could even look at the food not to even think about eating it. Yet, the sitter told me if I didn't eat it I wasn't getting any cake for my Birthday. I didn't care I wasn't feeling well. When I wouldn't eat she came over to me and held my head back, closed my nose off, and shoved the hot dog down my throat until I threw up. At that moment I was too sick to have any cake or gifts for my Birthday. However, my dad still gave me this really pretty turquoise and coral with silver ring for my Birthday. It was a horse head and I thought it was the most special thing in the world to me. It wasn't long after my dad gave me that ring that the sitter's daughter stole my ring and if I had not kept my silence about it, I feared what would have happened to me.

It was already hard enough to sit back and watch the sitter pocket the money our dad gave her for the bills, food, and medicine we needed. I had been stealing money from places the "sitter" took me to try help make the payments for our bills and food. When I had enough to send in a bill I just put the cash in the envelope and sent it in and dad never knew the difference of who paid the bills. I felt so much shame over this for most of my life until I understood that as a 12 year old, it was all I knew how to do and that I felt that I was doing the right thing (especially in the wife role). Through my recovery, I have had to learn how to let go of the shame that comes with stealing from so many people that year. I still did not understand what forgiveness was.

My teacher's name was Mr. Hayes. One day he came by and we were going over my homework papers. He was checking my math paper and I had almost every answer wrong. I was frustrated by my grade, yet, he was patient in trying to help me understand what I was doing wrong. However, as we sat in the living room going through this process of learning, the "sitter" came in the front door. My dad had been sitting in the kitchen drinking all morning and was getting drunk. She had brought a gift over to him. When she left a few minutes later, my dad came into the living room with this 18 inch hunting knife she had given him. He stood on the other side of the table and Mr. Hayes and I had stood up. I was terrified and grabbed Mr. Hayes hand and pulled him out the back door and told him to leave and not come back. I was sure that my dad was going to kill me that day. I ran and hid behind a neighbor's garage until I was sure my dad had passed out. I then went back in the house and took the knife and hid it so he would not find it. When he later asked where it was I lied to him and told him I didn't know what he had done with it. He thought he had put it somewhere before he passed out.

It wasn't long after this event that I ended up in the hospital for two weeks. During the time I was in there my dad never came up to see me. I saw and heard some horrific things while I was there. When I was released it was the "sitter" who came to take me home. On the way, she told me my dad was not feeling well and he was sleeping. I was not to bother him and to put my things up. When I finished putting up my belongings; I was told to get the house cleaned, supper for my sister, and to do the laundry. When we arrived at the house, I saw my dad sleeping on the couch, my sister was watching television, and the house had not been cleaned since I last cleaned it. The "sitter" left and went to her own family. I immediately checked on my dad. He was a severe diabetic and had been since he was 18 years old. I felt his skin and he was not able to be aroused and I knew he was in danger. So I went to get his insulin out of the refrigerator and give him a shot; however, the "sitter" had not gotten his insulin for him. So I took what was left in his bottles and gave him a shot. When I called her and told her there was a problem she yelled at me for not doing what I was told. At that moment I called the ambulance to take us to the hospital at that time. My sister and I rode in the ambulance with him. When we were at the hospital they called her and told her she was needed there. I knew I was going to be in trouble for disobeying her again but my dad needed help. His doctor came into this special room that they had put us in and she had already gotten there by that time and was furious with me. The doctor proceeded to tell us that it was a good thing I had called when I did because he was in a very bad condition. The doctor only gave our dad a 30% chance of surviving through the night. My sister began crying and I couldn't. The "sitter" became even angrier because I wasn't crying for my dad and smacked me across the face to try and make me cry, yet, I couldn't. The doctor kept her from hitting me again and took me outside the room. He knelt down in front of me and looked me in my eyes and asked why I couldn't cry. He said that most girls my age, when they find out their dad may not live do cry. But I told him, "I have a good God and He wouldn't take our dad away from us and leave us with a "sitter" like her. When my sister and I were are full grown and all of our babies are born and we are living on our own; our dad would die then." The doctor just looked at me and said, "I wish my faith was like yours but I believe in medicine." I didn't understand what faith was but I took it as something good.

The "sitter" did not allow us to stay at the hospital with our dad and took us back to her house with her. I was given a blanket and pillow to sleep on the floor where the dogs were and my sister slept in bed with one of her daughters. When the phone rang in the middle of the night; no one answered it so I ran to find out if it was the doctor. I was surprised that it was the doctor. He said he wanted me and my sister at the hospital as soon as we could get there. So I went to ask if we could go and she told me no that we would go later. I wasn't sure if my dad had passed away or what was going on. When she finally got up later that morning, we went to the hospital. The doctor was still there waiting for us. He knelt down in front of me and my sister and said, "Your dad is awake and asking for your girls." He took us in to see our dad and he looked really good by then. He told my dad and us girls that if he took care of himself that he would give my dad 5 years to live given the severity of his diabetes.

We lost our home again. This time we were sent to live with the "sitter", while our dad went to Bloomington to live out of the back of his truck and save some money for a new house. During this time, I began to wonder what was so wrong with me. Why can't I be like the other kids? Why can't I be treated as well as the other kids? I began believing I was really this bad person and I didn't know how to change. I began believing that I would always be the maid, the wife, and the mother and never be able to do what I wanted. By this time I had no voice and no choice. I just did what I was told and it was never enough and what I did was never good enough; there was always something wrong. I was only allowed to attend church when someone else was in a good mood or if my behavior was good enough to go. However, because I was made to clean the "sitter's" house, cook, to take care of all the animals and everyone's needs in the house; I found a way to keep my faith in spite of what they did or said. While my sister was allowed to sleep in bed with one of her daughter's, I was made to sleep on the floor where the dogs did in the other daughter's bedroom. At my head there was a dresser. I hid my Bible and a flashlight under it so at night I was able to read for a while after everyone was asleep. As long as I didn't make much movement where the dogs would attack my feet, no one woke up. My Bible and flashlight kept my faith alive and gave me hope in the darkest hours of my life.

In May of that year, her daughters had a party at the house. I was not allowed to participate in the party; however, I was supposed to serve of the snacks and drinks to the guests. At one point, I overheard a conversation between one of the boys and the sitter's daughter's talking about what his dad did for a living. The more I heard and thought about it, I began to think their dad may be able to help me get out of that home. So I waited until I believed it was the right time and I ran away with the hope that the boy's dad would help me. When everyone was asleep that night, I ran and went to their house. Their mom let me in to talk with the boys. When their dad came home that night, he sent them off to bed and took me into his and his wife's bedroom to drill me more. His voice was very stern and rough. He scared me to the point I couldn't ask for his help. I sat there in my silence and wanting to leave but I was not allowed to leave. He picked up this little magazine and at the top of it, it read, "Watch Tower." He wanted me to read it to him but I couldn't find my voice to say anything, I only felt the tears rolling over my cheeks. When his wife went to take a shower the boys were already in bed. Their dad grabbed my arm and took me to the living room in the front part of their house. There was a dim light in one corner, green carpet, and the curtains were pulled closed. While he raped me in the middle of the floor I felt myself leave my body and began watching what was happening to me from outside of the window. I tried to yell but I heard nothing. I wanted to die again but I wasn't. When he heard the shower shut off he pulled me up off of that floor and began to walk to their room again. On the way in there he says to me, "With my job I can make kids disappear." Without any direct words he strongly suggested that I not say anything to anyone about what happened. When his wife returned to the room he had once again insisted that I read to him that magazine. It had a lighthouse on the cover. The lighthouse was white with a black roof. Blue skies filled the page as seagulls flew through the air and water surrounded the lighthouse. That night I grew to hate lighthouses as much as I hated him. He sent me back to the sitter's house the next morning. The abuse grew even more intense as a result of what I had done.

I never quit looking for a way out of her house. The sitter made take the dress off my dad had bought me and put her daughters dress on; it was too small and when I sat down it rose up high on my legs. I was embarrassed by this dress but it didn't seem to matter to her. When we found out where I was supposed to go, she walked me all the way into the classroom. I felt even more humiliated when I saw there were no other girls in the class. I tried to walk out and she told me this class was for kids like me who couldn't be good. I was then physically turned around and sent back into class. I went in and set down my dress rode up high again and I was crying as I tried to keep pulling it down over my legs. One boy got up and took his wind breaker off and laid it over my lap and another took his outer shirt off and hung it on the back of my chair (looking back) trying to make me feel alright with what I had on.

This class was considered the misfits, outcasts, and troublemakers in the school. To me, in time, they became the best friends a girl could have. They had a lot of respect for me. They saw me come into class many times with a black eye, burn marks, and welts on me from the beatings I was getting. One boy and I had really begun to like each other a lot. He and I took off one day after school for some quiet time and although we never left the school grounds; it was quiet. I knew I would be in more trouble when I got back to the sitter's house but at that time I can't say that I really cared because escaping just seemed hopeless to me by then. He was the first boy I ever gave myself to. Yet, when I returned back to the house, she was waiting for me and my nightmare had ensued once again. This time instead of beating me she took me to the hospital and told them I had been raped. My dad eventually got back to Springfield and met us there. When they called the police and they questioned me I told them I had sex but I would not tell them with whom. When the doctor told them that there was evidence that I had sex but no evidence of rape my dad became angry. My hymen and been broken years earlier and had completely healed by then and the doctor shared this with the police officers which led them to believe that I had not been raped. After we got back to the house I had a belt taken to me for what I had done. The sitter and my dad made me choose which one would get to do the honors of it. After my dad left for Bloomington again that night the sitter told me if I took off again she was calling my Grandma to come and get me.

When I went to school the next day, I told the boys what had happened and they were upset. What I heard them say next left me with more hope than I had ever dreamed of. As I told them what the sitter had told me, one of the boys popped up with, "She just gave you your way out of her house." The planning then began to keep me safe and get me out of her home. We decided that when we all felt the time was right, I would not go home and they would stay with me. We knew this was going to be hard as we would have to let go of our friendships to set me free as I would be moving to the country and we wouldn't be able to see each other again. As hard as this was, we all believed if I stayed there much longer I would die there eventually. Yet, I had already felt like I was dead from living in fear. This had become such a way of life for me that I wasn't sure even living with my Grandma would change things, yet, as I was told, "It is worth a try."

The day came and we hung out on the school grounds until near dark and we were almost certain the sitter would have called the police to look for me. Then a couple of the boys walked me back to her house. We called my Grandma and gathered my things then waited on the front lawn for my Uncle and Grandma. The police held the sitter back from coming after me and the boys stood by me until I was leaving. Then I began a new journey.

A New Beginning

Life was different on the farm. My Grandma told me I was responsible for keeping my bedroom room clean and doing one other chore through the day. I was even able to sleep in a real bed. My Grandma and Uncle put a lock on the inside of my door so I could lock it if I wanted to and gave me until the new semester (about 2 months) before I would return to school, so I would have time to adjust. I was so engulfed in the routines of the 3 years prior to this change that it was very difficult for me to have so much time on my hands. I didn't know how to be a kid and I had no idea how to spend my time. I began taking walks, at first they were short and few and as I settled in my walks were longer and more frequent. I was starting to like the quiet of the home and loving even more the sounds of the earth as I walked. I was able to go to church every Sunday even if I wasn't good or what mood they were in. My faith was beginning to grow even though I still lived in fear of making a mistake or being bad. I wasn't even sure what it meant to be good or what it meant to be bad. By the time I was to return to school, I was allowed to attend a half day of school for the rest of the school year so as I continued to adjust it would be easier for me. The goal came to have me in school for the full day again beginning the first day of High School the following fall. That Summer I started to get to know more of my extended family and became close to a cousin as we worked in the fields together. My Uncle had allowed me to pick up helping in the fields to help me keep busy and to learn some other things for myself and when he paid me the first time; I felt really bad for it. He told me that if I was willing to work that hard I deserved to be paid and he was grateful that I would help with it.

On Christmas Eve, at the age of 13, I went to spend Christmas with my dad and sister at my dad's house. By this time I was reunited with my step mom; although, our relationship was still very strained, we were at least talking. She had given me a "grown up" jewelry box for Christmas. I was excited about this little thing that was given to me and wanted to show my dad. When I was at my dad's house I went into the bedroom to get the box out and my dad came in and set down next to me. As I pulled the box out of my suitcase he took it from my hand and laid me down on the bed again. I knew then he didn't care about my excitement over this gift. I told myself, Grandma and Uncle that I didn't want to be alone with him again. They respected my decision.

Over the next two years, I continued on with school but not without issues. Although, I never understood why I couldn't feel like I was a part of it, I did have a hand full of friends. My seizures were interfering as every time I had one the school would send me home. There was fear building up in those around me due to the seizures and how they were dealt with. I still had issues with incontinence and that hindered how I felt about myself and how others felt towards me. I took up getting to know the local disc jockeys on the phone to help fill that void in my life.

I began cutting my private areas trying to make myself less desirable; trying to get rid of the one thing so many seemed to want. For a while it seemed to help me release the pain with the pain. I watched blood flow from my body as if it were releasing me from what hurt me in that moment. When I finally figured out I could not get rid of it; I had become promiscuous and felt like I wanted to die most of the time. I was not aware that this was called depression or that there was help for it. I don't think my Grandma or Uncle knew what depression was either. At that time in my life I just knew that I was down and couldn't ever seem to feel good about much of anything.

By the time I was 15 and given permission to house date and my promiscuity had escalated and I was sneaking out of the house at night. I always felt good for that little bit of time; however, by the next morning I would feel worse and more lost than I had. Even though I never understood why I felt that way; I also knew that I wanted and needed to feel better and I believed that eventually I would be better.

I kept remembering being called a heifer and I thought it meant I was over eating. I became so self-conscious of my eating; I began taking my food into my bedroom and would crawl under the bed to eat my meals. By the time I was 16 I was able to change some of this behavior even though my fear remained of being called that name again. When I met my second actual "boyfriend"; I tried to quit seeing other guys and tried even harder to act like what I thought a kid was supposed to act at my age. However, too often, I still felt like a failure as everything in my life was a win or lose situation and I couldn't even win my dad's attention as my dad.

As time marched on I tried over and over to deal with things like I thought I was supposed to and when I realized I wasn't I began running away. Feeling like a failure I was looking for some way to succeed and if I could only find some way of being successful at something in my life, then maybe just maybe I could find some contentment in my life.

I was 16 years old when I found out I was pregnant with my first child. My baby's dad left for the Navy about a month prior to her birth and refused to acknowledge her. My Grandma had passed away in July and in August my Uncle had asked me to move out. I now had no one to turn to so I went to live in an unwed mother's home until my baby was born. After her birth I went to stay with my dad for a very brief period of time until I was able to get my own place to live.

Into Adulthood

I felt even more like a failure as there was so much I didn't know how to do. I felt things and yet I didn't know what I was feeling. I wanted help but I had no idea who to turn to. I was now living in the city and it was so much different than the farm. I didn't feel safe, I didn't hear the birds, or see the sunrise. I missed the smell of the fresh fallen rain and the openness of the land. There was no quiet in my mind anymore; all I heard were the drunks across the street, cars speeding up and down the streets, and neighbors arguing over who was buying the booze that night. My safe world had just become much like the world I once escaped.

About 3 months after I moved into my apartment I was pregnant again. By this time I was drinking, smoking pot, and doing some other street drugs, to try and kill the pain I felt inside. I hadn't even smoked cigarettes or tasted alcohol until this time in my life. When I was seven months pregnant I was standing at the cross roads with my baby. I was in premature labor and told that I was 45 minutes away from delivering her. The doctors were able to slow down the contractions but I had to get off the drugs and drinking. So I kicked the drinking and drugs to the curb to protect my baby. I saw my doctor as a parent telling me I had to do this not that it was a choice I had to make. This is how I viewed everyone in my life. They were someone just handing down orders to me and I had to follow them or else. The following year reality set back in.

I was pregnant for the third time and I was trying to keep my home as my home. I still cherished my family deeply and still lived inside this "fairy tale" thinking. I allowed my sister to come spend a couple weeks with me and I had set down the ground rules with her because I had a special needs baby in my home and did not want a lot of strangers coming and going in my house. It was like the second night or so when she was there she decided to bring home a group of people. I told her they couldn't stay as it was late and I needed to sleep while my girls were. She became angry and began beating me down again and kicked me until I lost my unborn baby. At first I thought I was just bleeding until my homemaker came by the next day and took me to the doctors and hospital for tests. We found out that I had lost my baby at that time. The doctors told me I could still have a baby and I could go ahead and try again.

In October I found out that I indeed was pregnant for the fourth time. This pregnancy was different for me. I seem to have more belly pain than usual with this one. I spent awhile in the Emergency Room one night checking for any issues the doctors could find. They thought there might be one or two but dismissed them as shadows in the sonogram. A family friend whom I entrusted my life and my girl's life with suggested I get a second opinion. However, I had no thought of how to go through this process so she took it upon herself to make all the arrangements. She set it up to take me to see the doctor she used to go to, she would pay for the visit, and even transport me to and from the visit since it was out of town. I thought this was nice of her to do at the time and had no real reason to question her judgment on it. I felt like I would have gotten into trouble if I had any ways since her and her husband had been licensed foster care parents.

When we arrived at the appointment she signed me in and paid for the visit. Later when they took me back the room looked pretty normal and everything seemed like it was supposed to be. The only thing I didn't understand is why they wanted to give me to valium to help me relax to make sure my baby was alright. When I woke up I was sitting in a green leather chair and this friend was nearby. The doctor came over later and said to me that he didn't even know how I got pregnant as there was so much damage to my uterus from my previous pregnancy. He told me that I would never be able to have another baby and inside this devastated me. I kept hanging on to the baby I was carrying.

It wasn't until we returned home that I found out that she had my baby aborted without my permission. A few years later, her and her husband would bring my girls home from a visit and my oldest daughter told me she was sorry that I had lost her little brother and sister. When I asked her how she knew that she told me that this friend had told her about the babies. I made some calls and did some checking into these facts to find out they were actually true. I had been carrying twins and she had them aborted because she didn't believe that I needed to be having any babies.

It is the reason why when I found out I was pregnant in December of 1984 that I refused to tell anyone but the father. He and I kept it a secret between us so that no one could harm our unborn baby. I was very sick during this time but as my dad always said to me, "Get up off your lazy a** and do what

I told you to do." So I did just that; I kept going until I could no longer go and I ended up in the hospital. By the time Summer came my OB doctor told me that I would not be able to have another child. To have another baby would kill me and my baby both. As I prepared to give birth I also prepared myself for this to be my last child. I was alright with it as I now had three children that I loved so much and felt like God had blessed me with that I needed no more. I knew any man who would love me would love my children as his own totally.

Seasons of Change

My husband and I were married in January 1994. He was 59 years old and I was 29 years old. He was a blessing on the wings of a dove. He loved my daughters like they were his own and there was no convincing him of anything different. We were together for almost 8 years before we were married and 5 years before he passed away.

Willie was my partner, confidant, and love of my life. He always seemed to know when to push me and when to back down from my moods. Many times he would challenge my fears so that I would overcome them one by one. Willie stood by me no matter how difficult things had gotten with me and was willing to take a chance if he thought he could help me face my worst fear.

One night before leaving for work he asked me why I always tore the pages out of books that had lighthouses on them, got sick in the stores when I would pass down an aisle where there lighthouses, or turn the TV channel just so I wouldn't have to look at them. With tears in my eyes I reluctantly told him about the rape that left me with such an effect on my life. I shared with Willie about a night prior to Mother's Day when a Juvenile officer raped me. The man sat me down trying to force me to read a "Watch Tower" magazine to him. I told Willie every detail of the cover of that magazine. I had connected the lighthouse on that cover to the rape and was unable to grow past it at that time.

After I shared this with my husband he began to understand something more about me. I recall feeling a little more secure with him as he didn't react to what I had told him but spent time asking questions about how I felt and tried to find a level of understanding others had not taken the time to find. Then he surprised me even more. Although the counselor I was seeing at this time was making slow progress with me, my husband decided to try and help in his own way.

In the early morning hour my husband came home from work early and woke me up. I saw a box sitting on my nightstand. He said to me, "I have something special for you. Before you get angry or upset with me I want you to hear me out." He then took the box off the nightstand and there stood a lighthouse water fountain. It was lit up and had fog horn sounds and the sounds of seagulls with flowing water. The tears began to flow and I felt so betrayed at first until he began telling me how he saw it. He said to me, "This Lighthouse is a lot like God. He stands firm through all the storms of our lives, shines a light when it's dark, protects the ships in the night, and each one has its own sense of beauty about it. I see you the same way. You are beautiful and stand firm in your faith. You protect our girls and shine a light in our lives. You do all the same things lighthouses do you just have a different way of doing it."

Not long after this our girls and their friends all started giving me lighthouses for gifts. My Birthday's, Christmas's, and sometimes for no reason I would get lighthouses. The more I received them the more I began to believe there was something good left in me. I began to believe there was still hope that things could change for the better.

After my husband passed away in 1999, I became worse. I became a Grandmother the following year and this made my heart jump with joy. Although this was difficult it was awesome to be a part of this with my daughters. I tried to go back to work for a while; but it was short lived. I became unable to think clearly or even comprehend half of what I was doing.

I had been hospitalized for gallbladder surgery with complications. A couple of weeks later since I was having suicidal ideations I was hospitalized again. It was during this time that I was then diagnosed with Bipolar Disorder, Borderline Personality Disorder, and Post-Traumatic Stress Disorder. I was already battling several physical health issues at this time as well. I went through the process of the doctors finding the right medications for me and right dosages. I felt like I was a new person. I was beginning to feel like I had always wanted to. I wanted to live and I began believing for the first time in my life that I could actually live.

During the months, while waiting for some insurance and some sort of income, I had done without my meds many times as I relied on State Agencies to help me acquire them. Many times I had already met my limit and there was no more funding to help me so I would be cycling inside my disorders rather rapidly.

When I had gotten my medications I had attempted suicide 9 months after I was diagnosed. While I was in the hospital, I noticed a brochure caddy on the wall. I began looking at these and I noticed a brochure that talked about classes that teach you about your mental illness(s). I knew this is what I have needed and more than anything it is what I wanted. Finally, there something that could help me to gain some understanding about what was happening to me and how to deal with it. Once I learn these things then maybe I could actually begin to live for the first time in my life. Maybe for the first time my dreams can come true. So I approached my doctor and asked her about the class. Although, it was not the class she felt was appropriate for me; she knew of a class that would be a good one for me to attend.

Through the efforts of many people I began attending the Westlake Center Group Therapy Program. When I first entered in the groups I had a false idea of recovery. I believed attending 6 days a week 8 hours a day, I would be able to return to work and I would be living. However, I was so wrong. I found myself facing things that I had not faced and dealing with issues so intense that it took me (what seemed like forever to overcome) months to learn to cope with and some of them I still battle with today.

A couple of years past while attending Westlake, I took my first trip to Rose Island Lighthouse alone. It commemorated the 9th Anniversary of my husband Willie's passing. He had wanted to take me to a Lighthouse so I thought this was a perfect place to go and the light was lit for him the night of the 5th. It was a calming and very serene place to enjoy the beauty around me. It is an Island of wonder to think and regain my thoughts and dreams to bring back home with me.

When I did return home I put together a small video of where I went and presentation of my experience. This began a whole new series of experiences for me. I had also put together a Consumer run group therapy class under the supervision of a therapist called the "Can You See Me?" class. This class was a combination class of all the classes we had at Westlake. Everything we were learning in them was brought into one class and some hands on learning were added as well. It made for an interesting and sometimes an intense class. It was a place where my experiences continued to help others open up and understand more of their own personal experiences. Some who were quiet began talking, some who thought they could do nothing started doing something and yet others were stepping up to help present the class. The teamwork presented through this class was remarkable and knocked the staff off their feet a couple of times. During our planning of special events when my class would do things they normally don't do, the staff would so often be awe of what was happening through the encouragement of what they have been given. This is the ultimate hope of all.

The excitement has built up in me over the years as word of my Inspirational Speaking has made its way around to many people. I have spoken at several church groups, the Regions 3 & 4 Recovery Conference, various Departments of Mental Health, and I am very open about my recovery with everyone.

I believe by being open about my recovery takes away the shame that others want to place on it. It tears down the stigmas and stereotypes to mental health issues. I am proud to be able to live as well as I am. I am proud to have even part of my dream come true.

Recovery is Discovery...
My Personal Experience

Recovery is the discovery of who I am,
what I want, and the desires of my own heart.
Recovery is the discovery
of my personal inner strength
which drives hope into open wounds
of what once was and what is and allows for one's
internal growth to become prominent and dominant
for the success of living out my dreams.
~Angela Willis~
2014

I serve God in the Harvard Park Baptist Church on the Music Committee, Public Relations Committee, I am currently serve on the Springfield Mass Transit District Advisory Committee, Molina Healthcare Advocate, I speak with training CIT (Crisis Intervention Training) police officers and I continue to develop "Breaking Sacred Ground" Presentations for churches so they may explore ways of tearing down stigmas and stereotypes associated with Mental Health issues, my "Journey to New Hope" Series continues to be developed and I continue to do my Inspirational Speaking whenever possible.

"If you can dream it,
You can do it."
~Walt Disney~

These are powerful words for recovery. It offers a form of continuous hope and says that all we need to do is dream of what we want. For everything we want we can reach.

"Keep your eyes on Heaven,
Reach for the stars,
Dreams really do come true,
It all begins with you."
~Angela Willis~
2008

In some countries we can't walk down the street talking on a cell phone, have central air, personal space, or have personal freedoms. In some countries the term recovery doesn't exist. In America we celebrate Thanksgiving, Christmas, Easter, The Fourth of July, and many others and we are able to celebrate our recovery as well because we have the freedom to choose to.

I continue to be blessed by a loving God who carries me and a support network that is there for me. I am certain without a doubt that you will be blessed as well.

Stand tall, stand proud of whom you are. For when you stand you are tearing down the walls of stigmas and stereotypes. You are giving hope to others who have not yet begun their journey to new hope or experienced the joy of being able to live their dream. There is no end to a journey into a dream as it continues on like a rainbow that we forever chase. Where there is a dream there is hope, where there is hope there is a dream. You have a voice and you have a choice to make it happen.

Thank you Lord, for the experiences of my past which give me strength for my today, thank you for my experiences of today, that give others hope for tomorrow. Amen.

Blessings, Angela

Thinking About Smiling
Rebecca Miller

Did you ever have to think about smiling? Think about how your cheeks rise, think about engaging the muscles and moving them upwards, think about whether the sides of your mouth are equally high, think about whether your lips are moving above your teeth, think about whether the smile is symmetrical or reaching your eyes?

Rebecca and Ceci visiting family in Seattle

A man looks at me in the elevator as I go up to the ICU recovery room for my candy striping duties at the hospital while in high school. "Smile!" he insists. I give him a half-hearted grin, no teeth, and wanly think, why am I doing this for you? Why are you invading my mental space? Why is it important to you that I smile? and, my own interpretation at the time, which was, wow, do I really look that down that someone needed to ask me to smile?[1] I probably did. My depression started in high school, around sophomore year, with a dull feeling of emptiness and inertia. I couldn't get motivated to do schoolwork, I lay in bed a lot, and generally moped and dragged and felt deadened. My mom thought it was the typical *storm unt drang* of adolescence until my younger brother reached my age and he was totally different.

---

[1] I will add here that there is a feminist take on this interaction as a form of harassment, recently taken on by an artist (see http://www.cnn.com/2014/04/06/living/street-harassment-art/).

I did better my senior year, finishing high school and leaving for college, but by second semester of my first year I had entered a new depth of despairing; thoughts of suicide, weight loss, crying and hand wringing. I made it, hanging on by my teeth, and went home for the summer. I decided not to return to college, which initiated some hand wringing for my parents, as they thought I would never go back.

I took a year off and went to live in Boston, where I took photography classes and worked at an upscale deli slicing prosciutto, dishing out pasta salad and making sandwiches. One morning, I got on the bus to work feeling just a bit angsty and unmoored; by the time my stop came, it was if a switch had flipped. I knew the script and my thoughts were down deep in the hole of dark depression. But this time I flipped around like an acrobat, going from despair to elation to anxiety. Several days later, after crying almost constantly, I arrived at work and declared it a new day. This feeling and revelation, that I could change my life for the better, lasted for about an hour, a bright glittering hour of possibility that soon transformed into dreary droning and sharp glaring confusion. I thought that the grocery store where I was working had been closed, and that the customers had been paid to come in and harass me. The music, usually upbeat contemporary jazz, turned into a slowed-down atonic nightmare soundtrack. I wandered and stared, and a coworker took me out on the loading dock to check in with me. I ended up slapping him for no logical reason; he, thankfully, had some understanding that things were not right, and he and my boss took me to the Cambridge Hospital ER. That night I ended up on the inpatient unit, running behind the nurses station, refusing to go to bed (I was afraid I would wake my already sleeping roommate) and finally, punching and fighting until 6 men held me down while a nurse shot Haldol in my behind. I ended up at McLean Hospital, in 4-point restraints and struggling to get my arms out. Now my parents were not so worried about college but whether their daughter would ever return as they knew her. My mom brought me creamed onions, mashed potatoes and cranberry sauce as that year, I spent Thanksgiving in the hospital.

My diagnosis was something I latched onto like a safety raft; I hung it around my neck like an ID badge. I was "bipolar". I called myself that, I identified with it, it wrapped around me like a blanket, muffling out any other parts of myself. I felt 'sick', I identified with being sick and I cast myself in that role. And I internalized a sense of being fragile and vulnerable. It was a slow process to start trusting myself again, especially to trust a mind that had betrayed me once before.

I wanted to go back to school, but I was afraid, nervous that I couldn't hack it, that I was too sick. The summer before returning to college, I took abnormal psychology at summer school, and wrote a paper on Bipolar Disorder in adolescence. "A graduate level paper" was the only comment my professor made on it, and that helped build my confidence as a student again. My identity shifted further when I restarted school, transferring to Barnard. There I found a community of queer folks; my self-image formed around being bisexual, being in a relationship with a woman, and being an activist. With a friend, I created a brochure about bisexuality and silkscreened tee shirts that said "Bi Power".

I researched bipolar disorder compulsively and decided my symptoms didn't quite fit after all. I broke up with a psychiatrist who refused to treat me unless I took Lithium, and I stopped the medication with the support of a new psychiatrist. I still struggled but made it through the next years of college, and was on track to finish classes a semester early. I had taken a graduate class in social factors and psychopathology, and had begun to consider graduate school for clinical psychology. I felt like maybe I could give back and help others. I was sternly warned not to reveal my history in my application or interview, "Not until you get in", said the professor. "Don't give them a reason to not take you." I took the advice to heart.

Once that last semester was complete, I picked up to move to San Francisco with a friend, and the journey cross country also took me back into the realm of psychosis; by the time we were in Tucson, I was feeling crazy again. I became obsessed with humor, and felt I had lost my sense of humor on the road to Cali. I only spoke in metaphor and was insisting things needed to be funny. When I was in the back of the cop car on the way to the ER, the officer said, "Are you thinking about killing yourself?" and I said "If I could find a fun way to do it". The admission paperwork at San Fran General had listed, "You said it would be fun to kill yourself". Not quite, but...

After a week inpatient and flying home with my mom to NJ, I started an intensive outpatient program. I was heavily drugged and still very paranoid, but able to drag myself into the program daily. Things started looking up a bit; my mom knew I was doing better when I started wearing socks with patterns and funny designs on them. I rebuilt my confidence through artwork, drawing in a sketchbook that I brought with me everywhere. I brought in work from my photography class to show my group therapy fellow travelers, and one day wore my 'Bi Power' t-shirt to IOP. I said, "Why can't bipolar disorder be the same? Why are there no parades for us? Or t-shirts? We need a new kind of activism". My group leader said, "Maybe that's what you can do. Are you up for doing it?" I wasn't quite sure. I wanted to apply to graduate school. And the advice of my professor rang in my ears. *Not until you get in.*

I got a job working as a secretary as I applied to psych related positions. Finally I landed an entry level Mental Health Assistant job on the inpatient unit at a local psychiatric hospital. My teeth were chattering with fear the first time I walked on the unit, and I clutched the keys to reassure myself that I could actually get back out. I couldn't believe that this time, unlike at Cambridge Hospital, I was supposed to walk behind the nurse's station. The imposter syndrome was strong, but I worked hard to learn my job and support people. I worked to empower others about their condition, leading psychoeducation groups, encouraging people to shop for a therapist and not just a car, and helping to start a community garden for the inpatients and outpatients.

I found inspiration in reading stories of others' experiences. Books like *An unquiet mind*, by Kay Redfield Jamison, Martha Mannings' *Undercurrents*, Lori Shiller's *The Quiet Room*, Scott Zwiren's *Godhead*, all gave me inspiration about the ability to survive and thrive.

And I went deep deep in the closet for many years, more so after starting graduate school in clinical psychology at Long Island University, Brooklyn. I shared my story with selected few; my advisor in graduate school, a few trusted supervisors, friends. But I struggled greatly with the idea of being 'out' more generally. I worried that the stigma and discrimination would fuel my own paranoia. "Are they talking about me?" I didn't want to add anything 'real' to my already ample imagined fears. I worried that I would put my career at risk. I kept waiting for the next goalpost, the next hurdle. I waited for graduation from graduate school. Then for internship to be over. Then to complete my postdoc. And then I was waiting for a more secure faculty position where I was working, at the Yale University School of Medicine. "Soon," I said, "soon".

And during that waiting time, other things happened. I bought a house, I made new friends, I joined a writing group. I became an aunt twice over. I went to France and milked goats. I adopted 3 cats. I gardened and learn how to knit. I taught others how to knit. I learned to cook steak on a charcoal grill. I became a single mother by choice, giving birth to an amazing daughter, Cecilia. I built a life.

And, and also, I found out I have Early Onset Parkinson's disease. Yes, Parkinson's. I was in shock and disbelief. Symptoms started at least 10 years prior to my diagnosis, but I had rationalized them away. I had had prior experiences with the medical system where my concerns had been minimized, and I had internalized the sense of being somewhat hypochondriacal. My shoulder problems, which are a common first symptom of PD, had been diagnosed 11 years earlier after a trip to the ER and subsequent rule out of MS. I had tingling in my right arm and leg, and my psychiatrist had suggested I go to the ER. I had an MRI and ended up being diagnosed with bursitis. Despite there being a real problem, I felt unentitled and I was certain that doctors saw me as anxious and 'overblowing' my physical symptoms because of mental illness. I was suspect, I successfully self-stigmatized, and I held back on telling most doctors about my psych hospitalizations and depression because I feared not being taken seriously. This discrimination and self-doubt led me to attribute the slight foot drag in my right foot, which went on for about 9 years, not to something neurological but to my own sense of being lazy. I thought the stiffness in my right side was due to longstanding mild scoliosis and my own distaste for exercise. So I chalked up the symptoms to other factors, kept it moving, and kept working.

Until it became too weird. Several months after my daughter was born, I noticed that I had to command my right hand to move when I went to pick up my daughter. "Move, hand, move," I would say internally. Maybe I was conflicted about raising my daughter, I thought, and it was coming out in physical ways. Maybe I was just a tired new mom. And then at an acupuncture appointment, I mentioned my symptoms, and threw in the foot drag too. "Go to a doctor!" said my acupuncturist. I did, not thinking too much of it.

Carpel tunnel maybe. Arthritis. Or something psychological. The first neurologist sent me to a movement disorder specialist. I didn't think much of it, until I mentioned my symptoms and the upcoming appointment to my psychiatrist. And when I saw the look of concern, nay alarm, on his face when I did finger taps for him, I worried too, and I googled my constellation of symptoms for the first time. Parkinson's. Parkinson's. Parkinson's was the only diagnosis that came up. Over and over again. And I learned that some seemingly unrelated things were also symptoms, like my reduced arm swing on one side, and the loss of my sense of smell (a common early sign, currently being researched), which had happened about 10 years prior but I had also rationalized away.

I made a promise to myself in the months between the initial prospect of Parkinson's and the actual diagnosis. I said if I do have this disease, then I am coming out about all of it. No more waiting, no more time to waste. No more hiding or awaiting the next goal post. It would be time. And I was pretty sure I had it, after consulting Dr. Google and seeing the possibilities (few, some others being even worse than PD), but PD is a diagnosis of rule outs – if they can't find anything else and the symptoms fit, then that's the diagnosis. There are a lot of things to rule out, (mitochondrial disorders, metabolic disorders, brain tumor, heavy metal accumulation, and lots more) so it takes a while. It was a funny experience, to find oneself wishing for a brain tumor. And also hoping that I was crazy and that this was part of some postpartum depression – there is a condition termed psychogenic Parkinson's[2] but after reading about it, that didn't seem to fit either. In some sense, I

---

[2] See Lang AE, Koller WC, Fahn S. Psychogenic Parkinsonism. *Arch Neurol*. 1995;52(8):802-810. doi:10.1001/archneur.1995.00540320078015. for more information

was very lucky; between when I brought the symptoms to a doctor's attention and diagnosis, it took only 5 months. One might argue 5 months plus 11 years but I'm going with 5 months. Other people go for years before a more definitive diagnosis is given.

At the specialist's office where I was finally diagnosed, the doctor said, "You definitely have Parkinson's Disease. But you need to take charge of your disease. Don't let it take charge of you." He wasn't the warmest of neurologists; "I can see you're getting upset", he said blandly from across the room after delivering the news and watching me tear up. But importantly, he said "Take Charge". He told me about a conference, The World Parkinson's Congress, happening in Montreal several months off. He encouraged me to get involved.

I googled it when I got home, and signed up. It was a unique conference with everyone there together; researchers, clinicians, caregivers, people with Parkinson's. There were workshops with varying levels of scientific rigor, roundtables where I met an ultramarathoner with Parkinson's, panels with doctors and astronauts with PD, and a buddy program which matched me with another young person recently diagnosed. I saw people like me walking around with foot drags and one arm not swinging. She has PD, I thought, she's like me. Seeing all these people living full lives and managing the illness was an inspiration. There was a renewal room with yoga, dance, exercise, and inspirational talks. And there was free massages and reiki.

What a contrast with the attitude, atmosphere and advice that I had heard with my mental illness diagnosis. At the time I was diagnosed with Bipolar Disorder in the early 90s, I thankfully never received the message of "You'll never work" or "You can't have a life", those devastating messages of hopelessness that many have heard. But there was still the sense conveyed that I was fragile, needing to reduce or minimize stress, and a kind of paternalism about the need to take medications "for the rest of your life". There was the sense of being damaged in some way, and needing to hide this fact from others. This was only reinforced by my professor in college telling me to keep my diagnosis a secret. And there was the sense that this was "all of me"; my diagnosis was all encompassing and all defining. I introduced myself when I shared my illness as "I'm bipolar", a semantic turn that spoke to how swallowed up I felt by the diagnosis. It took many years to gain distance from that attachment to the diagnosis and to the desire to define myself by such.

The process of accepting illness was easier with Parkinson's. Perhaps this was because I had been through the experience of working through a chronic illness diagnosis before; the stages of identity consumption around the illness, grief and depression, the process of re-imagining my life, and realizing what strengths and skills I still had. It took much less time to realize that "I'm still *me*" even with this illness. When I was diagnosed with Bipolar Disorder, I felt I *was* the disorder. With Parkinson's it felt much less of an all-consuming label, even though, ironically, I was much more open about the PD right away. I joined a Facebook group that provides incredible support and information to me. I came out to friends and coworkers. I raised $3500 and did the annual Unity Walk in NYC, coming together with hundreds of others with the disease, with family members and with researchers. I got active, took charge, and felt in control of the disorder. There is still fear about coming out – will people doubt my ability? Treat me differently? But overall the fear is much less.

And I did finally, after all those years, come out as a person with mental illness. It was a moment of liberation. I was ironically by that time in the position of Director of Peer Support at the local mental health center, but had been in the job a couple years before coming out. I struggled with the hypocrisy of supporting others in sharing their experience while keeping my own under tight wrap. I almost didn't take the job for that reason, but hoped that I could still help the program grow despite being in the closet myself. I debated for several months after making the decision of "if" then trying to decide "how". Do I drop it casually in a meeting, as one friend suggested? Do I make a big announcement? Send out a group email? I finally decided to let the peer supervisor know first, and then bring it up at a group supervision meeting.

I was amazed and humbled by the support I received from the peer staff. One person was left speechless. "I don't know what to say," she said. "Wow". The best part and most rewarding aspect was the fact that others took it as inspiration. "if you can do it, I can too". Which is one of the most powerful aspects of peer support; the living example of recovery and living a full life while having a mental illness.

I had to address, or felt obligated to address, why it had taken me so long. I was honest. I had worried about my own mental health, about my job, about discrimination. That was one of my biggest fears; that people would be angry at me for not coming out earlier. But, at least from what was shared with me, there was more appreciation for my sharing it. It brought our peer support team closer together, and helped me feel more authentic at work. I am grateful for the reception that my colleagues gave me, and their reception felt like a gift.

Coming out is an ongoing continuous process. The when and how still stumps me sometimes, but thankfully the 'if' question is forever put to bed. And now I feel I can acknowledge all parts of me, including the stiff, slow parts due to Parkinson's, the deep dark times due to depression, the chaotic speaking in metaphor times due to psychosis, the joyful times due to, well, life. One of the motivators for coming out about my Parkinson's disease was the fact that I had some outward obvious signs. Including a half smile – the right side of my face doesn't quite lift up in the same way anymore. I grin and feel my right cheek sag. But I know that I'm smiling inside.

Recovery Surfaces
Kyle D. Lloyd

In December 1976 while a senior at Southern Wells High School in Poneto, Indiana, I enlisted for the US Navy being advised to take advantage of the delayed entry program for Montgomery G.I. Bill benefits. My parents were ecstatic with this prospect as they urged me to consider any new living arrangements I could obtain after High School graduation.

Due to my high achievement on military entrance ASVAB test scores I qualified for Submarine Service and it thrilled me to go through all preparations and class work for the Submarine Sonar Technician Rate and attend Submarine School at Groton, Connecticut. This followed basic recruit training at Great Lakes USN Training Center in North Chicago, Illinois. My home port was Charleston, South Carolina and the USS *James Madison* SSBN627, a 16-missle Ballistic *Boomer* was my boat assignment and duty station. After a single patrol I passed ship's board exams for Submariner Qualification and received my Dolphin Pin and Deterrent Patrol insignia to wear beneath it. This 1st cruise exposed me to the exotic coast of Puerto Rico where the sea bed could be seen easily under our boat through crystal translucent waters.

Our second patrol aboard USS *James Madison* was a crew exercise and we accommodated several Naval Academy midshipmen for orientation and trial of submarine service. Come to think of it, I wished in hindsight that I had a trial run at submarining before taking the full bore DIVE! Mischief ran circles throughout this outing and several new young officers were pranked and spanked off the U.S. East Coast as we drilled and performed our Navy duties and showed them the ropes. To repair forward torpedo room, radio room, or operations room, some "middies" would be ordered to dash far aft to the machinery space with chits to collect parts or tools with names, such as, fallopian tubes, testicle wrenches, and other human anatomical names. The *Madison* made one more final port call in Charleston, long enough to clear the decks of all of midshipmen known as middies going ashore. Then we casted our lines off again to cruise up the U.S. Eastern Coastline to take USS *James Madison* into Norfolk shipyards for a major refit to put Trident missiles into her arsenal.

I was just a buffed 19 year old pup, beginning to get my sea legs firmed up, and well into my US Navy enlistment when mental illness struck me. At the Portsmouth Naval Regional Medical Center in the summer of 1979 I was psychiatrically triaged and hospitalized for approximately 9 months. The admission to the unit was quite traumatic for me. Two male escorts led me into the unit and then to the shower room; I was advised to remove all my clothing and wait for them to give me something to wear. They bagged each piece of my removed clothing in front of me, and then as I stood from head to toe totally nude, they produced a pair of light blue hospital pajamas for me and flat green and black sponge molded footie slippers.

Portsmouth Naval Regional Medical Center doctors diagnosed me with Schizophrenia Schizoaffective-type Disorder. In treatment, I stabilized with a round of Lithium and then when they seemed at a loss to readjust my behavior they proceeded to give me experimental Haloperidol drug therapy over the course of several months. After a short ramp up, I was taking two 2-ounce plastic cups full of liquid suspended Haloperidol at breakfast, lunch, and dinner or bed-time. This particular medication eventually made me feel a mental paralysis. My ability to read and adjust my eyes to make out print went away. A frenzy of frustration began to build and build as the staff rebuffed my complaints and concerns. I cannot remember the numbers of days that passed to bring me to a brink of despair, but in one instance I could no longer accept this anymore. One particular day I took a hold of my lunch time food tray and hurled it across the ward like it was a Frisbee™. This brought some attention to me right away.

Three well-built med techs tackled and shackled me in a strait jacket before I knew that food could not fly, at least according to the house rules here. I spent at least 3 hours in a seclusion room for this show of *inappropriateness.*

The setting at Portsmouth was an open-bay ward with approximately 24 psychiatric patients in cohabitation. The best way to visualize it would take a viewing of *One Flew over the Cuckoo's Nest.* On a couple occasions, the medication raised my temper to physical outbursts and I spent time in seclusion strapped to a bed tightly held in a strait-jacket. I observed other patients there too. Some were taken off the unit for their treatment(s) and sometimes they were taken by force and at times shackled to a gurney wheeled away from our ward space to endure something never mentioned nor spoken of – perhaps *ECT shock treatments –* that was my presumption.

The beds in the open bay ward were single twin size steel frames. The beds were evenly placed at about one for each at seven foot separations. With each bed was a small patient night stand where the open shelving could accommodate a clean set of pajamas, underwear, one clean bath towel, a wash cloth, and slippers. One shallow drawer within each stand accommodated patients' toiletries and minimal collection of personal items, perhaps a small amount of loose change a Bible, Rosary, or a religious necklace).

All the windows in our bay ward were open to full view from outside, no curtains or blinds; nothing to cover windows. If the expanse of the hospital grounds was not present, there would be no privacy whatsoever afforded us patients. Pedestrian strangers could have easily been voyeurs with a spectacular view. Many days in a row I paced endlessly around the ward and memorized the patterns of the floor tile placements, even so well I knew I was approaching the nurses' station and unit clerk's desk without even raising my head for checking. This was a time when patients were permitted to smoke on our unit and the air was nearly always cast with a mild haze along with billions of lofted carcinogenics.

I remember one of the male psych tech nurses wore make-up on his face, particularly eye liner, a beige base layer cover, and ruby colored lip gloss. His hair was professionally and impeccably styled while wearing white slacks and scrub tops with ironed hard creases. He constantly hovered about his beloved Spider plant hanging in the front corner of television lounge. His appearance could never inspire recovery of any sort mentally or physically. His value to this hospital must have been that he could trigger homophobes.

My symptoms included delusions of the *television telling me what to do* and *monitoring my thoughts and holding me hostage to its agenda*. And my recovery was delayed until I could gain personal insight to positive and negative symptoms associated with my SMI diagnosis. I also lacked any realization to consider even having a mental illness. When I was finally able to walk out of that hospital, the maintenance dose of Haloperidol and its refill prescriptions went into a trash can at the end of the sidewalk. Denial worked against me for several years to follow after leaving U.S. Navy's Submarine Service and becoming a civilian worker.

My family gathered around me after my departure from the Navy, and insisted that I had no mental illness, and that if I just *bucked-up some* and *got on with my life* I'd be just fine. Well, I tried this, but there were gradual and ever-present subtle symptoms that would not abate with passages of time, but some easily hid behind more or less self-medicating use of alcohol, a tobacco habit, and occasional marijuana use.

My life continued with this denial and I attained a Bachelor's of Science degree at Ball State University leading to a fair, but not very lucrative CAD designing and quality engineering career. I had a temporarily happy marriage that would last only 13 years before intimate relationship failure due partly to my blunted emotional responses and untreated symptoms. My career path followed a roller-coaster trajectory. Fulltime employment to downsized layoff. Temp Job to renewed Fulltime Employment with Benefits. Then catastrophe struck; I received a no-fault downsize layoff notice on August 31, 2001; less than 2 weeks before the 9-11 terrorist attack on New York, Washington, DC, and Pennsylvania.

After succumbing to homelessness, the NAMI Peer-to-Peer Course assisted me with sound and reasonable instruction and basic scientific knowledge which became effective for me to develop a personal recovery plan and take steps forward that were a very long time in coming. Succinctly worded, my *epiphany*. Since entering this program of recovery, I have strongly advocated for others with serious mental illnesses, and especially military veterans. I have also written grant requests and saw awards from them in support of fellow homeless veterans who also shared misfortunes in homeless situations.

Between 2004 and 2008 I served as Chairman for NAMI Indiana's Statewide Consumer Council Executive Committee, and proactively advocated for the passage of Parity Legislation and other public policy bills to support and protect the rights of individuals with mental health problems. I further developed and redefined myself with a new profession in the field as a Recovery Peer Specialist. I actively help others in their recovery as a Consumer/Provider by providing the services they need to live their daily lives and successfully stay in the community, and pursue their own goals. I am a role model of recovery and I willingly facilitate interested consumers with developing personal Wellness Recovery Action Plans (WRAP). Dr. Mary Ellen Copeland's WRAP is now an evidence-based practice.

Changing the mental health system is an evolutionary process that I am involved with and through my daily employment effort to shift medical models to Recovery and person-centered foci models. The changes that need to happen include eradicating stigma created by and propagated through media, and breaking down barriers to accessible care and treatment; also promoting social inclusion, and restoring dignity to individuals affected by serious mental illnesses and reconnecting patients to community, natural, and family supports.

I'm a champion for the cause with NAMI and have made several In Our Own Voice presentations to hundreds of people already. This program permits me to do public speaking where again I share my recovery story and model recovery to give family members and other persons living with serious mental illnesses hope for lives beyond a diagnosis. I also am a Peer-to-Peer 3rd Edition Facilitator and a qualified and experienced Family-to-Family Trainer. I'm rebuilding a local NAMI affiliate through a re-chartering process to become a full service leader affiliate with compliance to NAMI new National Standards of Excellence. Our team has got its work to do, but we'll soon see reforms in our community allowing much safer and streamlined services for those afflicted by serious mental health problems or brain injury.

Since 2010, I ascended much higher into Advocacy than I knew was possible by obtaining an appointment to the Indiana Protection and Advocacy Services or IPAS Commission. Presently, I continue to serve on this commission as its Vice Chairman. I participate in the NAMI

National Military and Veterans Council. In my everyday job at the Marion VA campus, I support my fellow Veterans and our new returning Veterans at VA Northern Indiana Health Care System, on our Mental Health Intensive Case Management Team.

Many of the veterans I serve have been disowned by their families, estranged from even parents, aunts, uncles, and spouses. Many of these veterans endure meager and marginal existence and some require highly structured living environments, but the care and support we show them sustains and encourages them. We are seeing recovery take root in many more Veterans' lives and my participation within this effort continues to fuel my torch-bearing advocacy and driving passion until all my brothers and sisters shall regain their places in returning home.

Coming Out Proud
Margaret E. Davenport

So here I was trying to park where authorities would not find me. Huddled beneath a sleeping bag, blankets and a hooded coat trying to survive New England's coldest winter. I had gone in a matter of days from being a middle class, stay at home mom, to childless and living in my car.

My husband at the time, decided he had enough of my pendulum swinging emotional state. He set in motion to divorce me, take custody of my daughters and our home. The feeling is like being pistol whipped over and over again without seeing the hand delving the blows or recognizing the reason why.

I poured out my grief at my mother's knees questioning my own existence. I always sensed that there was a peculiarity about me something that made me feel like an outsider, staring through windows panes at the rest of the world. The truth of my world was like a river, forceful, pounding like the Colorado jagged edges maiming me. When I wasn't crammed in my car, I was a patient at local hospitals either for physical or emotional health issues. At the time it did not matter to me what the doctors were treating, I was out of the cold. I had suffered frostbite so badly at one point that surgery was required to repair the damage.

I taped pictures of my girls to the dashboard of my car and sang them lullaby's snow fell outside my car. It gave me the sensation that I was still their mom. I had been diagnosed as dehydrated due to the fact that I drank very little water, because my car did not come with a bathroom. Nothing in life could have prepared for those dark nights without my beloved. Twisting in my soul was a monster like something from "Aliens", threatening at every turn to come busting out of its holding cell in my being. So I struggled with my body, mind and

heart all at once. The following poem was written to express
the anguish of feeling I would never be love.

When Longing Is Not Like Breathing
(Reading this poem now draws tears to my soul even still.)

I stand
in some darkened square
barely can the gravity hold up
what used to be defined as me
hardly do I hear
heart and voice cry
who will love me
body
soul
mind
who will love all of me
trains dragging chains of loneliness
utter back to me in voices
now familiar to m
caress the great beauty
of your thick brown lips
or say amen
just at your sigh
no one my flower
no one
now I bite hard on this needy tongue
till it bleeds
and red fusion covers once pearly teeth
it is heart I am tasting
heart is in consolable
I am devouring my unloved self
the truth
is in my eyes
in my arms

and in my bed
which I share and stare with emptiness

no one   no one no one
no one no one
no one

With the help of dedicated people I had intentionally out for help. I began to stand from crawling all the time, feeling sunlight against my skin reminding me of a certain hope that had long eluded me.

All my life I had waited to be at peace with myself but until I began to understand that I am not only loved but cherished. From the love of my children, the confidence they have in me to be their mother, made me look at myself differently. Unique, a gift and yes needed this is you. The moment I told my daughters that I would no longer harm myself at their request, was like lightening striking the key in Franklin's jar. I knew what had been clouded was clear. I was seen as priceless. A diamond is seen as precious whether it is in a sock draw, in the backyard buried beneath a shrub, or placed around a neck or on a ring. It is still like you, a diamond. If things hold such value, should not you. Today, I am trying to purchase a house and promote my poetry. My children are grown and live near me.

One last poem.

Knowing

I understand
that now is the time
to know
that the light shines on all of us

the instant
pure mercy embraces us
we become like stars
in a galaxy of human beings
created to resound
a perfect harmony
into the heavenly realm
yes
it is simple
we are transformed
so close your eyes
and do what stars do best
SHINE
SHINE
SHINE

Hope Isn't Quantifiable
David Castro

David Castro

I stood in my backyard, on the eve of my 30th birthday. My wife and a few friends looked on as I worked to start a campfire with one match. A colleague and fellow MFT intern asked in a tone between confused and entranced, "Why aren't you using paper or lighter fluid . " The fire was slowly catching— it had just rained.

I smiled. "I don't know, it's hard to put into words. Maybe, it reminds me, important things take time. That I can learn more from the longer process." Today life feels like the fire, working to reach critical mass, it's almost there. Life is really good. The reality I've worked to create around myself is one I love. It wasn't always this way. Eleven years ago hope became a dot on the horizon when I found out I had a mental illness. Life became very difficult.

I don't know how to tell you exactly how I found hope. It didn't come from an orange plastic cylinder, or in the pages of a book. It couldn't be measured with an assessment, but hope might just be the greatest indicator of my recovery. Igniting hope looked impossible, like trying to light a fire in a rainstorm, deep in the forest, with only one match. It started with a dream. "Maybe I could." Took careful preparation with friends and family. Letting go of fear, embarrassment, what other people would think when I failed. Knowing where to find it and store my dwindling energy. The first spark wasn't going to come from a degree, book, doctor, or gas can. I searched deep within myself to know when to strike my one match.

When the time came I smiled and intently watch it warm the carefully prepared tender. Smoke appeared and an orange glow grew brighter. Blowing my breath, my remaining life force into to. The peach branches started to smoke. Flickering against the wind, weather, and my fear. I marveled watching it grow. Knowing when to add larger pieces of wood and knowing when to let it burn until the fire grew large enough to warm myself. I learned to manage it, tend it, and share it. It is knowledge that could only come from lived experience.

Over the past eleven years I learned that I'm just one of many with mental illness.
We are all figuring out how to define recovery. Success doesn't mean becoming an eccentric artist, CEO, and Pop Icon rolled into one. Failure doesn't have to mean becoming a statistic in a freshman psych book. I get to be the person I am today, each day— as messy and glorious as it is. I am sharing my story, my lived experience, to honor those who shared their flame with me when recovery appeared impossible. Maybe, if my story is open and vulnerable enough it will help open a space in you to consider your attitude and beliefs towards all people. Perhaps it will help reduce internal stigmas and negative belief structures that we hold towards ourselves. It is your journey. Thank you for taking time to read my story.

I Was Normal, Until I Wasn't.

At 18 years old, my dad and I drove from the Central Valley to the edge of the Pacific Ocean. To my dorm room at UC Santa Barbara. We unpacked my gear hugged and said goodbyes. I was an average student, drank to decrease my insecurities, earned average grades, studied business economics, had a few friends and tried to figure out what to do with my life.

At 19 years old, a switch flipped about a week before I

left for my second year of college. I drove my car, stuffed
with my worldly possessions over the Grapevine.
Smoking a cigar and listening to a burned Bob Dylan mix-CD
as the sun set.
I rolled into the housing co-op and it was game on.

I ate very little. Soon 3 days had passed with no sleep.
My mind became more outgoing, creative, and alive than
anything I can describe. I watched as my friends' faces
shifted from excitement to wonder, concern and fear. Then I
drove 100 miles an hour to my Aunt & Uncles, south towards
Montecito. With a head filled with ideas and a trunk full of
relics of my journey to prove the incredible adventure I'd just
begun. I was going to be a millionaire with these ideas.

For an hour or so, my Uncle and I talked business. I
shared ideas with him at lighting speed. He took me on a
walk and then stopped. "David, before we go any further I
got to ask you, have you taken anything, drugs?" He said.

"No, I don't know why I feel so different." I replied.

"Could someone have some dosed you?" He asked.

"No, I don't think so, I just know what happening is
pretty amazing."

Later that night I tried to sleep in their guest bed. The
businesses that we had talked about had become real. All of
the people I knew were helping me to design, build, and ship
homes. We had designed them out of cargo containers and
were shipping around the world.

Save the world, give people cheap housing. I thought.
By 1 a.m. my Aunt, Uncle and I sat in a hospital waiting
room, with a 24 hour news cycle flashing images. I was
scared my project was going to be on the TV. As I lay on a
table in a quiet room. A nurse asked me to take a pill to help
me relax.

Then a woman sat in the corner and quietly asked,
"Where are you?, Who are the people who brought you
here?" and "What year is it?" I knew the answers and was

oriented, sort of. She gently said, "Your drug test came back negative."

"I know." I softly replied.

"Have your ever heard of Bipolar Disorder?"

"Once in a high school psych class."

"We think that is why you've been noticing so many changes." She said in a comforting tone. The gravity of that moment was lost on me.

The next thing I remember my Dad was standing in my Aunt and Uncle's living room. He drove me to the campus psychiatrist, who talked with both of us separately. She confirmed the bipolar diagnosis with both of us in the room. I had to withdraw from school and stand in lines at five different offices to do so. All the while popping pill after pill from sample packages the Doctor gave us. We packed up my room, broke my housing contact, and paid my rent. Then we drove past the rows of apartments and frat houses toward home.

Soon the sun dipped below the mountains and every oncoming car light had trails. They formed a circuit that snaked across the visible spectrum over the horizon. My Dad drove us in his white Ag truck over the grapevine. "How long till we get home?" I asked.

"Not long." He replied. Looking at the review mirror, I was overwhelmed with a deep sadness.

When we reached home, the valley heat almost knocked me over. The next few days were filled with my dad worked to find answers and treatment. He was an adept pathfinder through the tangle of systems we navigated.

Eventually I lay on a gurney in the middle of the ER, watching utter chaos. A girl I recognized from high school was shadowing a nurse. A woman died a curtain over from my bed. Moments later an old woman rolled by tied to a bed screaming about George Bush stealing her SSI. All the while a young security guard stood close— but not too close— to my gurney.

Then a man came over wearing a sweater and said, "You're going to be okay."

"I don't know, this is a pretty scary place." I replied.

"You're lucky, that woman over there is just garden variety crazy." Motioning to the woman yelling about SSI. "There isn't much we can do for her. We can fix you and you can get back to normal." I didn't realize I was broken, or knew what he meant by garden variety crazy.

A couple of days later I agreed to be admitted to the local Mental Hospital. Here I began to realize the difficult world I had entered. Within minutes I was loaded with cocktails of medications and began drawing voraciously. Over the next weeks my mind retreated to the agreed upon reality. That is the one that the normal's believe.

But normal wasn't what I felt anymore. The social worker had been half right. One week ago I'd been in a state of bliss, joy, expansive creativity, free of earthbound limits. A place most people have to take mind-altering substances just to catch a glimpse of. At UCSB I had an identity, even though I was surfing the surreally thin veil of reality. Now I was being pulverized, in every direction. Disoriented, I didn't know which direction to get air.

Now I slept in my childhood bedroom and took anti-psychotics with my 17 year-old brother, stepmom, and Dad taking shifts looking after me. I was labeled mentally ill, Bipolar I, with a recent psychotic episode. The level of internal stigma I felt marked me in a way I can't convey.

A month or two later, I looked in the mirror and saw a refection I no longer recognized. It's something you can only feel: every time someone used the word crazy it ground into my heart. Returning to UC Santa Barbara was quickly becoming another delusion. I felt that if I was lucky I'd live in my dad's house on SSI for the rest my life.

My vision was blurred; my hands and face trembled

from the Lithium. It was difficult to leave the couch, impossible to summon the energy to shower. I vomited so much that I had to keep a large blue cup in my car. I couldn't recognize my body in the mirror— I'd aged 10 years in 6 months. The meds were taking a heavy toll.

I was told to take the drugs or I'd end up hospitalized again. A powerful motivator to swallow the ever-increasing cocktail of drugs, regardless of the increasingly damaging side-effects. Fear works, for a while.

When I summoned the courage to ask the doctor what we could do about the he said, "I can give you more medication to decrease the side-effects." I felt like a test tube gone rotten.

One morning after vomiting yellow bile for the fifth time in four days, as I drove to a basic English class I was barely passing at the community college, I broke, for the first time since my mind had ran off the rails. I cracked, tears streamed down my face, as I pulled to the side of the road.

This is for the rest of my life. Bipolar Disorder doesn't go away. What if this is the best I got? I've done what they told me for six months, I feel worse than I've ever felt. I have 2 friends in a town I spent 18 years of my life in. Two week-long stays is the mental hospital have marked me as certifiable. My friends will graduate from UCSB in 2 years I'm getting C's at the JC. What happened?

What has this disorder and these drugs done to me?

I'm afraid, anxious, and depressed. My face twitches and my body shakes, adding to my self-consciousness. My vision blurred after reading 2 pages. I'm total unemployable and struggling in classes that should have been easy. Everywhere I go, I run into people I used to know.

When I returned home, my Dad hugged me. He gently reminded me of how far I'd come in six months. He held that glimmer of hope that things could get better.

What was most difficult during this period was how rapidly I went from being "normal" to "ill." In a matter of weeks my entire world shattered. People I'd known a year ago would run into me and barely recognize me.

Generally they would ask me two questions, "How are you?" and "What are you doing?"

I would replied "I fine how are you," but I knew that my twitching face showed the true answer: I feel awful, worse than I've ever felt. I'm mentally ill. I live at home and am trying to go to the community college.

Sometimes they would get up the courage to ask, "Are you okay, what happened?"

I would a repeat my stock footage lie. I mumble something about not liking UCSB. As my face trembled, my eyes tear up, and my hands shook. They tried to politely ignore it. I knew the real answers are covering my face like my Lamictal induced zits. I might say. "Yeah, it's been a rough few months."

The truth felt too horrible to discuss, most people couldn't handle the truth and I was certainly in no place to handle their responses. I knew that by describing the reality of a mental hospital, I would alienate myself and shatter their worldview. I didn't believe they had enough empathy, experience, or that they had been hit by enough failure and trauma to hear my story. I was afraid of what they would think, who they would tell, and they would say. I didn't have the strength yet to risk it, or to listen to their response.

Art Saves

Late one night I found oil paints and a blank canvas in my Dad's garage. I started painting, like I had channeled the Masters. The brushes turned tubes of paint into a heart fused with a white lightning bolt. I didn't know it but this was the beginning of my recovery: it was not a hobby, it was something I was driven to do.   After a month of painting, I told my mom about it. She had driven me to countless art lessons as a child. "Have you thought about showing your old art teacher?" she asked.

"I haven't seen her since middle school."

"She still has a studio, I can find her number"

"Okay," I said hesitantly.

During this time I was terrified of seeing anyone except my family and two compassionate friends, I'd known since preschool. I kept painting and about a month later, I summoned the courage to make the call.

She answered the phone. "I'd been hoping you would call."

My voice shook. "Can I come to the studio and show you some paintings?"

"I would love that." I ended the phone call and my face was twitching so hard my teeth were chattering.

Four days later I walk into her narrow studio, children's murals covered the wall and floor; artwork was stuffed in every corner. There was a line of drafting desks along one wall and a hint of turpentine and drying acrylic polymer wafted through the air. A portable AC hummed behind music playing from 1968. That studio became a home outside of home.

There I created art, worked with students, and was reminded of two incredibly important lessons she had taught me a long time ago:

1. There is no "I can't" in my studio. There is: I'm not ready, that looks hard, don't know how, I am scared, can I have help.

2. If you know one more thing than some else you can teach them, just make sure you help show them what they did

right.

In her studio I felt a little more normal. Over time the medication and depression started to level out. I gained about 70 pounds, shaved my goatee, got a haircut and showered most days. As the fog broke up pain my increased. I realized how far I had to go, how much I had lost. But I also could see how far I had come.

Now I had an answer to the question, "What are you doing?"

"I paint and make art. I'm a college student." I might tell them "I have bipolar disorder." If I feel it safe enough.

After about six months of consistent paint my Art teacher and another man with lived experience with mental illness encouraged me to enter my first art show at a local gallery. Winning 3rd and 4th place against seasoned artists built my confidence.

3 months later a friend and fellow traveler encouraged me to enroll in a ceramics class and other art classes at the JC. The ceramics professor was incredible. I learned I could do it, and he help build my skill and confidence as a student.

The professor taught me many important things, including: if you feel blocked - "Start anything." and "You can make it in the community college as an artist." But most importantly he would say "Keep filling your basket. Keep learning."

Art gave me:

Hope.

A place to be.

The ability to see that continuous hard work produces positive results.

A forgiving place and recognition that I couldn't make a mistake.

An opportunity for something I created to be valued,

even if only by me.

A physical finished product at the end of the day.

Finding those oil paints and painting probably cut years of pain, trauma and searching out of my recovery. I don't know where I would be without them.

Recovery in Vocation

A few weeks after my first art show I drove north and then east. Eventually, I turned off the highway down a road full of well-worn memories.

Two months earlier I had asked my camp director at a coffee shop, "Can I volunteer for the summer?" She had known me since I was a camper in second grade. I'd been on staff for two summers. She knew pieces of my story and about my new diagnosis. We both knew I was in no condition to work. She me gave the opportunity to volunteer. I had dared to hope that I would be hirable before the end of the summer.

As I coasted down the road on the edge of Giant Sequoias Trees glimmers of light reflected off of the lake. I hit a familiar curve. Both terrified and elated, my face twitched with fear and excitement; this place was a second home.

I had changed and I knew every summer was different as I nervously drove behind the dining hall. Staff training was already in session. My heart was rapidly beating in my throat. At a back door of the dining hall I could hear staff going over lost camper protocol.

A friend greeted me with a giant hug. She looked into me, "Something's different."

"It's been a hard year, I'll tell you about it soon." I said softly.

I went through the week of staff training, and shared my story with a few people. It was clear I was different and that my skills had drastically decreased from the previous summer. It felt so good to back, even if even making basic conversation was difficult.

The kids rolled in for their first week of camp. I was assigned to a cabin as a volunteer I role I had at 16 years old. It felt like a huge demotion not being a counselor.

I helped with a few special projects and taught kids to use boats at the waterfront. At the end that week, I felt up to the task of being a counselor. In an act of courage, I walked into the director's office. She could see the question on my face
I felt her answer before I asked it.

"David, you're not ready." She said compassionately. I disagreed with her and then collapsed in the chair in her office. She was probably right, but I couldn't accept it.

I held it together as I walked out of her office, but tears began streamed down my eyes as I slipped back to my cabin. Lying on the bed, I and cried till my pillow was soaked. It would be easier to go home. Maybe I'm not ready, I shouldn't be here. I looked through an open window at the lake I had spent parts of 14 summers.

If I can't make it here, I can't make it anywhere. Don't let Bipolar Disorder make you lose this place too. You've lost enough. Here is where I learn to figure this out.

I headed out of my cabin, and my grief turned to anger. A friend intercepted me and we took a walk on a little-used fire road above the camp. He said, "Do you want to try co-counseling? You talk for half the trip, and I listen. Then we switch."

He listened to me, and said almost nothing. With him as a witness I convinced myself to stay. I was welcome here, even if it didn't always feel that way. I could handle it, and there was a possibility of becoming staff, but not yet.

On the way back he talked and I listened to what was going on for him, it helped me feel valued and put us on equal footing.

Four weeks later the director said after the end of campfire. "You're ready for a cabin, I know those kids are going to have an incredible week."

I smiled: "Thank you, that means a lot."

I gave it my all for that week, leaving nothing on the table. They put the cook's 14-year-old child in my cabin, both as a support and because most counselors weren't able to connect with him. He told me years later how grateful he was for that week.

So was I. That cabin had an incredible week.

That summer marked an important turning point for me. I realized that no matter how hard things could get, there was a chance for my reality and skill set to rapidly change.

In six weeks I went from thinking I would never be employable to having a temporary job. I was not back to my former self, but I was on my way, and even thought I wasn't a perfect counselor, I had important things to offer.

It was also the first time I disclosed to most of the people around me that I had Bipolar disorder. It was the first time people I worked with knew my diagnosis. Through that I learned that many people had experience with the outside of reality. They may have had them through mental health, spiritual exploration or mind-altering substances. I also began learning my experiences were my own.

The next summer the friend who co-counseled me down the fire road and I were rowing a boat in the middle of the lake in the pre-season. He looked and me and said, "You know, they're going to ask you to be a lead counselor."

I smiled and replied, "You know, they're going to ask you to be program director." We talked while we rowed around the lake for over an hour. The director gave us both a big hug when we agreed to do it.

Porter College, Visual Art, and Banana Slugs
College, on my own – sort of.

Three years after I was diagnosed I had finished the
course work at the junior college and had been accepted into
UC Santa Cruz. My Dad and I drove to UCSC. On Campus
we were greeted by a redwood forest and views of the
Monterey Bay. Together we moved a truck full of gear up
five flights of stairs into my dorm room. Porter College - B5
South was my new address.

It was the transfer hall and I could see the Pacific
Ocean from my window. I was not an 18 year-old kid
anymore, but I had bipolar disorder. My stated major was
History. But, I had decided I was going to crash the art
department by portfolio review.

The first day I crashed a painting class and began
working hard. We had 24 hour access to the studio and I
practically lived there. Every time I was there when no other
student was, I imagined getting closer to passing the portfolio
review. I was not the most talented person in the class, but I
knew I could out-work them. They slept, partied, and showed
up late to class, while I painted as much as possible. I didn't
wait for inspiration, I just kept showing up. Kept Painting.

B5 South was an interesting assortment of people, like
most dorms halls. There were three girls from England. Two
Iraq war vets, a male porn actor. A refugee from hurricane
Katrina. We had fun and since most of us were 21 we could
drink in our dorms. We hid our friends who were not of age
in closets or under beds when Campus security knocked on
the door. It usually worked.

At UCSC it was the first time my health care was
totally my responsibility. I scheduled my appointment at the
campus health center, filled my prescription, and saw my
therapist. I was learned to manage my illness on my own.   I
also began to realize that the side effects had lessened, but my
mind was still fuzzy.

I was still gaining weight and I didn't know what to do. I wanted to be in control. I had begun to believe I had beaten Bipolar Disorder.

I also had several psychiatrist changes during this time. I began to lower my dosages of medication, and as the side effects decreased my quality of life increased. I become more reckless. I thought I could use my brain, education, and sheer will to manage this genetic variant. It became my belief that I could learn to handle this disorder with no medication. I just needed the right circumstance, training and enough time.

The time was coming, but not yet. I saw two options. Meds: a life with side effect, weight gain, and poor performance. No Meds: a difficult life built on peak performance, where my mind was unchained. Where I could become a successful artist and have my dreams come true. I was glossing over the fact that many historic figures lived incredibly tragic lives, often ending in suicide.

Even so these two unhealthy models persisted for many years. I was determined to be a superhero, not indigent and could see no middle path.

I hid my true medication regiment from my doctors and family for many years. The rates I had been prescribed had crippling side effects and early on I had learned not to ask for them to be lowered. During the summer of my last years at UC Santa Cruz, I put the plan into action.

At the end of the summer at camp I found an email from VSA Arts a national group that works with artists with disabilities. I opened it. It read "Your artwork has been chosen to be featured in the Smithsonian." Six months earlier I had applied for a show for emerging artists with disabilities.

I had 1 week to ship my artwork to Washington D.C. I took a deep breath and then got lost in the delusion of fame.

In August of the beginning of my final year of college, I begin noticing I was elevated. It's happening, I'm going to be a famous artist, this is incredible. Are you ready? – I don't know but I guess it time.

In September I sat on the edge of reality, on a bench overlooking the Monterey Bay. I noticed a few beautiful trees had been cut down. A building they were constructing would soon block this million-dollar view.

I hoped to make my last year at UC Santa Cruz, a good one. In 10 weeks you will be at the Smithsonian with your artwork hanging on the wall. Are you ready for this? Fame is coming.

Jailing the Spirit

A week later, in the middle of my second year of Resident Assistant training, I called my Dad, "Dad, it's bad."

"I'm coming, stay in your room." He said urgently.

Five hours later I was in the Doctor's office He was British and had gone to Oxford and Yale. I've got his number, does he have mine. We talk for about 20 minutes.

Then he talks with my dad alone. Minutes later he brings up back into the room and I asked the doctor "if I needed to be hospitalized, could it at least be voluntary. "

Then the doctor leaves and two police open the door. They let me know they will be transporting me to the hospital. We calmly and quickly walk through the campus health center, past students waiting for Adderall, VD tests, and birth control.

When we get to the patrol car, the officer says, "I have to handcuff you."

I turned around, he cuffs me and puts me in back seat. I looked out of the grated window of the patrol car with my arms behind my back at a grove of coastal redwoods and felt something I hope to never feel again.

I'm not a criminal, I have a mental illness, a health issue like diabetes, right? Except at that moment the difference was pretty imperceptible. I was now officially in the mental health/legal system with my first 5150, an involuntary confinement. I realize that I just became a marked citizen. Mental healthcare came in the form of handcuffs, backed up with a gun and taser.

I walk into the hospital, the handcuffs are taken off. I'm hungry, terrified, and minutes are feeling like hours. The staff projected strength and I match their energy.

"Can I have art supplies?" I asked

"No."

"How about a dry erase marker to draw on the white board?" I plead.

"No."

"No crayons or markers?"

"No, we go through gallons of paint with graffiti."

"I'm not going to paint your walls. I'm an art major I have art work in the Smithsonian. I'm going to Washington D.C. "

"Yeah, well you still can't have paint or markers. "

I realize the more I talk the more they will think I'm crazy. It does sound too fantastic to believe. "I'm hungry. Can I have some food or water?"

"We'll work on it," they say as they leave me at a table.

I wander the hospital, orienting myself to the common areas. The walls feel very old. Cameras from the 1970's are hanging in every corner. It begins to feel like a set. A man is watching the static between the TV channels. He speaks rapidly to no one in particular. He turns his head and stares intently at me.

"Come with me," he said in a clear, firm voice.

I hesitated. His voice and eyes softened. "Okay," I replied.

He takes me to his room; his walls are covered with drawings, and magazine images. He has individual packet crackers, cups of peanut butter, a juice packet. He offers them freely and we talk. Who is this man? I can't even get a cup of water. I wonder. He has a room full of food, art supplies, newspapers.

Soon the staff tries to give me pills. I ask them what they are giving me. The tell me to take it. I refuse and at that moment my tenuous grasp on reality disappeared.

I was surrounded and drug to a small room. This cycle repeated for four days.

On day five in the hospital I wake up with all four limbs tied to a bed. The man who greeted me at the door and was sitting on a chair.

"David, do you want to go back to school."

"Yes, more than anything, I need to get out by Friday." I said.

"That's three days from now. If you want to get out you have to follow the rules."

"What are they? I just keep getting surrounded and attacked by your staff."

He told me the rules: take your medicine; go to your room if we tell you to; if you resist going to solitary, we will put you in four-point. That was the last time I was put in four-point or solitary. That extra bit of care made the difference.

On Friday I was released. My mom picked me up. She was coming to visit, and was surprised they were going to release me. We went out for lunch and then to UC Santa Cruz.

At that moment I had no classes, no keys to my room or car, no ID, no job. I appeared at the Porter housing office and talked to my supervisor. She gave me a hug, a temporary ID and keys to my room. I emailed two professors in the Art Department then saw the psychiatrist. He cleared me to be back on campus. If one of these people had hesitated even for a day, I would have had to leave.

The real moment, the final hurdle, was the counseling office. Would they let me re-enroll? My Dad had made the right move by filling out the withdrawal paperwork a week earlier. Could I get them to overlook it?

At the counselor's office, I was pulled into a back office quickly. A counselor pulled out my file and was aware I'd been hospitalized.

"I've been cleared by the health center to reenroll, is it possible?"

"David, you were withdrawn from school."

"I know, I'd like to re-enroll."

The counselor looked me in the eyes. "How are you going to do this? It is a week into the quarter, and you have been dropped from all your classes."

I noticed a glimmer of hope in her eyes. I smiled. "I'm an art major. I was a T.A. for two professors, both of whom I've already emailed. A month from now I will have artwork in the Smithsonian. I will take 12 unites of classes from them, and pick up a PE class."

"You sure you can do this?"

"Yes, I know I can."

"Okay, I going to make this paper disappear."

As I was about to leave, she said, "You've got a lot of people who love you."

"Thanks, I know." I walked out of the office, hugged my mom and told her "I'm back in school. I just need classes."

She looked at me, astonished. "I don't know how you did that."

"Every person in those each of those offices knew me. Before I was hospitalized." The hospitalization in Santa Cruz was the most difficult, not because it was the hardest, but it was the first time I realized my mental illness made me a marked man in a legal system.

Learning that I live in a county where asking for medical care in my doctor's office meant a forced hospitalization, handcuffs, armed police, and the threat of force for non-compliance, is shattering to one's spirit. I held against my will for what I could have done, not any of my actions.

My perception of the mental hospital changed that trip. From a place where I went to get better. To a place where you are help against your will, drugged without informed consent and release as fast as possible. At several points I believe the staff used solitary confinement and restraints as the first course of action, not the last. There was little discussion, no therapy, privacy or humanity. The institution was adept at getting me back on the street, in a drug coma with a week's supply of medication. But it came at a great cost. There was no consideration made for the systemic trauma, dehumanization, and damage that it caused me, my support network and I am sure others with mental illness.

I still have moments when I remember how it felt to be in restraints, or locked in a room with no stimulus for what felt like an eternity. This pain was buffeted by and incredibly supportive College, especially the residential life staff. Within six weeks I had my job back as an R.A. My grades were in order and I was back on course to graduate on time.

I had been protected and ushered through the UC system by an incredible group of professors, academic counselors, mental health professionals, and residential life staff. I also had a few really close friends who sat up talking with me many nights. We took walks at Natural Bridges State Beach and in the redwood forest of the campus. I am grateful for that time.

VSA Arts, Washington DC, Patrick Kennedy and the Smithsonian

Seven weeks later my car was packed and parked under redwood trees. I walked to the art department, breathing in the fresh air, looking at the Pacific Ocean. I was not going to paint or attend the class, I was going to thank two professors. One who opened a space for me to paint, teach, and learn when to finish a painting. The other taught me to dream and put the pen to paper.

I gave Jennie a hug, saying, "Thank you. I couldn't have done this without you."

She smiled, "David I don't think much could have stopped you. In my career I never seen anyone come back from a crisis as fast as you did, no one. "

"Really?"

"No, not even close. Enjoy yourself!"

Then I walked to Frank's studio. He was finishing a lecture to twenty students and I sat on the floor and listened. We walked out and sat on the top of the picnic table. We had convened there for the previous seven weeks. He had advised me on my independent research project on non-profit art organization in Santa Cruz and the Central Valley, but today was not about work.

"So you're driving home, and then flying to Washington D.C."

"I'm leaving after we talk, car is already packed."

"David, enjoy this. Someday this will just be a line on a distinguished resume."

"Thank you Frank, I took your advice, bought a tie."

"Good, take a good look around see how Washington feels. In ten years you'll be 34, maybe America will be tired of lawyers by then."

I smiled. "You never know what ten years will bring. Thank you for all your help,

I don't know…" I started to say.

"David, it was you, you pulled this off. We just provided a space and a little structure. Don't ever forget that." He said jovially and slapped my shoulder.

I drove home, spent the night at my Dad's house, and had lunch with my Mom. We were all aware that this trip was going to be like throwing gasoline on my mania.

The next day we flew to Washington D.C., my art teacher, her grandson, and myself. I was closer to reality than I had been in months, but not quite on the ground. I knew this trip was going to be an extreme test. I was hoping that I could hold it together. We landed, took a taxi to the hotel, and dropped our bags off.

Then we found the Smithsonian's Dylan Ripley Center, a copper domed building. I smiled when I saw our show announcement poster in a large glass case. We took an elevator underground and walked to the exhibit. As I walked into the space that had the reverence of a cathedral. I was speechless. I slowly walked up to my painting hanging on the Museum wall. I breathed in and smiled,

"This is a minor miracle, I didn't think I would get to see this," I whispered as I touched my painting and suppress a hospital flashback. Then I smile, "it's okay."

I looked over at the museum guard and smiled as I touched my canvas on the wall of the Smithsonian. He started to walk up and then realized that my picture is on the bio next to the painting.

He smiled, "Go right ahead."

8 weeks ago, this sounded delusional to the orderly— I couldn't even have a crayon. Now I am here at the Smithsonian. I'd hit the pinnacle of the art world and was hit with a rush of endorphins. Breathe. I said to myself

The next evening we all gathered in the hotel lobby— fifteen artists, our VSA Arts state chaperons and caregivers, families, and friends. My mom, grandmother, art teacher, her grandson, a girl I'd known in grade school, and a chaperon from Marin county were all there.

We all rode on in bus to the building on Capitol Hill for the reception. I had a tic-tac container with 5 Ativans in my pocket in case things got too hard. For two hours I talked with people from all over the country: artists, arts organizers, politicians' aides. My local congressman sent two interns to talk with me and take pictures. It was an enjoyable evening.

I could tell I was beginning to spin. I was right on the edge of reality. Then Patrick Kennedy came into the room to give a speech. I noticed his hands were slightly shaking. He can't be nervous, I thought. He is trained to do this.

Then he discussed mental health parity, the law they had been working on and the importance of health care and art. Then In a moment I will never forget, he said, "It is our job as politicians to level the laws of the land for people with disabilities, it's your job to as artists with disabilities to go out and change peoples' attitudes."

I was almost in tears. At end of the speech people rushed him. I snuck up and realized that I had a giant sequoia pinecone in my pocket. I wanted to give it to him. It was odd, but I felt that it was important. I nodded to the director of VSA Arts. She smiled and nodded back as she guided Patrick around the room.

Eventually, she got to me. Visions of speaking before Congress flashed before me. I thanked him, handed him the tiny pinecone from the largest tree in the world, thanked him again, and told him I had bipolar disorder. He smiled, "So do I."

I was overwhelmed. Eventually I walked out to a balcony overlooking the Capitol, breathed, and used the pills in my tic-tac container. The girl from grade school came out and talked with me for a few moments. We went inside and then got on our buses.

At that time Patrick Kennedy was not as public about his mental health conditions as he is today. He helped me realize that I too could achieve great things. He helped me realize that as an artist I needed to someday share my story. It took years of experience, but slowly I learned to let go of the secrecy, fear and stigma that I'd been holding toward myself.

Graduation, Going Home

The next spring, two months before graduation, I'm was talking to the president of a local art organization. For months I'd been writing ideas down about how to bring art to my hometown. Dreaming of creating an arts non-profit. He was talking about leaving the board, and dissolving the non-profit. They had about a year's worth of operating expenses in the bank. "Why don't you hire a Director, see what they can do." I said offhand.

"Do you want to do it?"

"Hmm. Yeah, I think I would." I smiled, thinking to myself, "You might have just gotten yourself an arts job."

"We have to interview people, and figure out salary parameters."

"Talk with the board, and see what you can pull together. I can drive in for an interview most weekends. I graduate in June." Just like that, an unexpected phone call and I had the beginning of my dream job. Be careful what you wish for.

Two months later I stood in the quad of Porter College, on a cool misty June morning in a cap and gown. A slam poet was giving student address as tears slowly fell down my face. Them he launched into an incredible 5 minute poem.

Minutes later I was shaking hands, and walking across the stage. I hugged the woman who said yes, the woman who gave me the keys to my apartment and the chance go get my life back. To graduate on-time. We both cried tears of triumphant joy.

"Thank you" I said.

"You're welcome." And that was it: I'd graduated from UC Santa Cruz with a B.A. in Fine Art and a B.A. in History.

It took six years:

1 year at UC Santa Barbara.

2 years at Community College.

3 years at UC Santa Cruz.

3 hospitalizations, 4 majors, 2 Teaching Assistant positions, 2 years as an   Resident Advisor, and trip to the Smithsonian.

I was both elated and terrified about moving to my hometown. To add my energy to the small burgeoning Art scene.

Developing an Art Community and Letting Go

I drove home with a car stuffed with paintings and clothes. My Dad had picked up most of my gear when he had come for graduation a week prior. I had a house and more space than I knew what to do with. I spent the month setting up my studio, reconnecting, hanging out with friends I hadn't see much in years. As I planed the next move with the Art group.

The first board meeting was in early July. On the patio of the local microbrewery, four of seven board members were present. Accounting records were literally written from memory on the back of an envelope. The meeting lasted three hours. At the end of I was given boxes of ten year-old files stuffed in no particular order. At 24 years old I was an Executive Director of a non-profit that had just considered dissolving a month ago. I had no idea what I was in for.

Over the next two years, I learned an incredible amount. Directing an arts organization with no budget, no programs, and small board was a consistent struggle between old and new, between stagnation and growth. We put on events with incredibly small budgets, I called in favors and used many personal connections to pull them off.

In the first six months we created and Arts Street Fair with the Farmers' Market. We had about fourteen artists' booths and children's activities from four local non-profits.

By the second year we almost doubled the number of booths. People realize we existed and we were building momentum.

We did a collaborative public arts project with my art teacher and his Senior Studio class from UC Santa Cruz. They painted almost twenty banners that were 2 x 5 feet tall. We hung them in Downtown Visalia. Most importantly, we instituted proper accounting methods. We fixed longstanding IRS non-profit issues and wrote and received grants that brought money for the arts into the community.

Doing all of this in two years on a part-time position came at a high cost. We encountered a lot of adversity both internally and externally with other arts non-profits. My physical health also suffered. I gained weight. My diet consisted of coffee, fast food, and frozen dinners. My mental health was consistent, but the level of stress, anxiety, and frustration was rapidly increasing.

In order to get health insurance I picked up a second job working at a day program for adults with developmental disorders. It was 30 hours a week, on top of the 20-35 for the non-profit.

After about two years of working two jobs. I went on my first real vacation in two years – a few days after Christmas with my girlfriend. I'd been using my vacations days at the program to do events as the Director. Waking with the sun one morning in Monterey, while my girlfriend slept. I thought about the decision I'd been afraid to consider.

This isn't sustainable.

Is it time to let this dream go?

I'm tired of struggling and fighting to make the non-profit work.

There is no future in this struggle.

I had not touched a paintbrush in six months.

I was beginning to show signs of fatigue and poor physical health.

How long will my mental health hold at this rate?

I'd like to marry this woman lying next to me someday soon.

I've got to switch careers.

Three weeks later I sat down with my board president, fellow artist, and friend. We sat and drank beer at the same place this adventure began. "It's time for us to work to find my replacement." I told him.

"David, you gave it all you had, you did a good job."

"I feel really bad."

"The only thing I see is you did this in the wrong order. Most people take on a project like this in there 40's 50's or later." He said.

"Yeah, what was I thinking, 24 year old executive director."

"You were excited, and you did a lot of good. You also didn't know enough to evaluate what you were getting into, now you know a little more."

"Yes, thank you for joining me on the project."

This was a case where my experience and ability to push myself beyond the limits of what was healthy was double-edged. I was only able to accomplish what I did through the belief that I could. Most people would have looked at it and said it was impossible. They may have been right, but for two years our group had showed the community and the other arts groups what could be possible even with no budget, few resources, and a divided board.

It was a difficult experiences watching the remaining board and another Arts group I had worked closely with publically fight for scraps of funding we had worked so hard to bring to the community. After I left, things reverted back to the way they were before I started, and the organization faded away.

Heal Thyself: A Change in Course

I took a mental health day from work after making the decision to leave the council. Sitting at Starbucks with a book and my journal, I was totally exhausted. Two years of working 60 plus hour weeks at two stressful jobs had taken its toll. I had gained weight from too much fast food and no exercising and knew I'd maxed out my pay in the non-profit art world of my Ag town. I loved Art, but as my therapist helped me realize, I hadn't painted in months.

The jobs helped me scrape together an existence, but I would never thrive. As I wrote my mind on the page and considered the future. Someday I knew I wanted to marry my girlfriend. I'm not even painting, I need a change my career.

What's the common denominator in my jobs? I listen intently. I work well with people under stress, and have empathy for others. Could I meld art and therapy? Could they be separate? I wondered.

I'd been thinking about becoming a therapist from time to time, many people had told me I'd be good at it. I had been writing my story, waiting for the time when I would want to get it into a publishable format. A piece of me wanted to create training, ideas, and books that would help people with bipolar disorder. Do my part to shift the paradigm.

The next morning I drove to work deep in thought. I sat in the ceramics studio next to a woman who worked at day program for almost thirty years. She was burnt out, and retirement appeared far on the horizon. She turned to me unexpectedly, "Have you ever thought about going back to school?"

I smiled, "Yeah I've been it debating for a while, but I don't really want a Masters of Fine Arts."

"Ever think about becoming a therapist? I think you would be really good at it."

I almost started laughing. "Yeah, I spent all of

yesterday thinking about that!"

About forty days later, I was sitting in my first class at a for-profit college course. It was no UC Santa Cruz. I didn't have the desire to relocate for a public education. Most of my classmates were already in the mental health field. For four hours every Monday night from 6-10 for almost three years I took classes.

For seven months I worked the two jobs, went to school and ran on coffee and fast food. The UC had been a series of Olympic sprints, this program was an exercise in endurance.

Twenty-four months into the program, we were searching for trainee sites.

I had a singular goal an internship at the Community College Health Center I'd attended years ago. It was the closest thing to private practice I could get.

I'd put all my eggs in one basket. I applied a few places but had not actively cultivated multiple options. My friend and classmate was applying for the same position. I was terrified only one of us would get it. Luckily we were both chosen. It was nice having a friend and fellow student in the office next to me. I also had a supportive clinical supervisor.

About six weeks into work at the campus health center during my hour-long supervision, we started discussing our understanding of psychotropic medication and our feelings about its use. I realized that my level of understanding was higher than she expected, I'd been considering disclosing my mental health condition to her for weeks and it felt right.

"You know, the reason why I'm so aware of this is that I've taken many of these medications. I've been thinking about telling you this for some time. I was diagnosed with bipolar disorder about 9 years ago."

"I never would have known that."

"I know. I thought it was relevant to this conversation. I'm not totally open about it, but I don't hide it either."

"It is good to know, I'm glad you felt comfortable telling me."

"Do you think it is a problem? Do you have any concerns about it?"

She smiled, "You know, if you had told me the first day I would've been concerned, but after I've seen how you handle your position and your disclosure, I'm not concerned at all." It was in that vulnerability that a great semester of mentorship began.

Nine months later I was graduating from the for-profit college. I was entering an uncertain future. I was unemployed and had sent my application packet to four therapists who I thought might be interested in taking on interns. My goal was to work in private practice. Nothing less. I had six months before I would have student loan payments equal to two thirds my rent.

Three weeks later I was driving and picked up a phone call from a random number. It was one of the therapists in private practice. I pulled my car over and began talking with the woman who would later hire me in her private practice. Three months later I was seeing my first client in as a Marriage & Family Therapist Registered Intern.

Today

The girl I was dating is now my wife. We get each other. She is a school teacher, an incredible partner and friend who has seen me at my best as well as my most difficult moments. We love each other deeply.

Two years ago the idea of telling people my story was terrifying. I was asked to create trainings on storytelling for a Speakers Bureau in my hometown. As part of that training I shared my story.

Six years ago public speaking was impossible. I would shake uncontrollably. My face would tremble and my words would become jumbled. At my Master Program we had to give a lot of presentations. It helped me tremendously. Now I share my story in the community from time to time as part of the No Stigma Speakers Bureau. It helped launch me into the work I am doing for the Center for Dignity, Recover, and Empowerment, which I am grateful for. I created trainings to help support Speaker Bureaus and train people with mental illness to share their stories. We helped them weight the decision of sharing their experiences thru the Coming Out Proud Program which I help coordinator in Central California.

I feel incredibly lucky to be living my vision I had almost 5 years ago. I work to reduce stigma by sharing my story and helping empower others. I also see clients in a private practice as an MFT Intern.

I still get to experience moments of extreme creativity and performance. I paint, garden, and have started working in wood. Painting reminds me to dream expansively. Gardening helps me see that things worth doing need steady, consistent attention. Woodworking is teaching me that there are times when planning, measuring, and the right amount of tolerance are critical. My physical health is the best it has been since I was diagnosis. My wife and I have learned to cook, buy healthy local food, and eat out less. For the past three years I have worked with a physical trainer and practiced yoga. The improvement in my physical health has helped improve my mental health.

A Final Thought

Now I am sitting on my couch, next to wife, who is half asleep while, our cat paws at the sliding glass door. I thankful my family could be supportive of me at my most difficult hours. I am grateful for the incredible mentors and friends I've had along the way and all of those who looked out for me on my trips, to the outer realms.

I decided early on this was too hard to keep secret and

I need too much support. The people, who respected my experience, are the people I surround myself with. Over the years, I've learned I don't want to spend much time with people who treat me poorly and it is better to know sooner rather than later, someone's attitude. It saves a lot of time, energy, and heartache.

I'm still learning for each of my journeys to the edge of reality. Every day I work to recover my physically health and improve my mental health. Sometimes, I wonder, how did I get here? Life feels so good.

Then I remember it hasn't always been this way. It took a lot of help, a lot of hard work, and making the best bad options – until the choices got better. It has been 11 years since I was diagnosed, I've earned 3 college degrees, had 4 hospitalizations, I was fortunate to have family be there for me in superhuman ways. My Dad he always struck a healthy balance of support and autonomy, while being by my side at the most difficult moments of my life.

I had a group of mentors and incredible friends who are rooting for me. Married a caring wife and work to been a compassionate, loving husband. I thank them for their support and work to be as healthy as I can be.

I've learn it's possible that I may lose reality again. I hope it doesn't end in another hospitalization, but I don't fear it. These experiences have forged me into who I am today.

Each time I lost reality, I learned incredible things. Things that can't be taught, put in book, or even explained. After each trip I've been able to return faster, with less damage to my life. Even if hospitalization have become more difficult. I've learned to embrace hope & transcended struggle even in the darkest moments. Learned to love myself and to forgive and those that have cadged my body. While my spirit roamed free.

Trauma and pain can shatter, but can also teach empathy, compassion, & love. Through this journey I've learned things that no one can take away.   Lessons that are genuinely mine.   Sometime I wonder would it be easier to put this behind me, to let it go.   Then I remember courageous people shared their stories with me.   When I felt the most lost, people who helped instill hope.   I would not be able to do this today with them.

Perhaps you will consider sharing your experience. Thank you for reading my story.

A Flight From Despair: An Emergence
Carmen Lee

The dictionary defines recovery as reclaiming, recouping, or to win back and/or to restore. However, to be able to restore

something you must have had that experience previously and want to win it back. I, therefore, feel the need to use another word like inception, commencement, genesis, or better yet, emergence. Yes, emergence, since that is what happened to me.

Carmen Lee

I *gave birth* to myself at the age of 45. Up until that time, I was always in torment and depression, even as a young child. I thought everyone suffered this debilitating pain, confusion and despair, and that everyone was pretending. So, from the framework of my limited knowledge, I decided to become *the best pretender of them all.* And I was. I went to college, became an airline stewardess, married "Mr. Right" and had "Baby Right" and was in full pursuit of "The American Dream," just like everyone else. However, always, but always, there was this deep sense inside of indescribable gloom, turmoil and utter distress.

More and more often I was afflicted with paralyzing fatigue and had dark circles beneath my eyes. I was 23 years old, attractive, educated, traveling around the world, supposedly "flying high." Yet, all the time I thought that I must have an in- curable disease. Why else would I be this exhausted and depleted?

I tried to blend in, ignoring and denying the terror inside, but to no avail. At the age of 24, I gave up the fight and gradually slipped away into catatonia. For three years, in a hospital in Maryland, I lay on a thin mattress unable to communicate on any level. The doctors told my (then) husband that I would never be able to live outside of a hospital.

Over the course of years, I received multiple shock treatments, and when these weren't helpful, a pre-frontal lobotomy was recommended. However, my husband would not sign the papers *even though I so desperately wanted the surgery*. The omnipotent doctor figure said with this operation I would be able to raise my child, since I would no longer feel this immobilizing, helpless depression. (Little did I know that lobotomies don't turn out that way.)

Many of the present medications were non-existent in the late 60's. Thorazine and later, Mellaril, were the only two medications at that time. Eventually, though, by beginning to trust my doctor, I slowly started to speak and began two years of intense talk therapy, while still an inpatient. I became slightly better in time, but I've still been institutionalized over 20 years, collectively, since the age of 24. I've been stabbed and raped in a state hospital, chained with handcuffs to a metal gurney for 19 hours and left in my own feces and urine, without food and water, nor a caring soul - **all this because I had made a suicide attempt!**

This mental illness has consumed the greater part of my life. But you know something - I am better, much better! The professionals told me when I was in my late twenties that I'd probably get better when I was older. I thought to myself then, "Yippee, when I'm fifty I'll be better!" Of course, never believing I'd stay alive until the age of fifty. Living with such torment and despair, with suicidal ideation everyday of life, left me little energy to engage in imagining any kind of a positive future.

Erich Heckel, "Convalescent Woman," 1912-13, Oil

I see joy and feel pleasure now where there was none. I am in unison with myself, with my life, with my God, and I play a heck of a good game of tennis! I've acquired a sense of balance, so necessary for any kind of growth. I've attained a "wellness" that I thought was not possible. But most important, I am grateful that I did not become a bitter person. **Through all adversity, I have found that people get bitter or better.** No one ever stays the same.

I like who I am today and seldom look backward anymore. But, out of respect for this illness and the power it had over me in the past, I listen very carefully for signs and symptoms of this now dormant enemy. I take my medication and still have what I call my "stop days" to regroup and recoup. Perhaps, that's what recovery is all about – taking care of myself. I accept my limitations and use my skills and capabilities as well as I can. I live on a meager income and I don't like that either. It's no fun not to have the essentials one needs to live. **But, I'm rich, too, in so many ways.** On my good days (and I have many more of these), I function very well and I'm helping to make good things happen for myself and for others. Actually, this is when my real recovery began - when I found a purpose in life.

Several of us, all diagnosed with a serious mental illness, and tired of feeling ashamed of ourselves for something that is not our fault, have started to penetrate that prejudicial wall of false images. In October of 1990, we began the *Stamp Out Stigma (SOS) Program* - a public educational outreach program. Since then, the SOS teams have delivered over 2600 public presentations to diverse audiences throughout the Greater San Francisco Bay Area, at many national conferences and at international venues.

After giving a brief biographical-sketch of where we've been with mental illness, with a diagnosis, if it's appropriate, we focus on the needs of that particular audience. For instance, if it's to a higher school of learning, like UC Berkeley, San Jose State University and Santa Clara University, we emphasize what we need from a professional. For example, it is absolutely crucial to be able to work **together as a team** when solving problems. We also stress the importance of respect and dignity in a therapeutic relationship. We've really perfected our lists of what is helpful and what is not. They listen intently, and take notes as fast as they can. Hopefully, we 're erasing some of the great amount of stigma towards us that we have found in those who are supposed to serve us. If the presentation is to a police department, we focus on assisting the officers in developing more humane ways in their encounters with mentally ill people. With high school students, SOS makes the distinction between "growing up pains" versus having a mental health condition, while always offering available resources in the community.

At every presentation our sole aim is to educate, inspire, and connect with our audiences. A dialogue between the audience and the panelists is the most vital part of each

SOS and counter-balances the media's portrayal of how mentally ill people are viewed.

SOS goes to medical schools, schools of nursing, schools of psychology, high schools, college classes and various student-body functions, like *Health Day* where SOS has a booth with someone there to speak about mental health issues and hand out an SOS brochure. We are also a regular part of the five surrounding Bay Area Counties Suicide Prevention & Crisis Center's volunteer-training programs, and part of our own county's training program for their new psychiatric and psychology interns and resident doctors.

Stamp Out Stigma has been on several radio and TV shows, presented at mental health boards, boards of supervisors, fire departments, hospital administrators and civic clubs. The response to the SOS program has been overwhelmingly positive, with a great number of repeat presentations scheduled on a regular basis. In recent years, the SOS program has been replicated in many other communities nationwide and in London, England. In my opinion, there can't be enough of us doing this anti-stigma work. Stigma is the foremost deterrent on the road to recovery, as it affects everything from housing, to employment opportunities and personal relationships.

What a warm feeling it is to make a constructive contribution out of something that's been so terribly painful - what we're doing feels right and is right! The work we are doing is changing the face of the mental health system. We are changing attitudes and, perhaps, that's our most outstanding contribution. To reduce the stigma of a disease that already has caused tremendous suffering, gives those who suffer a wider network of caring and support in the world. *This is our gift.*

Research studies have found that most Americans think the worst things that can happen to a person are leprosy and insanity. Convicts stand on a higher ladder of acceptance than do mental patients. Because of society's discrimination, we must not chastise ourselves, as well, and think of ourselves as weak and morally faulty. A person has to be strong to endure the pain of mental illness and to cope with the illogical bigotry and prejudice from the insensitive and ill informed around us.

I'm a survivor and I had to first learn to survive before I could learn to live. With the help of my doctors, I began tracking the patterns in my thinking, my feelings and my actions. By doing this, I could see what got me into trouble. I then learned to interrupt those patterns **before** they became self-destructive, by doing something different and by getting help before I spiraled downward. I still have to do this occasionally and it really works. That's why in any forum I can get, I urge all who suffer from mental illness to use their doctors, trust one's own "gut feelings," be who you are and use your unique talents. **That doesn't mean that the illness can be an excuse for poor behavior**. A person with a mental health condition must take responsibility for their treatment, for "handling" their illness. It is that taking of responsibility that opens the way toward one's own recovery.

With over 20 years, collectively, of hospitalizations, I have never seen a single individual who is totally without a part of them that is either intact, well, or very well. It's all layered, though, with periods of psychosis, lack of self-esteem, confusion and turmoil. Somewhere, amid that chaos, however, is at least part of a person where there is hope and what some may call a core of wellness – something to work with – the start of emergence towards recovery.

My stay in the state hospital was terrifying. Committed because of a suicide attempt and under "observation" for 90 days on three different occasions, I was assigned to a ward with people from my own county. And no matter what your condition was, that was the ward in which you had to stay. It was absolutely the most impossible and inappropriate place for anyone's benefit. I don't think there was ever a time, during my three commitments, where there was a single person who could talk with me and make sense out of things. – certainly not the overworked staff, who really didn't care that much anyway. It was there that I began writing poetry so I could "talk" to myself, so to speak.

The first poem I wrote was titled, *"Desolation"* and it goes like this:

The trees are black, the forest gray
with ashy casts and foggy rays.
Can't the sunlight come through the air
And give some hope to the spirit there?
Then may we see the beauty that exists, can
sigh a moment and enjoy this long awaited bliss.

On death what do you have me do, when
everyday you force myself to talk to you?
I'm tired oh life and death combined.
Tell me what is really mine.
Do I have the sunlight coming through the fog?
Or will darkness always prevail, casting
shadows on my grave and longing for my fall?

Let me yield to the sweetness and the joy
of a forest shiny green and gold with
amber sounds coming through the leaves
yearning for my touch.
Hear me life, extend your hand and
guide me through until we find that
tender patch of precious blue.

This poem was written many years ago. Sitting here now writing, with a warm breeze sifting through the window screen and wild flowers blooming magnificently outside, I am grateful I failed at suicide. I am glad I didn't have a lobotomy. I am happy to be alive and thankful that I've found my "tender patch of precious blue."

Biography
Carmen Lee resides in Belmont, CA, a suburb of San Francisco. She directs the Stamp Out Stigma Program, serves as a member of the California Mental Heath Planning Council, The National Action Alliance for Suicide Prevention, Suicide Attempt Survivor Taskforce, the PIR Committee of the United State's Psychiatric Rehabilitation Association, and is a Board member for the Mental Health Association of San Francisco.
In her "spare" time, Carmen enjoys playing tennis, reading, writing and being in the great outdoors with her dog, *Ceely*.

From Stereotype to Recovery
Becky Brasfield

On the train there's a man with mental illness begging for money. He is laughing. His hair is matted. His clothes are filthy and hanging off his body. He is smelly and unkempt. A woman grabs her son and exclaims 'he needs to take his crazy pill.' The other passengers laugh, but try to calm her down. The man makes strange sounds and scares passengers who make faces at him before moving to another part of the train.

When I see this man, I have mixed feelings. I wish he would stop scaring the passengers because I think he is the reason why the general public is still so afraid of mental illness. But I also think I am looking at myself. I, too, scared people with my mania and psychosis, and had it not been for my family, I would have been homeless. This man and I have much in common, but what keeps me from acting out symptoms today is the unrelenting goal to recover and reclaim a life of hope, perseverance and success.

My recovery from mental illness is a miracle. It started with severe depression and anxiety as a child. I woke up every morning crying and asking God to kill me to put me out of my misery. I was hypomanic throughout my teenage years and young adulthood. I was a compulsive overeater during middle school and became obese. Then, I became an obsessive exerciser and near anorexic in high school. I kept wanting to lose 5 more pounds, and then another 5 more pounds, and then another 5 more pounds, but it was never enough. I was a cutter through the years. I suffered from attention deficits. I couldn't learn properly in classroom instruction even though I was smart. I wanted to drop out of the University of Chicago Laboratory School at 17 and get a GED just to leave home. I started drinking in college at the University of Illinois at Urbana-Champaign and became an alcoholic. I had social phobia and panic attacks. All of a sudden, I would be stricken by fear, have trouble breathing, and have to go home. I experienced symptoms of body dysmorphic disorder and agoraphobia and found it difficult to leave the mirror or the house. I became fixated on my nose and my facial profile and didn't want anyone to look at me. I became so incapacitated by depression that I could not muster the energy to walk across the room. I became a compulsive spender. I used my credit cards to buy clothes, alcohol, more clothes, useless household items, expensive meals and more books than I could store. I couldn't hold a job for more than a few months. I quit my college job at the bowling alley four times. I relied on family financial support to survive. I was on and off medications, some of which had horrible side effects. I gained 60 pounds, had a hand tremor, a twitchy eye, insomnia, night terrors and my symptoms of depression, mania, and anxiety still would not go away.

I never really believed any of the diagnoses I received. It's not that I didn't think I had a mental illness. I just didn't believe the evaluations assessed the big picture. However, one day I finally believed that I was an alcoholic and stopped drinking. Things got better quickly and I believed that a previous bipolar diagnosis had been in error, that it was actually the drinking sprees that caused my symptoms. So, I went off medication and was fine for a while, until I secretly started to believe that I was God. I didn't think anyone would understand my belief because I was in touch with reality well enough to know that people would think I was delusional if I told them. I had never had that kind of delusional thought before. Looking back, the only way I would have told anyone the truth is if I had heard someone like me talk about having had that symptom. This is why peer support and self-disclosure are so powerful. I couldn't have trusted someone without the lived experience of mental illness. It was far too easy for me to write off professionals. That's why I'm telling my story now.

My experiences in graduate school at the University of Illinois in Urbana-Champaign triggered a dangerous psychotic break. As an undergrad there, I studied psychology, but in graduate school I studied sociology. I was very respectful to faculty and had exceptional social skills. However, I walked into a sociology department with a great deal of problems. I was one of three students who left within a year. One student, "Tabitha[3]," immediately saw the red flags and applied to other graduate schools the minute she got there. "Tabitha" ended up getting into a very good sociology program at the University of Wisconsin. Another student, "Lisa," left after one semester. I was a good student and did good work in every class I took, but I was treated horribly. I thought that something was wrong with me until I talked to other students about my experiences.

Faculty criticisms didn't bother me. That's a part of academia and honing your skills to improve. I went to graduate school to learn. However, the behavior I encountered in the sociology department constituted actual abuse. I could have easily coped with a few misguided insults. For instance, one professor, "Dr. Irons" told me that my work was "social work" not sociology (intended to be demeaning) and that I might be better off in a social work program. That was disturbing to hear during my first week of class, but that didn't really bother me. However, "Dr. Irons" seemed to get some kind of ego-gratification from demeaning me. She took a paper I wrote for a pre-doctoral program and found everything she could to criticize it and did so in the most insulting way. I was still willing to accept her feedback as room for improvement, until she capped off the storm of belligerent criticism by flipping to a page, pointing to a

---

[3] The names of students, professors and clinicians are pseudonyms.

sentence, laughing (hysterically) out loud and saying "this is not even a sentence." In horror and shock, I looked at what she was pointing to and I had accidently omitted the word "is." After "Dr. Irons" yelled and laughed at me, I burst into tears which stopped her tirade. Then she told me "good luck with the rest of your tenure here" at which point I wondered why I had been accepted into the program. Looking back, I should have withdrawn from school after that encounter with "Dr. Irons" because it was the beginning of an experience that was so stressful and abusive that it triggered a psychotic break.

I had never experienced anything like that sociology department before. Personally, I felt that I was discriminated against as a Black woman and covertly kicked out of the program. I had a class in which a white professor, "Dr. Gibbons," coddled everyone in her classroom but challenged everything I said. She even literally screamed at me across the room about the "biggest flaw" in my work which stunned the entire classroom into silence. After class, students asked me if I was alright. I wasn't. I emailed "Dr. Gibbons" and told her that her comments felt insulting. "Dr. Gibbons" replied that she takes such concerns "very seriously" and was willing to meet with me to talk about it. I declined her offer. I found her conduct throughout the course to be inappropriate and felt that her response was disingenuous. "Dr. Gibbons" assured me that she's harder on students she thinks can get published in sociology journals and gave me an A. Every time I went to her class, she attacked everything I said until I just stopped talking in class.

Another professor, "Dr. Avery" gave me an A+, which I didn't even think was possible, but she wouldn't give me a letter of recommendation or respond to my email or voicemail after the course. I do not know why she failed to respond to me. I contacted her only once by email and by phone. I never said anything negative to her. I got along with all the students in our class. I did very good work. I didn't even exhibit any overt signs of mental illness. "Dr. Avery" followed up with *all* of the other students in my cohort and encouraged them to go to conferences. She told them that she would help them develop their work, but she wouldn't even respond to me. Two professors wouldn't do independent studies with me, and they certainly were under no obligation to work with me, but I was running out of options for support. Another professor in the department, "Dr. Gendahl" talked to me like I was a fifteen year old, illiterate black gang member. After I would share my perspective on theory, she would stop, spell things out slowly in very simple terms, and then tell me that I had misunderstood the concept, even though I had not. I stopped talking in that class too. After the semester was over, one of the other black students in "Dr. Gendahl's" class told me that he thought that she was racist and that he would never take another class in the sociology department again. He was a Doctoral student in educational policy studies. It was one of the most demeaning experiences of my life.

In the midst of this long series of events with all the stress of that unhealthy environment, I heard a voice in April 2008. It said, "You're not getting your PhD." It was not just the voice of my inner thoughts. It was an auditory hallucination. Typical of some people's early experiences with voices, it actually calmed me. At that point, I didn't care about not getting a PhD. I just wanted to get to a supportive place. I left school without pursuing the Master's degree that I had earned because the stress was so overwhelming. I returned home to Chicago and sought out treatment for my symptoms.

I went to therapy because I wanted help. However, the therapy was unsuited for me. I should have found a new therapist but I wasn't assertive enough to do so at the time. I needed a therapeutic approach that dealt with validating my stressful experiences in graduate school and empowering me while staying focused on the basic needs of work, income, and housing. "Timothy" meant well and did the best he could, but I felt like our sessions came straight out of an introductory counseling techniques manual. "Timothy" asked me to do a lot of activities that felt inappropriate for my issues, but I did everything he suggested. For example, I wrote out the things that upset me, tore up the paper and threw the pieces in the trash. I went home and looked in the mirror telling myself positive affirmations every day. I role played difficult situations in session. I did it all, however what I really needed was to feel heard so I could get comfortable enough to tell "Timothy" about all of my symptoms. That's why rapport is so important in therapy. "Timothy" and I just didn't have it. Thus, I was able to tell "Timothy" and my psychiatrist, "Dr. Strauss" about hearing the voice, but I was not willing to disclose thinking I was God, which was a delusion that would come and go.

"Dr. Strauss," my psychiatrist, insulted me during our first session and I knew that I would never go back to see him. If rapport between "Timothy" and I was bad, then it was horrible with "Dr. Strauss." "Dr. Strauss" asked me if I thought I had a special relationship with God and when I answered "yes", he snidely responded "that's quite grandiose, don't you think?" I didn't respond. Insulting me for being grandiose made me shut down and I was scared to tell him about the God delusion. I was mentally ill, not just full of a God complex of grandiosity and ego. I didn't tell "Timothy" about my God delusion either because I was upset that he wouldn't believe that my graduate school experience had been traumatic. He wouldn't validate something that hurt me deeply and that I knew was real. I was praying to God to help me, so deep down I knew that I wasn't God, but without medication I couldn't control the delusion. I didn't tell anyone because I didn't trust anyone to help me and I didn't want my experience in graduate school to be invalidated because I was "mentally ill."

I continued on with therapy without medication because I had a bad reaction to the anti-depressant that "Dr. Strauss" prescribed me. I felt very nauseous on the first day of taking it. I tried to fight through the nausea but it was unbearable and I told "Timothy" and "Dr. Strauss" I was going to stop taking it. "Dr. Strauss" didn't prescribe me an anti-psychotic, so at that point I was not on any medication at all. Then, a new issue surfaced. I told "Timothy" that I was uncomfortable going to therapy because someone I went to the University of Chicago with worked at "Timothy's" mental health agency. Every time I had a session with "Timothy," I saw "Jonathan" meet his clients in the waiting room and it was humiliating. The stigma of mental illness surfaced during my treatment. I felt like the "mentally ill" failure of my graduating class. I brought it up with "Timothy" to formally address the issue and he suggested that all three of us chat. I couldn't say no because, again, I wasn't assertive enough to do so. After the meeting, I told "Timothy" that it wasn't so bad, but it was a horrible experience and I set out to end the therapy as soon as I could get the courage to do so.

After about 9 months of therapy, I collaborated in a discharge plan with "Timothy" that ended treatment with no medication and no plan for a job or income. "Timothy" suggested that my department hadn't discriminated against me and that my perceptions were inaccurate. Hoping that "Timothy" was right and that I had been wrong about my experience, I contacted the Director of Graduate Studies of the sociology department and asked to submit a thesis to complete a terminal Master's degree. "Dr. Fisher" agreed. I terminated therapy and regained hope in my department. My Master's thesis passed, but the discrimination was not in my head. The sociology department had no intention of granting me my degree.

The sociology department not only failed to help me graduate, but they actively obstructed my degree conferral. The department took me off the graduation list twice. I had to get an administrative petition from a Dean in the Graduate College to get my degree. My department told me that I had been added to the May 2009 pending degree list. I thought that my degree had been awarded in May, but it was not. I was in Chicago and did not attend commencement in Champaign, Illinois, so I was not immediately aware of the problem. I applied for jobs in the summer of 2009. In August 2009, I was hired as a Research Data Analyst with a Master's degree on my resume. I assumed that my degree had been conferred. I would not have found out about the obstruction except that I needed to provide my new job with a confirmation of my Master's degree, which I had not received in the mail by September. That's when I found out that my degree had never been awarded. I had been placed on an August 2009 pending degree list and removed. I suspected the problem was intentional, but I gave the department the benefit of the doubt before jumping to conclusions. The department confirmed to me that I was on the October pending degree list, but somehow I was mysteriously removed again. After that I knew that the department wasn't going to grant me my degree, so I contacted the Graduate College to request that they award it.

Ultimately, the University of Illinois Registrar's office told me that "The petition you filed through the Graduate College was to retroactively award your degree for the October 2009 degree period. This was needed because your department had your name deleted from the October 2009 Pending Degree List." I asked the Graduate College to investigate the matter. I made complaints of systemic racism and sexism and explained that the Registrar's office informed me that the sociology department took me off the pending degree list. The Graduate College Dean attempted to explain away the situation and refused to investigate the matter.

Because of the stigma against mental illness, I have had a difficult time receiving validation for the real abuses I experienced in graduate school. During the later stages of my psychosis, I did experience a proliferation of conspiratorial ways of thinking. That might lead one to believe that everything I claimed to have experienced was merely a delusion, however, facts distinguish delusions from reality. I knew a man with a delusion that his father was the king of Germany. That assertion could be logically refuted using facts. I was demeaned and obstructed from graduating. That assertion can be confirmed using facts. For this reason, it was very important for me to ask the Registrar's office if there was any evidence that the department obstructed my degree conferral. Even I was shocked when they delivered the proof to me. That was not a delusion. The way I was treated in graduate school was not a delusion. I wasn't a "mentally ill" person that faculty members were avoiding due to a social skills problem. Racism and sexism still exist today and they occur in academia.

The experience in graduate school had a detrimental effect on my mental health. A year after having my degree obstructed and being denied an investigation into the matter, I ended up in Cook County jail. I lost hope and the strength to fight my illness. Schizoaffective disorder took over my mind. I was arrested for threatening a woman over email. The exact charge was Harassment through Electronic Communications. Out of respect for the victim and her family, there isn't much I can say about the incident, other than in a manic rant of writing, I sent 5 or 6 emails to my former employer and threatened the wife's life if she didn't leave her husband. I was not attracted to the husband. I wasn't angry with the wife. I had not had any contact with them for several years, but the idea that they had wronged me just popped into my head. A delusional storyline developed in my head about me saving the husband from his wife. I deeply regret the fear and harm I caused them, but I was definitely not in my rational mind at the time.

I was in jail for five months while the case proceeded. I was in delusional state for the duration of the case. I told myself that I had wanted to go to jail and was trying to get into prison. That denial protected me from the reality that my mental illness caused me to lose control of my rational mind and landed me in jail. I was trying to cognitively assert some semblance of control over a situation that was totally out of control. I told myself and the court-ordered forensic psychologist that I was studying the criminal justice system for a project into understanding its processes and rooting out its problems. She must have believed me because she found me fit to stand trial after I told her that delusion and turned into my house arrest electronic monitor to force jail officials to put me in residential jail. I certainly learned a great deal about the criminal justice system, but I was not there to do research. I was sick, and in denial of my mental illness. Studying the criminal justice system was my "reasonable explanation" for what I had done.

New delusions of being persecuted came up because of the arrest but at some point, there was an end to the delusion that I was God. There was a point when I really didn't want to be in jail anymore and I couldn't lie to myself that I was on a mission to understand the criminal justice system. I wanted to get out of jail and go home, but I couldn't willpower my way out of it. Finally, my mind accepted that I couldn't be God if I was powerless over the situation. I plead guilty to the charge and released the same day. Unfortunately, I was released without any diagnosis or any medication. About a month after I was released, the reality of the damage I had done hit me and I tried to kill myself in June, 2011. I had reached the point at which the pain of living surpassed the hope for better days. However, within minutes of my attempt, I knew I would not die and a terror, like none I have ever experienced, came over me. I checked myself into an emergency room. When I was transferred to Chicago Read Mental Hospital, I was put on medication, regained my will to live and began true recovery.

Eventually, I came out of the denial that I had intentionally researched the criminal justice system. I started to accept the severity of my illness. I was put on an anti-psychotic/mood stabilizer after my suicide attempt and remain on medication to this day. Today, I have no denial about the experience and feel excessively remorseful to everyone involved. It has been difficult to face, but honesty has been my way out.

"Mental Illness" is a stigmatized term because it connotes the idea that 'it's all in my head.' For me, mental illness is a medical illness that affects my mental health. I truly believe that I have a mental illness, but I also feel I have a "brain disorder." I have Schizoaffective Disorder. Without medication, I cannot function. No amount of psychotherapy can prevent mania, depression, paranoia, or psychosis in me. I need medication. I understand that this is not true for everyone, but it is true for me.

I have recovered my rational mind and my ability to function, but it is very difficult to recover from a felony conviction associated with mental illness. You would never know that I had Schizoaffective Disorder if you met me. With medication, I have no symptoms, but today, I live with multiple stigmas for having Schizoaffective Disorder and having a criminal record. What employer wants to hire me? What university wants to admit me? What landlord wants to rent to me? Truth be told, I'm not even sure I would give me a chance without knowing me. Why not choose someone else with no criminal history and no mental illness? People tell me to get my record sealed or expunged, but there is a lot of misinformation about criminal record sealing and expungement. Some people still think charges miraculously vanish from your record after a certain amount of time passes. This is not the case. Others think that anyone can get their record expunged. The only remedy I have for expungement is by being granted Executive Clemency by the Governor of Illinois. The more time that passes beyond the criminal offense, the greater the chance of clemency. In the meantime, I actively wait. I realize that I am facing an uphill battle and to participate in school, work, and life, I will have to present an upside that outweighs the "risk." That is the reality I live with and the stigma that I have to overcome.

Because of the severe and comprehensive effects of my mental illness, as well as my commitment to mental health advocacy, I choose to be open about my mental illness. In many ways, I no longer have a choice about being out about it. I have to be honest about it professionally because applications ask and I won't lie. It's not fair to anyone involved and being dishonest is not something that I can do. It was not my intent to commit a crime, but I do have to be responsible for it. The way I show that I am remorseful is to be honest, up front, and responsible about my healthcare and well-being. When I was sick, I acted out in ways that I regret, and I attempt to atone for it through healthy living today.

Living with mental illness in this society is one of the most difficult things you can do. Disclosing mental illness has risks and benefits and it's important to weigh them before making a decision to disclose personal health information. Once, I was very upset about breaking up with my boyfriend and started crying. A relative who knew about my illness immediately asked me, "did you take your medication?" I felt stigmatized for having a mental illness. Every time I show emotion, does it have to have something to do with mental illness? The stigma of mental illness can make it unsafe to disclose in some circumstances. I don't want my behavior to be constantly scrutinized for signs of mental illness.

A highly functional and very successful person with a mental illness in this society may have more to lose (personally) than gain by disclosing one's mental illness. For this reason, we do not have many high profile positive role models of people who have overcome their mental illness. We know they exist, but without being *out and proud*, we lose the ability to overshadow the negative stereotypes with their stories. The negative stereotypes of people with mental illness usually focus on individuals at their worst: acting out violent criminal behavior, scaring people, extremely bizarre behavior, homelessness, and images of patients in hospital robes. Certainly, these depictions are parts of the lives of many people with mental illness, but the proliferation of these images contribute to the notion that no one feels good about "being mentally ill." We need more success stories. Without positive role models for recovery and triumph over the illness, the images scale is weighted in the wrong direction.

I lost my freedom, my home, my career and many of my friends due to mental illness. Yet, with the smallest amount of hope I managed to rebuild my life. With hard work and determination, anything is possible. Today, I volunteer with multiple mental health agencies. I advocate for mental health legislation. I provide peer support. I'm a part of community of mental health advocates who are committed to advancing the treatment of mental illness. I still live with lingering consequences of my mental illness, but today those consequences do not impede my progress. I have the strength of my peers and recovery to overcome any obstacles I may face. Therefore, instead of cowering to the stigma of mental illness by remaining silent, I choose to share my story. Wherever I go, the face of mental health recovery will go. Pride in my accomplishments has replaced the shame of my mental illness because I have successfully transformed my life from stereotype to recovery.

A Vision of Recovery
Kevin Coyle

Kevin Coyle

During my junior year in college I summoned up the courage to come out about my illness. After a weeklong hospital stay, I met with my roommates in a restaurant a stone throw away from my college. These were close friends that I have known for two years, friends I thought I could trust. Indeed, we often exchanged jokes, played ping pong in the basement of Pangborn Hall, and watched more movies than I can remember. I told them about my delusions and that I was receiving treatment for my mental illness. That proved to be a mistake, one that would haunt me for years.

Shortly after my disclosure I couldn't get into my dorm. At first, I thought that it was something wrong with my card, but I later discovered the painful truth. My roommates became scared and told the dean of student affairs everything I shared. The dean then shut me out of my dorm and changed the lock to my room because I was deemed a threat to the campus. All this was done without informing me. Finally we had a meeting with the Vice President.

In that meeting there was the director of learning services. She was easy going and full of jokes, but when it came to standing up for my rights, she was tough and unwavering. She stood up for me when it came time to procure sign language interpreters for my classes and the many incompletes or extensions I needed to finish courses.

Her presence made a difference in that meeting. My access was finally restored, but the incident destroyed the trust I had in others.

My psychologist referred me to On Our Own, a wellness and recovery center for persons with mental illnesses. There I found a staff member who would listen to my story. As a man who also has a mental illness, he could relate. As an organization for and by people with mental illnesses, On Our Own served as a counter-weight that helped mitigate the effects of self-stigma that I would later face.

In 2008 I moved into a group home for deaf individuals. What happened during those early years is a blur, but what I do remember was how I felt. Before I became diagnosed with schizoaffective disorder, I swam on a club swim team for eight years, performed juggling and magic shows during high school, and was inducted into the National Honor Society. Even with mental illness I graduated from college with honors. Stuck in the group home, I felt like I was leaving all my past behind me. What had I to be proud of? Yes, I had a degree, but was held back from achieving my dreams by circumstance and situation. Most of the group members there had been stuck in the program for 10 to 30 years. I thought that I would suffer the same fate.

Although the organization exist smack dab in the city, we were isolated from not only the hearing world, but the deaf community. Instead of focusing on our own individual aspirations and dreams, they addressed us as a collective giving workshops on what they thought was best for us. The organization operated primarily as a social club, not as a forward looking rehabilitation program.

Besides a lack of vision was a lack of understanding about mental illness. One time when I went to Wal-Mart with a staff member, I felt like I was in a dream. I was so overwhelmed that all I wanted to do was lay down. I was in the throes of another psychotic episode, but the staff did not display any empathy or understanding. He complained about how he had two people to watch over, as if I was being a burden to him. Sometimes the stigma was more subtle like addressing us like children in a different way than they would to other people or talking amongst themselves without including us in the conversation.

I have experienced much stigma in my life, but I believe change is possible. The solution cannot happen overnight. Changing one's worldview radically is a slow process. The difficulty arises when new information runs counter to what we see, hear, and experience in our own families, communities, and social networks. It is easier to ignore it than to reconcile and synthesize two conflicting ideas. To think things through requires a lot of mental effort and an openness to the possibility that one is wrong. It requires that we be self-critical.

Before there can be empathy, there must be understanding. When someone falls and hurts themselves on the sidewalk, our heart goes out to them because we know what it is like to suffer. When people see someone acting strange on the street, they don't know how to respond, yet psychosis is also painful. It is hard to explain to someone what it is like to experience these things. The National Alliance for Mental Illness' Family to Family class for family members, does a useful exercise that gives participants a bird's eye view into the minds of those who suffer from voices in their heads. In the activity some people have to follow instructions given to them while others say different things in the background such as reading the weather report over and over again. It is exercises like these that can help participants relate to the sufferer.

Even with the best programs, the real change must come from within. Two effective tools for transformation are self-advocacy and reinforcement. I do not necessarily mean going down to Annapolis or Washington D.C. to voice concerns. Advocacy can happen in our families, businesses, and small social networks. The biggest hurdle to self-advocacy is fear and intimidation. When we say how we feel in a calm, but firm way it can have an impact.

Hearing the truth from one person can be effective, but it can be even more so when that message is repeated from multiple people that they respect or view equal to themselves. Even when people do not change, voicing our concerns is liberating. It breaks the cycle of self-stigma. No longer do we have to stuff our anger inside of us. By speaking out we can be set free.

Recovery is an act of the imagination. It requires foresight, the ability to envision a better tomorrow. The hardest part is always the beginning. Ten years ago when I was struggling with delusions, hallucinations, and depression I had a hard time separating myself from my illness. I still struggle, but becoming mentally healthy helped me regain confidence in myself. With medicine and doctors, I have been able to cope with my symptoms. One technique that has helped me time and time again is doing my research or engaging with people in conversations. Not only does it focus my mind, it turns my attention away from myself and my problems.

Even with the support of On Our Own and my family I felt like a child. Living in the group home it didn't dawn on me that people my age could have not just jobs, but careers. I too was victim of self-stigma. It is only now that I am starting to realize my potential as a grown man of 30 years old.

Another thing that has helped is my faith in God. Through him I have found a purpose for my life that transcends all suffering. In my writing and my living I try to uplift others who are struggling and bear witness to Jesus. I am not perfect, but this reason for living carries me through my struggles. With God I know I am never alone. I can always turn to him for wisdom and guidance. He is with me through and through. In the fellowship of friends or in a service at church, my strength is renewed me to face the challenges of the coming week.

Coming out about mental illness is a scary thing. We do not know how others will react. They may turn against us, like my roommates did to me, but if we can find those special people who will listen to us it can make all the difference in the world. As I learned at On Our Own, being heard is a powerful thing. It tells us that we are not alone and that there is a light at the end of the tunnel. It is good to find someone who will listen to you not just once, but many times. It is even better if we can find a network of people. I found this at On Our Own Inc. and through my parent's involvement with the National Alliance on Mental Illness. Beyond mental health organizations, we can expand and start new networks of care and support. The biggest hurdle is stigma. There are many great educational programs, but the best tool comes from ourselves. By standing up and speaking out or by writing articles, we can make a difference. Indeed, this is what the Coming Out Proud book is all about.

Those of us with mental illness carry labels and stereotypes, but it is my hope that people who stigmatize us will eventually see us as equal human beings no different than they. To capture this vision I wrote a poem.

Just Look at Me

Just look at me
What do you see?
What do you see in this mirror called me?
A man who is too sick to be free?
Free to lead,
Free to go
Free to be?

Just look at me?
What do you see?
A reflection of yourself?
You, the human?
You who struggle through
You who climb mountains and brave the seas?
Searching for hope like me?

Changing My Mind
Keith Mahar

Keith Mahar

For a number of years I wanted to hide that I was diagnosed with a severe mental illness and had experienced a traumatic life-altering episode of psychosis in Toronto. Fortunately, I changed my mind.

Today, I am a mental health advocate, social worker and activist living in Australia, where I am employed to assist individuals with their mental health recovery. Ironically, part of this support includes sharing relevant aspects of my own lived experience of bipolar disorder.

There were a number of obstacles that had to be overcome for me to rebuild my life, but stigma was by far the biggest one that I faced. To be more precise, internalized stigma was the most damaging. I was effectively paralyzed by shame. Furthermore, I was totally demoralized and felt hopeless because I accepted the false stereotype that people with severe mental illness cannot recover.

Upon reflection, my decision to stop trying to hide my experience of mental illness set me free to rebuild a satisfying life. However, there is no universal recipe when it comes to disclosure. I've learned that it is an individual's choice whether to disclose, with whom to disclose, and also how much to share. This is the part of my experience of mental illness and recovery that I wish to share.

Growing Up

I was born in Montreal in 1962, six months after my grandfather had died of pneumonia while being treated for mania in a psychiatric institution in the city. My father developed symptoms of bipolar disorder during my childhood, but he was not diagnosed for years, and my family experienced periods of financial hardship. I was tested for ulcers at age 11 but the doctor determined that my frequent abdominal pain was due to stress. Over time I periodically experienced symptoms of anxiety but I did not tell anyone. My parents' marriage ended while I was in Grade 9 and the following year my father was briefly homeless. However, I put on a brave public face which effectively hid my feelings of sadness, fear, embarrassment and anger.

From the outside, it was not obvious that I was having any problems. I had lots of friends, enjoyed playing baseball and football with them on weekends, and finished high school in 1980 without apparent difficulty. In fact, my teachers placed me on their honor list and my classmates selected me as the outstanding male graduate in the class. But at 17 years old I felt worn out and wanted to reinvent myself. Three months after high school graduation, I left my family and friends in Montreal to study business at the University of New Brunswick. At university, I repeatedly earned a position on the Dean's List for my academic performance and was elected president of an on-campus residence, primarily for my ability to throw decent parties. During 3rd year I experienced a brief period of elevated energy, confidence and creativity, which was followed by a loss of motivation and energy. I dismissed the mild mood swings as being normal for someone my age and dropped out of university for a semester to recharge my batteries. Recharged, I returned to university and was awarded a Bachelor of Business Administration with Distinction, the highest academic category.

At 22 I was hired by a Canadian subsidiary of a Fortune 500 company, bought my first real estate property and started following a disciplined savings and investment plan. Two years later I started a corporate career in the Canadian broadcasting industry. Shortly after turning 31, I was hired by a broadcasting company for my knowledge of the cable television industry, to manage corporate relationships and negotiate distribution agreements for its specialty television networks across Canada. It was a wonderful job for me as I was part of a skilled and enjoyable team at a highly innovative broadcasting company.

At that point I thought I had my life all figured out. My plan was to remain with my employer until I turned 40 and was able to afford to retire from corporate life to an alternative lifestyle. I wanted a simple existence which permitted me more freedom to travel and join a group like Amnesty International or Greenpeace. But my plan for 'Freedom 40' was hijacked by mental illness.

Onset of Symptoms and Activism

In July 1994, three months before my 32nd birthday, I began to have difficulty sleeping properly during a stressful period. However, I did not go to the doctor because I felt fine otherwise. By mid-August I started to feel absolutely fantastic. Despite less and less sleep, my energy and productivity increased and I felt more creative and confident. Early one morning I erroneously concluded that sleep was highly over-rated.

In hindsight, this period was a window of opportunity for me to seek professional help before it was too late, but I was unaware of all the symptoms of bipolar disorder. In spite of my family history of mental illness, I somehow felt immune to the possibility of losing control of my mind, my primary asset. Nevertheless, by the beginning of that September, I was suffering from mild psychosis. My perception of reality had become impaired by highly seductive delusions of grandeur, that I was destined to change the world.

While in this mental state, I decided to fix the Canadian broadcasting system. During my career I had lost faith in the integrity of the Canadian Radio-television and Telecommunication Commission (CRTC) and the quality of decisions by this federal regulator. As a result, I quit my job to undertake this project in the public interest. In the process of conducting regulatory research, I discovered evidence that officials at the CRTC had adopted a scheme to unjustly enrich influential corporations by allowing several million Canadians to be over-charged for cable television service by close to $600 million over five years. After a couple of lawyers agreed to help me pursue the issue, things got really interesting.

In March 1995 I held a Parliament Hill press conference in Ottawa with three members of parliament and my lawyers. The MPs and I called on the federal government to investigate the matter. As a result, questions were directed to the Prime Minister the next day in the House of Commons, but the well-documented case of wrongdoing was not pursued. It was abundantly clear to me that corporate power had silenced elected representatives and that the democratic process had been undermined.

After the federal government did not investigate the matter, I decided to try to personally resolve the legal right of consumers to rate refunds, and simultaneously pressure the government to democratically reform the CRTC. During May 1995, as part of the strategy, my legal team initiated a lawsuit on my behalf against the largest cable television company in Canada, a company that was part of the corporate empire controlled by Ted Rogers. The billionaire was definitely not a soft target for such activism – some described him as Canada's Rupert Murdoch. (Years later, journalist Caroline Van Hasselt wrote in *High Wire Act*: "Ted Rogers is like the great white shark, which tears into its prey until its needs are sated.")

Mahar v. Rogers Cablesystems Ltd. became the front-page lead story in *The Toronto Star*, and a columnist for *The*

Globe and Mail supported my challenge against the cable television industry and the federal regulator, writing that I was "charging head-long into battle with two of the most powerful opponents in the country." It seemed as though I had finally found my purpose in life. I had become a social activist.

In response to my actions against the unjust corporate enrichment scheme, my industry opponents effectively undermined my credibility by initiating a smear campaign against me personally. Journalists reported that I had been described as a nut, fanatic, crank and fruitcake - despite my campaign being based upon documented facts that were simple to verify. The smear campaign was so intense that a couple of journalists felt it necessary to defend me in the press.

> "Keith Mahar is not nuts. Nor is he a fanatic or secret agent for the telephone companies, who are allegedly paying him to sabotage the cable industry." (Antonia Zerbisias, *The Toronto Star*, 9 July 1995)

> "Predicatably, Mahar has been characterized variously as a "crank" and "a fruitcake" by his opponents, but I think he's something much more rare, namely, an angry consumer who's fed up with being victimized by monopolistic capitalism and a compliant, business-friendly government regulatory agency." (John Haslett Cuff, *The Globe and Mail*, 11 July 1996)

Despite the allegations that I was "nuts" and my case had no merit, the corporation I sued retained a legal team headed by one of Canada's top barristers. With this lawyer's assistance, the corporation won a precedent-setting decision on jurisdiction in October 1995 that stopped the court from ruling on the merit of my legal case. However, weeks later I won a precedent-setting decision on costs. The judge designated me as a public interest litigant and determined that my lawsuit had been in the public interest and had "raised a genuine issue of law of significance to the public at large." (Mahar v Rogers Cablesystems Ltd. continues to shape costs jurisprudence in public interest litigation cases in Canada and internationally.)

I was determined to pursue the case further in the Federal Court of Appeal and remember thinking at the time that I would never be in a bigger battle in my life, but I was soon proved wrong.

Depression and Psychosis

The legal issues that I raised in 1995 remain unanswered to this day because in May 1996 my campaign was rudely interrupted by a life-threatening episode of depression – the first severe depression in my life, at the age of 33. It came on really fast, and hit exceptionally hard. Feelings of courage and hope were replaced by terror, futility and pure misery. One day I found myself on the bedroom floor, curled up in the fetal position struggling to cope with the agony of the moment. That afternoon, I was diagnosed with bipolar disorder and felt ashamed. In addition, I was frightened that I would never be able to work again and my old fear of being poor resurfaced with a vengeance. During that period sleep was extremely difficult and thoughts of suicide dominated my waking hours.

A psychiatrist told me that it was impossible for me to resume my role as a social activist due to stress being a major trigger to relapse of mental illness. However, in the process of trying to hold powerful opponents accountable, I had discovered my own political voice, and I was exceptionally motivated to finish my campaign In fact, the struggle had profoundly shaped how I perceived myself as a person. The thought of stopping was heartbreaking, precisely at a time when I required a dose of hope. Ultimately, I ignored the psychiatrist's warning.

Unfortunately, I returned to my campaign too early, pushed myself far too hard, and my mental health quickly started to deteriorate. Soon symptoms of both mania and depression surfaced and played a tug of war with my mind, dragging me to uncharted territory and resulting in uncharacteristic behavior. I was lost and my life was rapidly unraveling. Making a critical error in judgment, I abruptly stopped taking my prescribed medication just as it was needed most – an incredibly stupid decision, born out of impaired thinking due to my illness, ignorance, anger and ego. In short order, my mind was racing beyond belief and I was propelled into the stratosphere of major psychosis where logic and reason totally abandoned me.

Loss of Self

On 14 November 1996, in the midst of this psychotic episode, I handed out hundred dollar bills to panhandlers in the city, convinced that I was somehow responsible for their plight. Though I am not a religious person, as I walked down Toronto's Yonge Street that cold fateful afternoon, I thought that God wanted me to demonstrate my faith that the truth was the only thing required to change the world, by walking the earth naked for the rest of my life. I thought that this action would eradicate poverty and end human suffering in the world. With this mission in mind, I set off to Ted Rogers' office hoping to find a solution to the CRTC issue. Unfortunately, changing the world is not quite so simple. Furthermore, a Rogers Communications Inc. employee witnessed my 'March for Freedom', ensuring catastrophic damage to my reputation that same afternoon.

After being transported by police to a Toronto psychiatric hospital, I was treated with medication and discharged two weeks later. But the most damaging consequences of the episode were not readily visible. My prolonged campaign had placed considerable strain on my relationship, a situation that was made significantly worse by my symptoms of severe mental illness and uncharacteristic behavior. By the time I was discharged from hospital, my long-term relationship was over and my reputation was destroyed. Furthermore, I was publicly humiliated, privately ashamed, and suffering from profound feelings of grief and loss. My self-esteem, confidence and self-respect were at rock bottom. In effect, I no longer knew who I was, and I had absolutely no idea how to go on. I was totally lost.

I wanted to disappear, so I did. I drifted for a period of time in a dark mood, spending that Christmas by myself in the Dominican Republic. I spent the next Christmas alone in South Africa. In between I travelled in the United States, Europe and Africa, thinking about life and death, while trying in vain to make sense of how things had gone so wrong. While I kept moving, anxiety always managed to find me.

During that time, I was unable to imagine a future that was worth living. I was convinced that I was never going to work or enjoy life again.

I was wrong.

From Canada to Canberra

Fortunately, I did not encounter any major drama while outside Canada (although I did come face to face with a large black mamba snake and a male lion over a 24-hour period, while on foot in Botswana's Okavango Delta) and returned to Toronto in early 1998. Later that year, I was hesitant to accept an invitation to a friend's party fearing discovery by strangers of my mental illness or that I did not have a job, but I forced myself to go anyway. That seemingly small decision forever changed my life, as it was there that I met my current partner Gail, an Australian citizen who was living in Toronto. Love, however, is not a cure for mental illness and I continued to struggle with symptoms of bipolar disorder and anxiety, in addition to intense feelings of shame and a loss of identity.

Furthermore, I was torn. I dearly wanted to revive my social justice campaign against the federal regulator and corporations, but did not pursue the matter because of the humiliation I felt, knowing that my opponents in industry and government, as well as journalists, were aware of my psychotic episode.

Defeated, directionless and extremely anxious that I might bump into someone from my former industry, I stagnated in Toronto. It felt as though I was stuck in my own Waterloo. My unhappiness was adversely affecting my relationship, so we decided to make a fresh start and moved to Australia in October 2001 - our flight landed on my 39th birthday. It was not an easy decision, as my family and many of our long-term friends live in North America.

One of my original objectives of immigrating to Australia was to hide my mental illness from as many people as possible. But of course the fact that you are now reading about my experience with bipolar disorder demonstrates that I changed my mind.

Benefits of Disclosure

Once again, a major shift in the focus of my life occurred from just one small step in the right direction. By chance, in early 2002 I saw a poster for Mental Illness Education ACT (MIEACT, with ACT standing for the Australian Capital Territory) on a bulletin board at the University of Canberra. The non-profit organization needed volunteers to share their 'lived experience' of mental illness with high school classes as part of its school education program. I found the idea of using my story of mental illness to try to help young people and reduce the stigma of mental illness appealing. I wish that I had known more about mental illness earlier in life.

I decided to become a mental health advocate. This was a decision which felt far more natural than trying to hide my experience, and which ultimately permitted me to rebuild my life as a person diagnosed with a severe mental illness.

Joining MIEACT proved an instrumental step in my recovery. Meeting other people with mental health issues who I respected helped me accept my own mental illness and put it into its proper social context. I also felt productive and part of the community again, while the reaction of high school students to my personal story helped me to feel more positive about myself.

All of this activity soon opened other doors. In September 2003 I was invited to be an inaugural member on a bipolar disorder reference group for "Beyondblue", the Australian national depression initiative. Two months later I was elected President of MIEACT.

Momentum and Transformation

I finally felt confident enough to put together a resumé and search for part-time employment. Given the massive gap in my employment history, I struggled over how exactly to address the issue with potential employers. Finally, I made the decision to disclose my mental health issues and approach employers who might be less likely to discriminate against me. The strategy worked. I was hired for one day a week by the Mental Health Council of Australia in January 2004, at the age of 41. One day per week probably does not sound like much to most people, but I felt like I had won the lottery. It was my first job in years, and the psychological rewards of employment far outweighed the financial gain, especially in terms of the social interaction with staff and the benefit of working to my sense of identity.

Importantly, I started to feel more and more like my old self, only far more secure in who I was than before my mental health problems. No longer was I ashamed to be someone living with a mental illness, which had been a major barrier to my recovery, and my ability to dream of a satisfying future returned.

After careful consideration, I decided to become a social worker and in February 2005 started studying part-time for a Bachelor of Social Work at the Australian Catholic University, a public university that is open to students of all beliefs. I did experience a couple of anxiety attacks in class during my first month in the course, but I was determined not to let mental illness stop me from achieving my goal to be a social worker, so I persisted. Soon I felt comfortable. The staff and students were friendly, and the small campus was a perfect setting for my return to university after a twenty-year hiatus. The course proved far more interesting to me than business had been. I especially related to the profession's commitment to social justice and social change. Since I do not possess a strong aptitude for writing, I adopted a policy of starting academic papers early to reduce their stress, which worked out well.

Later in the same year Gail and I bought a house in Canberra close to a reserve, a perfect location to walk our dog and watch kangaroos. After experiencing the stress of moving four times in four years, settling down felt wonderful.

During August 2006 I became an Australian citizen. The citizenship ceremony in Canberra was quite moving and my status as a citizen left me with a heightened sense of belonging, which served to cement the fact that Australia is my home. That realization was thought-provoking in itself, however, because the month before that ceremony I had become an uncle, and my nephew was in Canada. This reality made me once again acknowledge the ongoing cost of rebuilding my life.

On November 13th 2006 I completed a three-month field placement in case management at a youth detention centre as part of my university program. Before starting I was unsure whether I would be able to carry out a full-time schedule because I had not worked comparable hours in more than a decade. Nevertheless, it ultimately proved to be an extremely positive and rewarding experience, highlighting the possibility of a future career in a challenging and important field. Moreover, the comments and actions of my clients and colleagues convinced me that I had made the right career choice to become a social worker.

The day after that field placement finished was my last day of university for the year; it was also the tenth anniversary of my episode of major psychosis in Toronto. I reflected on my battle against severe mental illness, coming to the conclusion that I had finally made peace with my mind. I also realized that I had never felt more satisfied or content in life. At that moment, I made the decision to start celebrating my recovery from bipolar disorder each year on November 14th, my former day of shame.

I completed my degree a year later, earned a position on the Dean's List, and started working for the territory government in February 2008 as a case manager in youth justice – after disclosing my mental health issues during the interview process.

At my request, I was employed three days a week. The main reason that I wanted to work part-time for the statutory agency was to reduce the risk of relapse, while increasing my capacity to work more hours in the future. In addition, I did not want to reduce my involvement in mental health advocacy. In fact, I actually wanted to increase the amount of time that I was able to commit to mental health advocacy.

Consolidation and Contagious Recovery

While at university, Professor Albert Bandura's work on human learning and the ability of 'social models' to enhance the self-efficacy of other people caught my attention. Specifically, I was inspired to consider ways to raise awareness of recovery and generate hope for individuals with mental health issues and their families.

At the International Initiative for Mental Health Leadership in March 2009, I launched a website to progress the creation of an online community channel for people with mental health issues: Mentalympians®. In its related press release, the Mental Health Council of Australia described my initiative as a "creative approach to promoting awareness of recovery [and] a world first website which is all about mental health recovery and resilience."

Two months later, I had the opportunity to consolidate my passion for mental health with earning a living, which was simply too temping to turn down. As a result, I left youth justice to start working 4 days a week at Woden Community Service, as a peer support worker in a national recovery-oriented program funded by the Australian Government and delivered across the country by community organizations.

Hope has been identified as a catalyst for recovery, and a growing body of evidence suggests that it is possible for workers with a lived experience of mental illness to effectively assist other individuals experiencing mental illness in their recovery. I had a feeling that the role, program and community organization were going to be an excellent fit for me, and my feelings turned out to be correct. I am still employed in that same role, although I started working 5 days a week in 2011 (my first full-time employment since 1994). My health supports my belief that the job is a good fit. While I still periodically experience anxiety, I haven't experienced depression since 2008, or psychosis since 2004. Moreover, in the first five years in my present role I missed less than two days a year on average for all types of sick leave.

In 2013 the Mental Health Council of Australia published a strategic publication addressing a range of issues, including an article I wrote regarding the peer workforce. In that publication - *Perspectives: Mental Health and Wellbeing in Australia* - I describe the dynamic of peer workers helping to inspire hope by sharing their own lived experience as "contagious recovery". I also note that a key feature of peer support is reciprocity, and that I am inevitably inspired by the people with mental health issues that I support. In short, it is a highly satisfying and rewarding job to help people with mental health issues in their recovery process.

Working openly as a person with a lived experience of mental illness has also given me more flexibility and freedom to try to raise awareness of recovery and reduce stigma. For example, I've shared parts of my story in the media (radio, television and in the press), as well as to public servants, mental health workers and a parliamentary committee examining education and employment. To my surprise, I was acknowledged in the Australian Senate in 2011 by a senator who was at a function where I shared my story to help launch a resource to assist tertiary education graduates with mental health issues successfully transition into employment.

I turned 52 during 2014 and find myself far more patient than when I was a young man, which is reflected in my approach to Mentalympians®. While I was able to establish an international advisory group for the project, including a number of prominent mental health advocates, I was unsuccessful in securing funding to progress the initiative. Although I consider that such an online community channel holds significant potential, I put the project on hold a couple of years ago. I decided to devote my spare time and energy to other areas in mental health, and to wait for a good opportunity to present itself in order to resume developing the initiative.

By adopting a longer-term vision for what I want to accomplish, the amount of stress is significantly reduced, thereby increasing both the sustainability of my efforts and the probability of success. It's similar to one of Aesop's Fables – The Tortoise and the Hare. I used to approach major life tasks like a sprinter, rather than a marathon runner. But I've learned that a slow and steady approach is far better for me in terms of managing my mental health, which, in turn, unquestionably helps me to achieve my goals in the end.

The Promise and the Present

There are numerous definitions of mental health recovery, but none have been more influential that the one penned by William Anthony, who defines recovery as "a deeply personal, unique process of changing one's attitudes, values, feelings, goals, skills and/or roles. It is a way of living a satisfying, hopeful, and contributing life even with limitations caused by the illness. Recovery involves the development of new meaning and purpose in one's life as one grows beyond the catastrophic effects of mental illness."

I totally embrace the concept that recovery inherently involves a process of personal change and growth. However, I think that it is important to acknowledge that recovery can also involve a person maintaining some of their attitudes, values, feelings, goals, skills and/or roles. For example, at the same time that it is fair to say I've established myself as a mental health advocate in Australia, I am still pursuing the outstanding governance issue in Canada.

There is considerable interest in the increasing concentration of wealth in the world, including as a result of the recent publication of *Capital in the Twenty-First Century* by French economist Thomas Piketty. The CRTC scheme serves as a compelling case study of the democratic process being abused by government officials to unjustly enrich members of a powerful economic elite. But my interest in this particular case of wealth redistribution is inherently personal. I made a promise to myself during the depths of my severe depression in 1996 to not let go of my campaign, and that promise helped me hold on to life in those darkest days.

I successfully returned to the matter in September 2004, by sending then Prime Minister Paul Martin information and documents regarding the issue, on the tenth anniversary of my departure from the Canadian broadcasting system. While his government opted to not address the matter, I was satisfied that I had updated the issue and started a new paper trail for accountability.

More importantly, I adopted a long-term and sustainable campaign approach, reducing its priority in my day to day activities to a manageable time commitment – essentially conducting the campaign in parallel with my studies, volunteering, work and family commitments over the subsequent years.

As documented on my website www.onemedialaw.com, which I have created to support my campaign, I appeared at a CRTC public hearing in Canada on February 7th 2008 and briefly addressed the outstanding affair on the public record. Hours later, my related press release was covered by several international online news sources, including Reuters, CNBC and Forbes. As a result of my direct action, the following day questions were raised in the House of Commons. Once again, the Canadian government did not pursue the well-documented issue. However, as a more mature, experienced and patient social activist, I adopted a different approach than in I did in the mid-1990s. Rather than putting my life on hold to challenge industry and government, I left Canada and started my new job at youth justice the following week in Australia.

My legal counsel in Canberra subsequently provided information on my allegations of government corruption and numerous related documents to Prime Minister Stephen Harper in 2010. This correspondence is also posted on my website, as well as copies of documents related to the unjust corporate enrichment scheme that were destroyed by CRTC officials several years ago - after my lawyer had first sent information on the matter to Mr. Harper.

While it is my belief that the CRTC affair warrants a public inquiry, my website permits others to review and judge the issue for themselves. This time I am under no delusion. It is entirely possible that the facts of the case will never be properly addressed by the Canadian government. On the other hand, I think a public inquiry into the affair might naturally and positively raise awareness of mental health recovery, if journalists report that my original opposition to the unjust corporate enrichment scheme was interrupted by severe mental illness and that I resumed my campaign after my mental health improved.

In any event, I plan to continue to pursue this scandal until it is logically concluded, or I am no longer in a position to address the matter. Furthermore, it is safe to say that I am not going to change my mind. After all, I am a social activist.

> "The two most powerful warriors are patience and time."
> -Leo Tolstoy (*War and Peace*, 1869)

No Purple Hearts in This War
Katherine Tapley-Milton

As I lay on the couch lifeless and miserable, I had no idea what was happening to me. Surely, to feel this badly I must be dying. My mother insisted that I make an appointment to see the doctor, because she thought I must need vitamins. I had gone from a fairly normal, bouncy fourteen year old to a fifteen year old who could not move off of the couch. When I saw the doctor, I ended up crying in his office and he told me that my problems were emotional. After that I embarked on a quest to find out why I was feeling the way I did. I read every psychology book that I could get my hands on and I changed religions every week. Through all my reading I found a name for what I had – bipolar mood disorder. This is an illness in which a person alternates between periods of mania such as rapid speech, verbosity, grandiosity, and frenetic activity followed by periods of depression that involve feelings of bleakness, sadness, inactivity, and feeling suicidal.

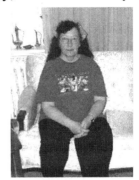

Katherine Tapley-Milton

It was in grade nine when the full brunt of mental illness really hit me. The previous year in grade eight I had been on the student council and had friends that I did things with. However, by the next year I had become obsessed with suicide, withdrawn, and deeply depressed. I was in so much mental anguish that I tried a series of overdoses. First I bought two bottles of over the counter sleeping pills at the drug store. I took all the pills and went to bed, thinking that I would never wake up again. It was a tremendous shock when I woke up the next morning. Having failed, I planned another attempt some months later. I felt I could not stand another five minutes of deep depression, so I went to the medicine cabinet and raided it. There were three hundred pills, which I counted out, mainly aspirins, but also prescription medications that my father and mother had lying around. That night I went into the bathroom and painfully swallowed all the pills. The medication burned my oesophagus badly, but I was determined to make an end of myself. I went to bed at nine o'clock and prepared to die. However, the image of my horse with nobody to ride her haunted me. I got up around one o'clock and awakened my parents. They did not believe that I had taken all three hundred pills, though they got up and poured salt water down my throat to make me vomit.

The next day I was sweating profusely and my hands turned black and puffy. I was very weak and ill. My father came and hugged me and told me that he loved me, but I knew that love was not enough to spring me from the prison of my mind. My parents made an appointment with a psychiatrist for me; he was a choleric man who swore at me a lot. He prescribed lots of Valium and told me that I was just going through a bad adolescence. In those days one did not tell anyone that you were seeing a psychiatrist, because it would have been a disgrace. As it was I felt that my family was ashamed of me. My parents were confused as to why a healthy, happy teenage girl had become depressed and morose, refusing to go out with any of her friends, and attempting suicide. My mother always maintained that the psychiatrist made me worse, and I guess she was right. He was a quack and had an uncontrolled temper. Everyone who went to my high school either accused me of being on street drugs or said that I was crazy.

I was experiencing bipolar mood swings and began to feel an invisible force was pursing me, around corners and up the stairs. I saw a family doctor that my friend had recommended. The man told me that I was a hopeless case and would never get my B.A. or amount to anything. He advised me to join a convent. In retrospect I think that doctor did me a favor, because he made me so angry that I wanted to succeed academically to prove him wrong. In the 1970's I enrolled in Mount Allison University and studied to get a B.A. with an area of concentration in psychology, sociology, and history. It was a gigantic struggle to get the essays and exams done while suffering from hallucinations, panic attacks, anxiety, and extreme insomnia, but I graduated on the Dean's list.

Hallucinations, voices, and extreme mood swings were thought to be symptomatic of bipolar illness. It is very hard to describe to a non-mentally ill person what auditory or visual hallucinations are like. Some people have tried and ended up with bizarre descriptions that don't make sense to most people. Over the years there has been quite a bit of confusion over my diagnosis – whether I am schizo-affective or have bipolar illness with borderline personality disorder. However, the various mental illnesses have overlapping symptoms. It is not uncommon for a mental health consumer in New Brunswick to have up to eight different diagnoses given by different doctors.

After I got my B.A., I enrolled in Tyndale Seminary in Willowdale, Ontario to study for a Master of Theological Studies degree. Within the first twenty-four hours of being there I contacted the school psychologist and met him in a classroom. He said, "You want to jump out of that window don't you?" I was surprised that my suicidal intentions were so obvious. The psychologist insisted that I be evaluated at the North York hospital, so I complied. They wanted to admit me, but I was so driven to get my degree that I convinced the doctor to let me go back to the seminary.

The first year of my masters degree was very turbulent. I was in a manic state and suffered from hallucinations that were a mixture of the most gruesome things a human being could conjure up -- skulls, dead soldiers, corpse- like creatures, and a mishmash of nightmarish scenes. During the second year of the program I slipped into a severe, numbing depression. I could not feel the hot water in the bathtub, I felt spaced out, dead, and emotionless. I should have taken some antidepressants, but I had refused them because I didn't believe in taking pills at the time. . The things that helped me survive university were seeing the psychologist once a week and my determination to succeed academically. Also, I was fortunate to have some professors and friends help me. The psychologist at the seminary heard me say that I just wanted to go back home to the Maritimes and forget getting my masters degree. I only had half a credit left to go and I was so depressed that I didn't care anymore. However, he insisted that I finish my degree. He talked to the dean of students and they allowed me to do a minithesis at home. I did go home to Atlantic Canada and worked really hard on the paper. The dean gave me an A+ on it and I finally graduated. It was a proud day when I got my Master of Theological Studies degree. I had done it in a psychotic state yet made the dean's list. After I finished my education I embarked on a career as a freelance writer. For the last twenty-five years I have been a writer and poet. I have been published in over one hundred periodicals and have just finished a book on my life experience with mental illness titled, "Mind Full of Scorpions" which is listed on Amazon. I've always had the belief that handicapped persons should live as normal a life as possible, so I drive a car and participate in our activity group events such as having coffee together, doing crafts, or going to movies.

Twelve years ago I met my husband, Dave, on an Internet site titled, "Adam Meet Eve".

Dave suffers from a neurological illness called Dystonia, which causes neck spasms. Having experienced illness he is sympathetic to my health issues. Dave pledges his loves for me despite my recurring episodes of mental illness. Together we watch videos when we are both down, take nature walks, discuss theology, and visit family.

As I have gotten older I don't have many manic episodes anymore, I mainly struggle with depression and some psychotic symptoms. Since I also suffer from fibromyalgia I feel depression from my physical pain and disability as well as from mental illness. In order to control my illness I have to take antidepressants, mood stabilizers, and anti-psychotic medications, which unfortunately have side effects of weight gain and thirst. However, I find pleasure in relating to other mentally ill persons, attending our activity group, cooking, gardening, and writing for periodicals. There are about five different women that I talk to on a regular basis. Some are older than I am and have a lot of life experience. Then there are others who suffer mental illness and physical pain like me. I have known these friends for decades and we have been through a lot together. At times I still get into suicidal crises and need help from the crisis center or the mental health clinic. However, I'm trying to get on with my life and have carved a niche out for myself as a mental health critic, having written for a local mental health magazine for the last thirty-five years. I have written articles about every facet of the mental illness and the mental health care system. My articles have been about what it is like to suffer from mental illness; the dangers of shock therapy, the abuses in psychiatric hospitals, what it is like to be in a clinical trial at Yale University, an interview with Patch Adams, the life story of someone who was sexually abused, and many other mental health topics.

What I find frustrating about having a mental illness is the invisible nature of it. People who are in a hospital bed, wrapped in bandages, confined to a wheelchair, or are on crutches are generally considered ill and get sympathy. However, when it comes to having a mental illness people judge you and think you suffer from a weak will or lack of self-control instead of realizing that the illness is not your fault. After years of struggling, I know that I'll never get a purple heart for my war against the dragon of depression. However, at the age of fifty-nine, my goal is to try and get more humane treatment for those suffering from mental illness and to raise awareness of this agonizing affliction. My psychologist has said that my advocacy has helped many clients that he sees and that staff may think twice before abusing patients in a psychiatric hospital. It has not only been my voice that has achieved this, but he says that my voice is the strongest among the lot.

I think that after decades of suffering, my pain has given me the gift of showing mercy. Because of my mental illness I am moved to help individuals that normal people would ignore. Suffering compels me to help those who are in extreme need. I write to a needy child in Africa and to send shoe boxes filled with toys and school items to the Third World. My husband and I visit the local penitentuary every Sunday to work with inmates in the chapel program. Many of them have mental illness like bipolar mood disorder, schizophrenia, personality disorders. I have been a prison volunteer for twenty years. My husband and I also reach out to mentally ill persons that I know. You might say that I am a wounded healer.

Biographical Note
Katherine Tapley-Milton lives with her husband, Dave, and five cats in Atlantic Canada. She graduated from Mount Allison University with a B.A. in the areas of psychology,

sociology, and history and has a two year Master of Theological Studies degree from Tyndale Seminary in Willowdale, Ontario. Katherine has been a freelance writer for the last 35 years and has been published in hundreds of periodicals. Her books "Mind Full of Scorpions"; "Devotions With Your Cat"; and "The Adventures of Sir Lancelot the Cat"; are already published, and "Old Boats and Old Quotes"; and "The Adventures of the Three Mouse-Breath-Kateers" are soon to be published. Her hobbies include cooking, organic gardening, writing, reading historical romances, doing crafts, and hanging out with her cats.